IT SHOULDN'T
HAPPEN TO A VET

'There is a very fine dividing line between looking a real smart vet on the one hand and an immortal fool on the other.' . . . The words of his boss acquired an increasing significance and reality for young James Herriot during his early years in veterinary practice. The diverse and unpredictable natures of his animal patients made it seem inevitable that he should run into all kinds of trouble and dilemma. Most of his predicaments, although highly amusing in retrospect, were not so funny to him at the time, but at least he was living and working amidst the wild beauty of the Yorkshire dales which he loved. In this book he takes the reader with him as he struggles to deal with the ailments of the various species—from racehorses to kittens—which are his province. He soon realizes that it is not only the animals—it is also their owners he has to learn to deal with: often it is they who cause him most exasperation, although at the same time they can be so utterly charming! James Herriot's narrative is infused not only with the fascinating atmosphere of his beloved Yorkshire dales and the authentic flavour of some of the colourful characters who live there, but also, not least of all, with his own innate sense of humour.

Also by
JAMES HERRIOT

★

IF ONLY THEY COULD TALK

IT SHOULDN'T
HAPPEN TO A VET

★

JAMES HERRIOT

**THE
COMPANION BOOK CLUB
LONDON**

This edition, published in 1973 by
The Hamlyn Publishing Group Ltd,
is issued by arrangement with
Michael Joseph Ltd.

THE COMPANION BOOK CLUB

The Club is not a library; all books are
the property of members. There is no
entrance fee or any payment beyond the
low Club price of each book. Details of
membership will gladly be sent on
request.
Write to:
    The Companion Book Club,
Borough Green, Sevenoaks, Kent.

---

*Made and printed in Great Britain
for the Companion Book Club
by Odhams (Watford) Ltd.*
600871584
2.73/258

To
DONALD and BRIAN SINCLAIR
Still my friends

Chapter One

I COULD SEE that Mr Handshaw didn't believe a word I was saying. He looked down at his cow and his mouth tightened into a stubborn line.

'Broken pelvis? You're trying to tell me she'll never get up n'more? Why, look at her chewing her cud! I'll tell you this, young man—me dad would've soon got her up if he'd been alive today.'

I had been a veterinary surgeon for a year now and I had learned a few things. One of them was that farmers weren't easy men to convince—especially Yorkshire Dalesmen.

And that bit about his dad. Mr Handshaw was in his fifties and I suppose there was something touching about his faith in his late late father's skill and judgment. But I could have done very nicely without it.

It had acted as an additional irritant in a case in which I felt I had troubles enough. Because there are few things which get more deeply under a vet's skin than a cow which won't get up. To the layman it may seem strange that an animal can be apparently cured of its original ailment and yet be unable to rise from the floor, but it happens. And it can be appreciated that a completely recumbent milk cow has no future.

The case had started when my boss, Siegfried Farnon, who owned the practice in the little Dales market town of Darrowby, sent me to a milk fever. This suddenly occurring calcium deficiency attacks high yielding animals just after calving and causes collapse and progressive coma.

When I first saw Mr Handshaw's cow she was stretched out

motionless on her side, and I had to look carefully to make sure she wasn't dead.

But I got out my bottles of calcium with an airy confidence because I had been lucky enough to qualify just about the time when the profession had finally got on top of this hitherto fatal condition. The breakthrough had come many years earlier with inflation of the udder and I still carried a little blowing-up outfit around with me (the farmers used bicycle pumps), but with the advent of calcium therapy one could bask in a cheap glory by jerking an animal back from imminent death within minutes. The skill required was minimal but it looked very very good.

By the time I had injected the two bottles—one into the vein, the other under the skin—and Mr Handshaw had helped me roll the cow on to her chest the improvement was already obvious; she was looking about her and shaking her head as if wondering where she had been for the last few hours. I felt sure that if I had had the time to hang about for a bit I could see her on her feet. But other jobs were waiting.

'Give me a ring if she isn't up by dinner time,' I said, but it was a formality. I was pretty sure I wouldn't be seeing her again.

When the farmer rang at midday to say she was still down it was just a pinprick. Some cases needed an extra bottle—it would be all right.

I went out and injected her again.

I wasn't really worried when I learned she hadn't got up the following day, but Mr Handshaw, hands deep in pockets, shoulders hunched as he stood over his cow, was grievously disappointed at my lack of success.

'It's time t'awd bitch was up. She's doin' no good laid there. Surely there's summat you can do. I poured a bottle of water into her lug this morning but even that hasn't shifted her.'

'You what?'

'Poured some cold water down her lug 'ole. Me dad used to get 'em up that way and he was a very clever man with stock was me dad.'

8

'I've no doubt he was,' I said primly. 'But I really think another injection is more likely to help her.'

The farmer watched glumly as I ran yet another bottle of calcium under the skin. The procedure had lost its magic for him.

As I put the apparatus away I did my best to be hearty. 'I shouldn't worry. A lot of them stay down for a day or two —you'll probably find her walking about in the morning.'

The phone rang just before breakfast and my stomach contracted sharply as I heard Mr Handshaw's voice. It was heavy with gloom. 'Well, she's no different. Lyin' there eating her 'ead off, but never offers to rise. What are you going to do now?'

What indeed, I thought as I drove out to the farm. The cow had been down for forty-eight hours now—I didn't like it a bit.

The farmer went into the attack immediately. 'Me dad allus used to say they had a worm in the tail when they stayed down like this. He said if you cut tail end off it did the trick.'

My spirits sagged lower. I had had trouble with this myth before. The insidious thing was that the people who still practised this relic of barbarism could often claim that it worked because, after the end of the tail had been chopped off, the pain of the stump touching the ground forced many a sulky cow to scramble to her feet.

'There's no such thing as worm in the tail, Mr Handshaw,' I said. 'And don't you think it's a cruel business, cutting off a cow's tail? I hear the R.S.P.C.A. had a man in court last week over a job like that.'

The farmer narrowed his eyes. Clearly he thought I was hedging.

'Well, if you won't do that, what the hangment are you going to do? We've got to get this cow up somehow.'

I took a deep breath. 'Well, I'm sure she's got over the milk fever because she's eating well and looks quite happy. It must be a touch of posterior paralysis that's keeping her down.

9

There's no point in giving her any more calcium so I'm going to try this stimulant injection.'

I filled the syringe with a feeling of doom. I hadn't a scrap of faith in the stimulant injection but I just couldn't do nothing. I was scraping the barrel out now.

I was turning to go when Mr Handshaw called after me. 'Hey, Mister, I remember summat else me dad used to do. Shout in their lugs. He got many a cow up that way. I'm not very strong in the voice—how about you having a go?'

It was a bit late to stand on my dignity. I went over to the animal and seized her by the ear. Inflating my lungs to the utmost I bent down and bawled wildly into the hairy depths. The cow stopped chewing for a moment and looked at me enquiringly, then her eyes drooped and she returned contentedly to her cudding.

'We'll give her another day,' I said wearily. 'And if she's still down tomorrow we'll have a go at lifting her. Could you get a few of your neighbours to give us a hand?'

Driving round my other cases that day I felt tied up inside with sheer frustration. Damn and blast the thing! What the hell was keeping her down? And what else could I do? This was 1938 and my resources were limited. Thirty years later there are still milk fever cows which won't get up but the vet has a much wider armoury if the calcium has failed to do the job. The excellent Bagshaw hoist which clamps on to the pelvis and raises the animal in a natural manner, the phosphorus injections, even the electric goad which administers a swift shock when applied to the rump and sends many a comfortably ensconced cow leaping to her feet with an offended bellow.

As I expected, the following day brought no change and as I got out of the car in Mr Handshaw's yard I was surrounded by a group of his neighbours. They were in festive mood, grinning, confident, full of helpful advice as farmers always are with somebody else's animals.

There was much laughter and legpulling as we drew sacks under the cow's body and a flood of weird suggestions to which I tried to close my ears. When we all finally gave a concerted heave and lifted her up, the result was predictable; she just hung there placidly with her legs dangling whilst her owner leaned against the wall watching us with deepening gloom.

After a lot of puffing and grunting we lowered the inert body and everybody looked at me for the next move. I was hunting round desperately in my mind when Mr Handshaw piped up again.

'Me dad used to say a strange dog would allus get a cow up.'

There were murmurs of assent from the assembled farmers and immediate offers of dogs. I tried to point out that one would be enough but my authority had dwindled and anyway everybody seemed anxious to demonstrate their dogs' cow-raising potential. There was a sudden excited exodus and even Mr Smedley the village shopkeeper pedalled off at frantic speed for his border terrier. It seemed only minutes before the byre was alive with snapping, snarling curs but the cow ignored them all except to wave her horns at the ones which came too close.

The flash-point came when Mr Handshaw's own dog came in from the fields where he had been helping to round up the sheep. He was a skinny, hard-bitten little creature with lightning reflexes and a short temper. He stalked, stiff-legged and bristling, into the byre, took a single astounded look at the pack of foreigners on his territory and flew into action with silent venom.

Within seconds the finest dog fight I had ever seen was in full swing and I stood back and surveyed the scene with a feeling of being completely superfluous. The yells of the farmers rose above the enraged yapping and growling. One intrepid man leaped into the mêlée and reappeared with a tiny Jack Russell hanging on determinedly to the heel of his wellington boot. Mr Reynolds of Clover Hill was rubbing the cow's tail between two short sticks and shouting 'Cush! Cush!' and as I watched helplessly a total stranger tugged at my sleeve and whispered: 'Hasta tried a teaspoonful of Jeyes' Fluid in a pint of old beer every two hours?'

It seemed to me that all the forces of black magic had broken through and were engulfing me and that my slender resources of science had no chance of shoring up the dyke. I don't know how I heard the creaking sound above the din— probably because I was bending low over Mr Reynolds in an attempt to persuade him to desist from his tail rubbing. But at that moment the cow shifted her position slightly and I distinctly heard it. It came from the pelvis.

It took me some time to attract attention—I think everybody had forgotten I was there—but finally the dogs were separated and secured with innumerable lengths of binder twine, everybody stopped shouting, Mr Reynolds was pulled away from the tail and I had the stage.

I addressed myself to Mr Handshaw. 'Would you get me a bucket of hot water, some soap and a towel, please.'

He trailed off, grumbling, as though he didn't expect much from the new gambit. My stock was definitely low.

I stripped off my jacket, soaped my arms and pushed a hand into the cow's rectum until I felt the hard bone of the pubis. Gripping it through the wall of the rectum I looked up at my audience.

'Will two of you get hold of the hook bones and rock the cow gently from side to side.'

Yes, there it was again, no mistake about it. I could both hear and feel it—a looseness, a faint creaking, almost a grating.

I got up and washed my arm. 'Well, I know why your cow won't get up—she has a broken pelvis. Probably did it during the first night when she was staggering about with the milk fever. I should think the nerves are damaged, too. It's hopeless, I'm afraid.' Even though I was dispensing bad news it was a relief to come up with something rational.

Mr Handshaw stared at me.

'Hopeless? How's that?'

'I'm sorry,' I said, 'but that's how it is. The only thing you

12

can do is get her off to the butcher. She has no power in her hind legs. She'll never get up again.'

That was when Mr Handshaw really blew his top and started a lengthy speech. He wasn't really unpleasant or abusive but firmly pointed out my shortcomings and bemoaned again the tragic fact that his dad was not there to put everything right. The other farmers stood in a wide-eyed ring, enjoying every word.

At the end of it I took myself off. There was nothing more I could do and anyway Mr Handshaw would have to come round to my way of thinking. Time would prove me right.

I thought of that cow as soon as I awoke next morning. It hadn't been a happy episode but at least I did feel a certain peace in the knowledge that there were no more doubts. I knew what was wrong, I knew that there was no hope. There was nothing more to worry about.

I was surprised when I heard Mr Handshaw's voice on the phone so soon. I had thought it would take him two or three days to realize he was wrong.

'Is that Mr Herriot? Aye, well, good mornin' to you. I'm just ringing to tell you that me cow's up on her legs and doing fine.'

I gripped the receiver tightly with both hands.

'What? What's that you say?'

'I said me cow's up. Found her walking about byre this morning, fit as a fiddle. You'd think there'd never been owt the matter with her.' He paused for a few moments then spoke with grave deliberation like a disapproving schoolmaster. 'And you stood there and looked at me and said she'd never get up n'more.'

'But ... but ...'

'Ah, you're wondering how I did it? Well, I just happened to remember another old trick of me dad's. I went round to t'butcher and got a fresh-killed sheep skin and put it on her back. Had her up in no time—you'll 'ave to come round and see her. Wonderful man was me dad.'

Blindly I made my way into the dining-room. I had to consult my boss about this. Siegfried's sleep had been broken by a 3 a.m. calving and he looked a lot older than his thirty-odd years. He listened in silence as he finished his breakfast then pushed away his plate and poured a last cup of coffee.

'Hard luck, James. The old sheep skin, eh? Funny thing— you've been in the Dales over a year now and never come across that one. Suppose it must be going out of fashion a bit now but you know it has a grain of sense behind it like a lot of these old remedies. You can imagine there's a lot of heat generated under a fresh sheep skin and it acts like a great hot poultice on the back—really tickles them up after a while, and if a cow is lying there out of sheer cussedness she'll often get up just to get rid of it.'

'But damn it, how about the broken pelvis? I tell you it was creaking and wobbling all over the place!'

'Well, James, you're not the first to have been caught that way. Sometimes the pelvic ligaments don't tighten up for a few days after calving and you get this effect.'

'Oh God,' I moaned, staring down at the table cloth. 'What a bloody mess I've made of the whole thing.'

'Oh, you haven't really.' Siegfried lit a cigarette and leaned back in his chair. 'That old cow was probably toying with the idea of getting up for a walk just when old Handshaw dumped the skin on her back. She could just as easily have done it after one of your injections and then you'd have got the credit. Don't you remember what I told you when you first came here? There's a very fine dividing line between looking a real smart vet on the one hand and an immortal fool on the other. This sort of thing happens to us all, so forget it, James.'

But forgetting wasn't so easy. That cow became a celebrity in the district. Mr Handshaw showed her with pride to the postman, the policeman, corn merchants, lorry drivers, ferti- lizer salesmen, Ministry of Agriculture officials and they all told me about it frequently with pleased smiles. Mr Hand- shaw's speech was always the same, delivered, they said, in ringing, triumphant tones:

14

'There's the cow that Mr Herriot said would never get up n'more!'

I'm sure there was no malice behind the farmer's actions. He had put one over on the young clever-pants vet and nobody could blame him for preening himself a little. And in a way I did that cow a good turn; I considerably extended her life span, because Mr Handshaw kept her long beyond her normal working period just as an exhibit. Years after she had stopped giving more than a couple of gallons of milk a day she was still grazing happily in the field by the roadside.

She had one curiously upturned horn and was easy to recognize. I often pulled up my car and looked wistfully over the wall at the cow that would never get up n'more.

Chapter Two

SIEGFRIED came away from the telephone; his face was expressionless. 'That was Mrs Pumphrey. She wants you to see her pig.'

'Peke, you mean,' I said.

'No, pig. She has a six-week-old pig she wants you to examine for soundness.'

I laughed sheepishly. My relations with the elderly widow's Peke was a touchy subject. 'All right, all right, don't start again. What did she really want? Is Tricki Woo's bottom playing him up again?'

'James,' said Siegfried gravely. 'It is unlike you to doubt my word in this way. I will repeat the message from Mrs Pumphrey and then I shall expect you to act upon it immediately and without further question. The lady informed me that she has become the owner of a six-week-old piglet and she wants the animal thoroughly vetted. You know how I feel about these examinations and I don't want the job scamped in any way. I should pay particular attention to its wind—have it well galloped round a paddock before you get your stethoscope on it and for heaven's sake don't miss anything obvious like curbs or ringbones. I think I'd take its height while you're about it; you'll find the measuring stick in . . .'

His words trailed on as I hurried down the passage. This was a bit baffling; I usually had a bit of leg-pulling to stand ever since I became Tricki the Peke's adopted uncle and received regular presents and letters and signed photographs from him, but Siegfried wasn't in the habit of flogging the joke to this extent. The idea of Mrs Pumphrey with a pig was unthinkable; there was no room in her elegant establishment for livestock. Oh, he must have got it wrong somehow.

But he hadn't. Mrs Pumphrey received me with a joyful cry. 'Oh, Mr Herriot, isn't it wonderful! I have the most darling little pig. I was visiting some cousins who are farmers and I picked him out. He will be such company for Tricki—you know how I worry about his being an only dog.'

I shook my head vigorously in bewilderment as I crossed the oak-panelled hall. My visits here were usually associated with a degree of fantasy but I was beginning to feel out of my depth.

'You mean you actually have this pig in the house?'

'But of course.' Mrs Pumphrey looked surprised. 'He's in the kitchen. Come and see him.'

I had been in this kitchen a few times and had been almost awestruck by its shining spotlessness; the laboratory look of the tiled walls and floors, the gleaming surfaces of sink unit, cooker, refrigerator. Today, a cardboard box occupied one corner and inside I could see a tiny pig; standing on his hind legs, his forefeet resting on the rim, he was looking round him appreciatively at his new surroundings.

The elderly cook had her back to us and did not look round when we entered; she was chopping carrots and then hurling them into a saucepan with, I thought, unnecessary vigour.

'Isn't he adorable!' Mrs Pumphrey bent over and tickled the little head. 'It's so exciting having a pig of my very own! Mr Herriot, I have decided to call him Nugent.'

I swallowed. 'Nugent?' The cook's broad back froze into immobility.

'Yes, after my great uncle Nugent. He was a little pink man with tiny eyes and a snub nose. The resemblance is striking.'

'I see,' I said, and the cook started her splashing again.

For a few moments I was at a loss; the ethical professional man in me rebelled at the absurdity of examining this obviously healthy little creature. In fact I was on the point of saying that he looked perfectly all right to me when Mrs Pumphrey spoke.

'Come now, Nugent,' she said. 'You must be a good boy and let your Uncle Herriot look at you.'

That did it. Stifling my finer feelings I seized the string-like tail and held Nugent almost upside down as I took his temperature. I then solemnly auscultated his heart and lungs, peered into his eyes, ran my fingers over his limbs and flexed his joints.

The cook's back radiated stiff disapproval but I carried on doggedly. Having a canine nephew, I had found, carried incalculable advantages; it wasn't only the frequent gifts—and I could still taste the glorious kippers Tricki had posted to me from Whitby—it was the vein of softness in my rough life, the sherry before lunch, the warmth and luxury of Mrs Pumphrey's fireside. The way I saw it, if a piggy nephew of the same type had been thrown in my path then Uncle Herriot was going to be the last man to interfere with the inscrutable workings of fate.

The examination over, I turned to Mrs Pumphrey who was anxiously awaiting the verdict. 'Sound in all respects,' I said briskly. 'In fact you've got a very fine pig there. But there's just one thing—he can't live in the house.'

For the first time the cook turned towards me and I read a mute appeal in her face. I could sympathize with her because the excretions of the pig are peculiarly volatile and even such a minute specimen as Nugent had already added his own faint pungency to the atmosphere in the kitchen.

Mrs. Pumphrey was appalled at the idea at first but when I assured her that he wouldn't catch pneumonia and in fact would be happier and healthier outside, she gave way.

An agricultural joiner was employed to build a palatial sty in a corner of the garden; it had a warm sleeping apartment on raised boards and an outside run. I saw Nugent installed in it, curled up blissfully in a bed of clean straw. His trough was filled twice daily with the best meal and he was never short of an extra titbit such as a juicy carrot or some cabbage leaves. Every day he was allowed out to play and spent a boisterous hour frisking round the garden with Tricki.

In short, Nugent had it made, but it couldn't have happened to a nicer pig; because, though most of his species have an unsuspected strain of friendliness, this was developed in Nugent to an extraordinary degree. He just liked people and over the next few months his character flowered under the constant personal contact with humans.

I often saw him strolling companionably in the garden with Mrs Pumphrey and in his pen he spent much of the time standing upright with his cloven feet against the wire netting, waiting eagerly for his next visitor. Pigs grow quickly and he soon left the pink baby stage behind, but his charm was undiminished. His chief delight was to have his back scratched; he would grunt deeply, screwing up his eyes in ecstasy, then gradually his legs would start to buckle until finally he toppled over on his side.

Nugent's existence was sunny and there was only one cloud in the sky; old Hodgkin, the gardener, whose attitude to domestic pets had been permanently soured by having to throw rubber rings for Tricki every day, now found himself appointed personal valet to a pig. It was his duty to feed and bed down Nugent and to supervise his play periods. The idea of doing all this for a pig who was never ever going to be converted into pork pies must have been nearly insupportable for the old countryman; the harsh lines on his face deepened whenever he took hold of the meal bucket.

On the first of my professional visits to his charge he greeted me gloomily with 'Hasta come to see Nudist?' I knew Hodgkin well enough to realize the impossibility of any whimsical wordplay; it was a genuine attempt to grasp the name and throughout my nephew's long career he remained 'Nudist' to the old man.

There is one memory of Nugent which I treasure. The telephone rang one day just after lunch; it was Mrs Pumphrey and I knew by the stricken voice that something momentous had happened; it was the same voice which had described Tricki Woo's unique symptoms of flop-bott and crackerdog.

'Oh, Mr Herriot, thank heavens you are in. It's Nugent! I'm afraid he's terribly ill.'

'Really? I'm sorry to hear that. What's he doing?'

There was a silence at the other end except for gasping breathing then Mrs Pumphrey spoke again. 'Well, he can't manage . . . he can't do . . . do his little jobs.'

I was familiar with her vocabulary of her big jobs and little jobs. 'You mean he can't pass his urine?'

'Well . . . well . . .' she was obviously confused. 'Not properly.'

'That's strange,' I said. 'Is he eating all right?'

'I think so, but . . .' then she suddenly blurted out: 'Oh, Mr Herriot, I'm so terribly worried! I've heard of men being dreadfully ill . . . just like this. It's a gland, isn't it?'

'Oh, you needn't worry about that. Pigs don't have that trouble and anyway, I think four months is a bit young for hypertrophy of the prostate.'

'Oh, I'm so glad, but something is . . . stopping it. You will come, won't you!'

'I'm leaving now.'

I had quite a long wait outside Nugent's pen. He had grown into a chunky little porker and grunted amiably as he surveyed me through the netting. Clearly he expected some sort of game and, growing impatient, he performed a few stiff-legged little gallops up and down the run.

I had almost decided that my visit was fruitless when Mrs Pumphrey, who had been pacing up and down, wringing her hands, stopped dead and pointed a shaking finger at the pig.

'Oh God,' she breathed. 'There! There! There it is now!' All the colour had drained from her face leaving her deathly pale. 'Oh, it's awful! I can't look any longer.' With a moan she turned away and buried her face in her hands.

I scrutinized Nugent closely. He had halted in mid gallop

and was contentedly relieving himself by means of the inter-mittent spurting jets of the normal male pig.

I turned to Mrs Pumphrey. 'I really can't see anything wrong there.'

'But he's . . . he's . . .' she still didn't dare to look. 'He's doing it in . . . fits and starts!'

I had had considerable practice at keeping a straight face in Mrs Pumphrey's presence and it stood me in good stead now.

'But they all do it that way, Mrs Pumphrey.'

She half turned and looked tremblingly out of the corner of her eye at Nugent. 'You mean . . . all boy pigs . . . ?'

'Every single boy pig I have ever known has done it like that.'

'Oh . . . Oh . . . how odd, how very odd.' The poor lady fanned herself with her handkerchief. Her colour had come back in a positive flood.

To cover her confusion I became very business-like. 'Yes, yes indeed. Lots of people make the same mistake, I assure you. Ah well, I suppose I'd better be on my way now—it's been nice to see the little fellow looking so well and happy.'

Nugent enjoyed a long and happy life and more than ful-filled my expectations of him; he was every bit as generous as Tricki with his presents and, as with the little Peke, I was able to salve my conscience with the knowledge that I was really fond of him. As always, Siegfried's sardonic attitude made things a little uncomfortable; I had suffered in the past when I got the signed photographs from the little dog—but I never dared let him see the one from the pig.

Chapter Three

ANGUS GRIER, M.R.C.V.S., was never pretty to look at, but the sight of him propped up in bed, his mottled, pop-eyed face scowling above a pink quilted bed jacket was enough to daunt the bravest. Especially at eight in the morning when I usually had the first of my daily audiences with him.

'You're late again,' he said, his voice grating. 'Can ye no' get out of your bed in the morning? I've told you till I'm tired that I want ye out on the road by eight o'clock.'

As I mumbled apologies he tugged fretfully at the counterpane and looked me up and down with deepening distaste. 'And another thing, that's a terrible pair o' breeches you're wearing. If you must wear breeches to your work, for heaven's sake go and get a pair made at a proper tailor. There's nae cut about those things at all—they're not fit to be worn by a veterinary surgeon.'

The knife really went in then. I was attached to those breeches. I had paid thirty shillings for them at the Army and Navy Stores and cherished a private conviction that they gave me a certain air. And Grier's attack on them was all the more wounding when I considered that the man was almost certainly getting my services free; Siegfried, I felt sure, would wave aside any offers of payment.

I had been here a week and it seemed like a lifetime. Somewhere, far back, I knew, there had been a brighter, happier existence but the memory was growing dim. Siegfried had been sincerely apologetic that morning back in Darrowby.

'James, I have a letter here from Grier of Brawton. It

seems he was castrating a colt and the thing threw itself on top of him; he has a couple of cracked ribs. Apparently his assistant walked out on him recently, so there's nobody to run his practice. He wants me to send you along there for a week or two.'

'Oh no! There's a mistake somewhere. He doesn't like me.'

'He doesn't like anybody. But there's no mistake, it's down here—and honestly, what can I do?'

'But the only time I met him he worked me into a horrible rubber suit and made me look a right chump.'

Siegfried smiled sadly. 'I remember, James, I remember. He's a mean old devil and I hate to do this to you, but I can't turn him down, can I?'

At the time I couldn't believe it. The whole idea was unreal. But it was real enough now as I stood at the foot of Grier's bed listening to him ranting away. He was at me again.

'Another thing—my wife tells me you didna eat your porridge. Did you not like it?'

I shuffled my feet. 'Oh yes, it was very nice. I just didn't feel hungry this morning.' I had pushed the tasteless mass about with my spoon and done my best with it but it had defeated me in the end.

'There's something wrong with a man that canna eat his good food.' Grier peered at me suspiciously then held out a slip of paper. 'Here's a list of your visits for this morning. There's a good few so you'll no' have to waste your time getting round. This one here of Adamson's of Grenton—a prolapse of the cervix in a cow. What would you do about that, think ye?'

I put my hand in my pocket, got hold of my pipe then dropped it back again. Grier didn't like smoking.

'Well, I'd give her an epidural anaesthetic, replace the prolapse and fasten it in with retention sutures through the vulva.'

'Havers, man, havers!' snorted Grier. 'What a lot of

twaddle. There's no need for a' that. It'll just be constipation that's doing it. Push the thing back, build the cow up with some boards under her hind feet and put her on to linseed oil for a few days.'

'Surely it'll come out again if I don't stitch it in?' I said.

'Na, na, na, not at all,' Grier cried angrily. 'Just you do as I tell you now. I ken more about this than you.'

He probably did. He should, anyway—he had been qualified for thirty years and I was starting my second. I looked at him glowering from his pillow and pondered for a moment on the strange fact of our uncomfortable relationship. A Yorkshireman listening to the two outlandish accents—Grier's rasping Aberdeen, my glottal Clydeside—might have expected that some sort of rapport would exist between us, if only on national grounds. But there was none.

'Right, just as you say.' I left the room and went downstairs to gather up my equipment.

As I set off on the round I had the same feeling as every morning—relief at getting out of the house. I had had to go flat out all week to get through the work but I had enjoyed it. Farmers are nearly always prepared to make allowances for a young man's inexperience and Grier's clients had treated me kindly, but I still had to come back to that joyless establishment for meals and it was becoming more and more wearing.

Mrs Grier bothered me just as much as her husband. She was a tight-lipped woman of amazing thinness and she kept a spartan board in which soggy porridge figured prominently. It was porridge for breakfast, porridge for supper and, in between, a miserable procession of watery stews, anaemic mince and nameless soups. Nothing she cooked ever tasted of anything. Angus Grier had come to Yorkshire thirty years ago, a penniless Scot just like myself, and acquired a lucrative practice by the classical expedient of marrying the boss's daughter; so he got a good living handed to him on a plate, but he also got Mrs Grier.

It seemed to me that she felt she was still in charge—probably because she had always lived in this house with its memories of her father who had built up the practice. Other people would seem like interlopers and I could understand how she felt; after all, she was childless, she didn't have much of a life and she had Angus Grier for a husband. I could feel sorry for her.

But that didn't help because I just couldn't get her out of my hair; she hung over my every move like a disapproving spectre. When I came back from a round she was always there with a barrage of questions. 'Where have you been all this time?' or 'I wondered wherever you'd got to, were you lost?' or 'There's an urgent case waiting. Why are you always so slow?' Maybe she thought I'd nipped into a cinema for an hour or two.

There was a pretty full small animal surgery every night and she had a nasty habit of lurking just outside the door so that she could listen to what I was saying to the clients. She really came into her own in the dispensary where she watched me narrowly, criticizing my prescriptions and constantly pulling me up for being extravagant with the drugs. 'You're putting in far too much chlorodyne—don't you know it's very expensive?'

I developed a deep sympathy for the assistant who had fled without warning; jobs were hard to come by and young graduates would stand nearly anything just to be at work, but I realized that there had been no other choice for that shadowy figure.

Adamson's place was a small-holding on the edge of the town and maybe it was because I had just been looking at Grier but by contrast the farmer's lined, patient face and friendly eyes seemed extraordinarily warming and attractive. A ragged khaki smock hung loosely on his gaunt frame as he shook hands with me.

'Now then, we've got a new man today, have we?' He looked me over for a second or two. 'And by the look of you you're pretty fresh to t'job.'

'That's right,' I replied. 'But I'm learning fast.'

Mr Adamson smiled. 'Don't worry about that, lad. I believe in new blood and new ideas—it's what we want in farming. We've stood still too long at this game. Come into t'byre and I'll show you the cow.'

There were about a dozen cows, not the usual Shorthorns but Ayrshires, and they were obviously well kept and healthy. My patient was easy to pick out by the football-sized rose-pink protrusion of the vaginal wall and the corrugated uterine cervix. But the farmer had wasted no time in calling for assistance; the mass was clean and undamaged.

He watched me attentively as I swabbed the prolapse with antiseptic and pushed it back out of sight, then he helped me build a platform with soil and planks for the cow's hind feet.

When we had finished she was standing on a slope with her tail higher than her head.

'And you say that if I give her linseed oil for a few days that thing won't come out again?'

'That's the idea,' I said. 'Be sure to keep her built up like this.'

'I will, young man, and thank you very much. I'm sure you've done a good job for me and I'll look forward to seeing you again.'

Back in the car, I groaned to myself. Good job! How the hell could that thing stay in without stitches? But I had to do as I was told and Grier, even if he was unpleasant, wasn't a complete fool. Maybe he was right. I put it out of my mind and got on with the other visits.

It was less than a week later at the breakfast table and I was prodding at the inevitable porridge when Grier, who had ventured downstairs, barked suddenly at me.

'I've got a card here frae Adamson. He says he's not satisfied with your work. We'd better get out there this morning and see what's wrong. I dinna like these complaints.' His normal expression of being perpetually offended deepened and the big pale eyes swam and brimmed till I was sure he was going to weep into his porridge.

At the farm, Mr Adamson led us into the byre. 'Well, what do you think of that, young man?'

I looked at the prolapse and my stomach lurched. The innocuous-looking pink projection had been transformed into a great bloated purple mass. It was caked with filth and an ugly wound ran down one side of it.

'It didn't stay in very long, did it?' the farmer said quietly.

I was too ashamed to speak. This was a dreadful thing to do to a good cow. I felt my face reddening, but luckily I had my employer with me: he would be able to explain everything. I turned towards Grier who snuffled, mumbled, blinked his eyes rapidly but didn't say anything.

The farmer went on. 'And you see she's damaged it. Must have caught it on something. I'll tell you I don't like the look of it.'

It was against this decent man's nature to be unpleasant, but he was upset all right. 'Maybe it would be better if you would take the job on this time, Mr Grier,' he said.

Grier, who still had not uttered an intelligible word, now sprang into action. He clipped the hair over the base of the spine, inserted an epidural anaesthetic, washed and disinfected the mass and, with an effort, pushed it back to its place. Then he fastened it in with several strong retention sutures with little one-inch lengths of rubber tubing to stop them cutting into the flesh. The finished job looked neat and workmanlike.

The farmer took me gently by the shoulder. 'Now that's something like. You can see it's not going to come out again now, can't you? Why didn't you do something like that when you came before?'

I turned again to Grier, but this time he was seized by a violent fit of coughing. I continued to stare at him but when he still said nothing I turned and walked out of the byre.

'No hard feelings, though, young man,' Mr Adamson called after me. 'I reckon we've all got to learn and there's no substitute for experience. That's so, Mr Grier, isn't it?'

'Aye, och aye, that's right enough. Aye, aye, rightly so,

rightly so, there's no doubt aboot that,' Grier mumbled. We got into the car.

I settled down and waited for some explanation from him. I was interested to know just what he would say. But the blue-veined nose pointed straight ahead and the bulging eyes fixed themselves blankly on the road ahead of us.

We drove back to the surgery in silence.

Chapter Four

IT WASN'T LONG before Grier had to return to bed; he began to groan a lot and hold his injured ribs and soon he was reinstalled upstairs with the pillows at his back and the little pink jacket buttoned to the neck. Whisky was the only thing that gave him relief from his pain and the level of his bedside bottle went down with remarkable speed.

Life resumed its dreary pattern. Mrs Grier was usually around when I had to report to her husband; beyond the bedroom door there would be a lot of whispering which stopped as soon as I entered. I would receive my instructions while Mrs Grier fussed round the bed tucking things in, patting her husband's brow with a folded handkerchief and all the time darting little glances of dislike at me. Immediately I got outside the door the whispering started again.

It was quite late one evening—about ten o'clock—when the call from Mrs Mallard came in. Her dog had a bone in its throat and would Mr Grier come at once. I was starting to say that he was ill and I was doing his work but it was too late; there was a click as the receiver went down at the other end.

Grier reacted to the news by going into a sort of trance; his chin sank on his chest and he sat immobile for nearly a minute while he gave the matter careful thought. Then he straightened up suddenly and stabbed a finger at me.

'It'll not be a bone in its throat. It'll only be a touch of pharyngitis making it cough.'

I was surprised at his confidence. 'Don't you think I'd better take some long forceps just in case?'

'Na, na, I've told ye now. There'll be no bone, so go down and put up some of the syrup of squills and ipecacuanha mixture. That's all it'll want. And another thing—if ye can't find anything wrong don't say so. Tell the lady it's pharyngitis and how to treat it—you have to justify your visit, ye ken.'

I felt a little bewildered as I filled a four ounce bottle in the dispensary, but I took a few pairs of forceps with me too; I had lost a bit of faith in Grier's long-range diagnosis.

I was surprised when Mrs Mallard opened the door of the smart semi-detached house. For some reason I had been expecting an old lady, and here was a striking-looking blonde woman of about forty with her hair piled high in glamorous layers as was the fashion at that time. And I hadn't expected the long ballroom dress in shimmering green, the enormous swaying earrings, the heavily made up face.

Mrs Mallard seemed surprised too. She stared blankly at me till I explained the position.

'I've come to see your dog—I'm Mr Grier's locum. He's ill at the moment, I'm afraid.'

It took a fair time for the information to get through because she still stood on the doorstep as if she didn't know what I was talking about; then she came to life and opened the door wide. 'Oh yes, of course, I'm sorry, do come in.'

I walked past her through an almost palpable wall of perfume and into a room on the left of the hall. The perfume was even stronger in here but it was in keeping with the single, pink-tinted lamp which shed a dim but rosy light on the wide divan drawn close to the flickering fire. Somewhere in the shadows a radiogram was softly pouring out 'Body and Soul.'

There was no sign of my patient and Mrs Mallard looked at me irresolutely, fingering one of her earrings.

'Do you want me to see him in here?' I asked.

'Oh yes, certainly.'

She became brisk and opened a door at the end of the room. Immediately a little West Highland Terrier bounded across the carpet and hurled himself at me with a woof of delight. He tried his best to lick my face by a series of mighty springs and this might have gone on for quite a long time had I not caught him in mid air.

Mrs Mallard smiled nervously. 'He seems a lot better now,' she said.

I flopped down on the divan still with the little dog in my arms and prised open his jaws. Even in that dim light it was obvious that there was nothing in his throat. I gently slid my forefinger over the back of his tongue and the terrier made no protest as I explored his gullet. Then I dropped him down on the carpet and took his temperature—normal.

'Well, Mrs Mallard,' I said, 'there is certainly no bone in his throat and he has no fever.' I was about to add that the dog seemed perfectly fit to me when I remembered Grier's parting admonition—I had to justify my visit.

I cleared my throat. 'It's just possible that he has a little pharyngitis which has been making him cough or retch.'

I opened the terrier's mouth again. 'As you see, the back of his throat is rather inflamed. He may have got a mild infection in there or perhaps swallowed some irritant. I have some medicine in the car which will soon put him right.' Realizing I was beginning to gabble, I brought my speech to a close.

Mrs Mallard hung on every word, peering anxiously into the little dog's mouth and nodding her head rapidly. 'Oh yes, I do see,' she said. 'Thank you so much. What a good thing I sent for you!'

On the following evening I was half way through a busy surgery when a fat man in a particularly vivid tweed jacket bustled in and deposited a sad-eyed Basset Hound on the table.

'Shaking his head about a bit,' he boomed. 'Think he must have a touch of canker.'

I got an auroscope from the instrument cupboard and had begun to examine the ear when the fat man started again.

'I see you were out our way last night. I live next door to Mrs Mallard.'

'Oh yes,' I said, peering down the lighted metal tube. 'That's right, I was.'

The man drummed his fingers on the table for a moment. 'Aye, that dog must have a lot of ailments. The vet's car seems always to be outside the house.'

'Really, I shouldn't have thought so. Seemed a healthy little thing to me.' I finished examining one ear and started on the other.

'Well, it's just as I say,' said the man. 'The poor creature's always in trouble, and it's funny how often it happens at night.'

I looked up quickly. There was something odd in the way he said that.

He looked at me for a moment with a kind of wide-eyed innocence, then his whole face creased into a knowing leer.

I stared at him, 'You can't mean . . .'

'Not with that ugly old devil, you mean, eh? Takes a bit of reckoning up, doesn't it?' The eyes in the big red face twinkled with amusement.

I dropped my auroscope on the table with a clatter and my arms fell by my sides.

'Don't look like that, lad!' shouted the fat man, giving me a playful punch in the chest. 'It's a rum old world, you know!'

But it wasn't just the thought of Grier that was filling me with horror; it was the picture of myself in that harem atmosphere pontificating about pharyngitis against a background of 'Body and Soul' to a woman who knew I was talking rubbish.

In another two days Angus Grier was out of bed and had apparently recovered; also, a replacement assistant had been engaged and was due to take up his post immediately. I was free to go.

Having said I would leave first thing in the morning I was out of the house by 6.30 a.m. in order to make Darrowby by breakfast. I wasn't going to face any more of that porridge.

As I drove west across the Plain of York I began to catch glimpses over the hedge tops and between the trees of the long spine of the Pennines lifting into the morning sky; they were pale violet at this distance and still hazy in the early sunshine but they beckoned to me.

And later, when the little car pulled harder against the rising ground and the trees became fewer and the hedges gave way to the clean limestone walls I had the feeling I always had of the world opening out, of shackles falling away. And there, at last, was Darrowby sleeping under the familiar bulk of Herne Fell and beyond, the great green folds of the Dales.

Nothing stirred as I rattled across the cobbled market place then down the quiet street to Skeldale House with the ivy hanging in untidy profusion from its old bricks and 'Siegfried Farnon M.R.C.V.S.' on the lopsided brass plate.

I think I would have galloped along the passage beyond the glass door but I had to fight my way through the family dogs, all five of them, who surged around me, leaping and barking in delight.

I almost collided with the formidable bulk of Mrs Hall who was carrying the coffee-pot out of the dining-room. 'You're back then,' she said and I could see she was really pleased because she almost smiled. 'Well, go in and get sat down. I've got a bit of home-cured in the pan for you.'

My hand was on the door when I heard the brothers' voices inside. Tristan was mumbling something and Siegfried was in full cry.

'Where the hell were you last night, anyway? I heard you banging about at three o'clock in the morning and your room stinks like a brewery. God, I wish you could see yourself—eyes like piss-holes in the snow!'

Smiling to myself, I pushed open the door. I went over to Tristan who stared up in surprise as I seized his hand and began to pump it; he looked as boyishly innocent as ever except for the eyes which, though a little sunken, still held their old gleam. Then I approached Siegfried at the head of the table. Obviously startled at my formal entry, he had choked in mid-chew; he reddened, tears coursed down his thin cheeks and the small sandy moustache quivered. Nevertheless, he rose from his chair, inclined his head and extended his hand with the grace of a marquis.

'Welcome, James,' he spluttered, spraying me lightly with toast crumbs. 'Welcome home.'

Chapter Five

I HAD BEEN AWAY for ony two weeks but it was enough to
bring it home to me afresh that working in the high country
had something for me that was missing elsewhere. My first
visit took me up on one of the narrow, unfenced roads which
join Sildale and Cosdale and when I had ground my way to
the top in bottom gear I did what I so often did—pulled the
car on to the roadside turf and got out.

That quotation about not having time to stand and stare
has never applied to me. I seem to have spent a good part of
my life—probably too much—in just standing and staring
and I was at it again this morning. From up here you could
see away over the Plain of York to the sprawl of the Hamble-
ton Hills forty miles to the east, while behind me, the ragged
miles of moorland rolled away, dipping and rising over the
flat fell-top. In my year at Darrowby I must have stood here
scores of times and the view across the plain always looked
different; sometimes in the winter the low country was a dark
trough between the snow-covered Pennines and the distant
white gleam of the Hambletons, and in April the rain squalls
drifted in slow, heavy veils across the great green and brown
dappled expanse. There was a day, too, when I stood in
brilliant sunshine looking down over miles of thick fog like
a rippling layer of cotton wool with dark tufts of trees and
hilltops pushing through here and there.

But today the endless patchwork of fields slumbered in the
sun, and the air, even on the hill, was heavy with the scents
of summer. There must be people working among the farms
down there, I knew, but I couldn't see a living soul; and the

peace which I always found in the silence and the emptiness of the moors filled me utterly.

At these times I often seemed to stand outside myself, calmly assessing my progress. It was easy to flick back over the years—right back to the time I had decided to become a veterinary surgeon. I could remember the very moment. I was thirteen and I was reading an article about careers for boys in the Meccano Magazine and as I read, I felt a surging conviction that this was for me. And yet what was it based upon? Only that I liked dogs and cats and didn't care much for the idea of an office life; it seemed a frail basis on which to build a career. I knew nothing about agriculture or about farm animals, and though, during the years in college, I learned about these things I could see only one future for myself; I was going to be a small animal surgeon. This lasted right up to the time I qualified—a kind of vision of treating people's pets in my own animal hospital where everything would be not just modern but revolutionary. The fully equipped operating theatre, laboratory and X-ray room; they had all stayed crystal clear in my mind until I had graduated M.R.C.V.S.

How on earth, then, did I come to be sitting on a high Yorkshire moor in shirt sleeves and wellingtons, smelling vaguely of cows?

The change in my outlook had come quite quickly—in fact almost immediately after my arrival in Darrowby. The job had been a godsend in those days of high unemployment, but only, I had thought, a stepping-stone to my real ambition. But everything had switched round, almost in a flash.

Maybe it was something to do with the incredible sweetness of the air which still took me by surprise when I stepped out into the old wild garden at Skeldale House every morning. Or perhaps the daily piquancy of life in the graceful old house with my gifted but mercurial boss, Siegfried, and his reluctant student brother, Tristan. Or it could be that it was just the realization that treating cows and pigs and sheep and horses had a fascination I had never even suspected; and this brought with it a new concept of myself as a tiny wheel in the great machine of British agriculture. There was a kind of solid satisfaction in that.

Probably it was because I hadn't dreamed there was a place like the Dales. I hadn't thought it possible that I could spend all my days in a high, clean-blown land where the scent of grass or trees was never far away; and where even in the driving rain of winter I could snuff the air and find the freshness of growing things hidden somewhere in the cold clasp of the wind.

Anyway, it had all changed for me and my work consisted now of driving from farm to farm across the roof of England with a growing conviction that I was a privileged person.

I got back into the car and looked at my list of visits; it was good to be back and the day passed quickly. It was about seven o'clock in the evening, when I thought I had finished, that I had a call from Terry Watson, a young farm worker who kept two cows of his own. One of them, he said, had summer mastitis. Mid-July was a bit early for this but in the later summer months we saw literally hundreds of these cases; in fact a lot of the farmers called it 'August Bag'. It was an unpleasant condition because it was just about incurable and usually resulted in the cow losing a quarter (the area of the udder which supplies each teat with milk) and sometimes even her life.

Terry Watson's cow looked very sick. She had limped in from the field at milking time, swinging her right hind leg wide to keep it away from the painful udder, and now she stood trembling in her stall, her eyes staring anxiously in front of her. I drew gently at the affected teat and, instead of milk, a stream of dark, foul-smelling serum spurted into the tin can I was holding.

'No mistaking that stink, Terry,' I said. 'It's the real summer type all right.' I felt my way over the hot, swollen quarter and the cow lifted her leg quickly as I touched the tender tissue. 'Pretty hard, too. It looks bad, I'm afraid.'

Terry's face was grim as he ran his hand along the cow's

back. He was in his early twenties, had a wife and a small baby and was one of the breed who was prepared to labour all day for somebody else and then come home and start work on his own few stock. His two cows, his few pigs and hens made a big difference to somebody who had to live on thirty shillings a week.

'Ah can't understand it,' he muttered. 'It's usually dry cows that get it and this 'un's still giving two gallons a day. I'd have been on with tar if only she'd been dry.' (The farmers used to dab the teats of the dry cows with Stockholm tar to keep off the flies blamed for carrying the infection.)

'No, I'm afraid all cows can get it, especially the ones that are beginning to dry off.' I pulled the thermometer from the rectum—it said a hundred and six.

'What's going to happen, then? Can you do owt for her?'

'I'll do what I can, Terry. I'll give her an injection and you must strip the teat out as often as you can, but you know as well as I do that it's a poor outlook with these jobs.'

'Aye, ah know all about it.' He watched me gloomily as I injected the Coryne pyogenes toxoid into the cow's neck. (Even now we are still doing this for summer mastitis because it is a sad fact none of the modern range of antibiotics has much effect on it.) 'She'll lose her quarter, won't she, and maybe she'll even peg out?'

I tried to be cheerful. 'Well, I don't think she'll die, and even if the quarter goes she'll make it up on the other three.' But there was the feeling of helplessness I always had when I could do little about something which mattered a great deal. Because I knew what a blow this was to the young man; a three-teated cow has lost a lot of her market value and this was about the best outcome I could see. I didn't like to think about the possibility of the animal dying.

'Look, is there nowt at all I can do myself? Is the job a bad 'un do you think?' Terry Watson's thin cheeks were pale and as I looked at the slender figure with the slightly stooping shoulders I thought, not for the first time, that he didn't look robust enough for his hard trade.

'I can't guarantee anything,' I said. 'But the cases that do best are the ones that get the most stripping. So work away at it this evening—every half hour if you can manage it. That rubbish in her quarter can't do any harm if you draw it out as soon as it is formed. And I think you ought to bathe the udder with warm water and massage it well.'

'What'll I rub it with?'

'Oh, it doesn't matter what you use. The main thing is to move the tissue about so that you can get more of that stinking stuff out. Vaseline would do nicely.'

'Ah've got a bowl of goose grease.'

'O.K. use that.' I reflected that there must be a bowl of goose grease on most farms; it was the all-purpose lubricant and liniment for man and beast.

Terry seemed relieved at the opportunity to do something. He fished out an old bucket, tucked the milking stool between his legs and crouched down against the cow. He looked up at me with a strangely defiant expression. 'Right,' he said. 'I'm startin' now.'

As it happened, I was called out early the next morning to a milk fever and on the way home I decided to look in at the Watsons' cottage. It was about eight o'clock and when I entered the little two-stall shed, Terry was in the same position as I had left him on the previous night. He was pulling at the infected teat, eyes closed, cheek resting against the cow's flank. He started as though roused from sleep when I spoke.

'Hello, you're having another go, I see.'

The cow looked round, too, at my words and I saw immediately, with a thrill of pleasure that she was immeasurably improved. She had lost her blank stare and was looking at me with the casual interest of the healthy bovine and best of all, her jaws were moving with that slow, regular, lateral grind that every vet loves to see.

'My God, Terry, she looks a lot better. She isn't like the same cow!'

The young man seemed to have difficulty in keeping his

39

eyes open but he smiled. 'Aye, and come and have a look at this end.' He rose slowly from the stool, straightened his back a little bit at a time and leaned his elbow on the cow's rump.

I bent down by the udder, feeling carefully for the painful swelling of last night, but my hand came up against a smooth, yielding surface and, in disbelief, I kneaded the tissue between my fingers. The animal showed no sign of discomfort. With a feeling of bewilderment I drew on the teat with thumb and forefinger; the quarter was nearly empty but I did manage to squeeze a single jet of pure white milk on to my palm.

'What's going on here, Terry? You must have switched cows on me. You're having me on, aren't you?'

'Nay, guvnor,' the young man said with his slow smile. 'It's same cow all right—she's better, that's all.'

'But it's impossible! What the devil have you done to her?'

'Just what you told me to do. Rub and strip.'

I scratched my head. 'But she's back to normal. I've never seen anything like it.'

'Aye, I know you haven't.' It was a woman's voice and I turned and saw young Mrs Watson standing at the door holding her baby. 'You've never seen a man that would rub and strip a cow right round the clock, have you?'

'Round the clock?' I said.

She looked at her husband with a mixture of concern and exasperation. 'Yes, he's been there on that stool since you left last night. Never been to bed, never been in for a meal. I've been bringing him bits and pieces and cups of tea. Great fool —it's enough to kill anybody.'

I looked at Terry and my eyes moved from the pallid face over the thin, slightly swaying body to the nearly empty bowl of goose grease at his feet. 'Good Lord, man,' I said. 'You've done the impossible but you must be about all in. Anyway, your cow is as good as new—you don't need to do another thing to her, so you can go in and have a bit of rest.'

'Nay, I can't do that.' He shook his head and straightened his shoulders. 'I've got me work to go to and I'm late as it is.'

Chapter Six

I COULDN'T HELP FEELING just a little bit smug as I squeezed the bright red rubber ball out through the incision in the dog's stomach. We got enough small animal work in Darrowby to make a pleasant break from our normal life around the farms but not enough to make us blasé. No doubt the man with an intensive town practice looks on a gastrotomy as a fairly routine and unexciting event but as I watched the little red ball roll along the table and bounce on the surgery floor a glow of achievement filled me.

The big, lolloping Red Setter pup had been brought in that morning; his mistress said that he had been trembling, miserable and occasionally vomiting for two days—ever since their little girl's ball had mysteriously disappeared. Diagnosis had not been difficult.

I inverted the lips of the stomach wound and began to close it with a continuous suture. I was feeling pleasantly relaxed unlike Tristan who had been unable to light a Woodbine because of the ether which bubbled in the glass bottle behind him and out through the anaesthetic mask which he held over the dog's face; he stared moodily down at the patient and the fingers of his free hand drummed on the table.

But it was soon my turn to be tense because the door of the operating room burst open and Siegfried strode in. I don't know why it was but whenever Siegfried watched me do anything I started to go to pieces; great waves seemed to billow from him—impatience, frustration, criticism, irritation. I could feel the waves buffeting me now although my employer's face was expressionless, he was standing quietly at the end of the table but as the minutes passed I had the growing impression of a volcano on the bubble. The eruption came when I began to stitch the deep layer of the abdominal muscle. I was pulling a length of catgut from a glass jar when I heard a sharp intake of breath.

'God help us, James!' cried Siegfried. 'Stop pulling at that bloody gut! Do you know how much that stuff costs per foot? Well it's a good job you don't or you'd faint dead away. And that expensive dusting powder you've been chucking about—there must be about half a pound of it inside that dog right now.' He paused and breathed heavily for a few moments. 'Another thing, if you want to swab, a little bit of cotton wool is enough—you don't need a square foot at a time like you've been using. Here, give me that needle. Let me show you.'

He hastily scrubbed his hands and took over. First he took a minute pinch of the iodoform powder and sprinkled it daintily into the wound rather like an old lady feeding her goldfish, then he cut off a tiny piece of gut and inserted a continuous suture in the muscle; he had hardly left himself enough to tie the knot at the end and it was touch and go, but he just made it after moments of intense concentration.

This process was repeated about ten times as he closed the skin wound with interrupted silk sutures, his nose almost touching the patient as he laboriously tied off each little short end with forceps.

When he had finished he was slightly pop-eyed.

'Right, turn off the ether, Tristan,' he said as he pulled off half an inch of wool and primly wiped the wound down.

He turned to me and smiled gently. With dismay I saw that his patient look was spreading over his face.

'James, please don't misunderstand me. You've made a grand job of this dog but you've got to keep one eye on the economic side of things. I know it doesn't matter a hoot to you just now but some day, no doubt, you'll have your own practice and then you'll realize some of the worries I have on my shoulders.' He patted my arm and I steeled myself as he

42

put his head on one side and a hint of roguishness crept into his smile.

'After all, James, you'll agree it is desirable to make some sort of profit in the end.'

It was a week later and I was kneeling on the neck of a sleeping colt in the middle of a field, the sun was hot on the back of my neck as I looked down at the peacefully closed eyes, the narrow face disappearing into the canvas chloroform muzzle. I tipped a few more drops of the anaesthetic on to the sponge and screwed the cap on to the bottle. He had had about enough now.

I couldn't count the number of times Siegfried and I have enacted this scene; the horse on his grassy bed, my employer cutting away at one end while I watched the head. Siegfried was a unique combination of born horseman and dexterous surgeon with which I couldn't compete, so I had inevitably developed into an anaesthetist. We liked to do the operations in the open; it was cleaner and if the horse was wild he stood less chance of injuring himself. We just hoped for a fine morning and today we were lucky. In the early haze I looked over the countless buttercups; the field was filled with them and it was like sitting in a shimmering yellow ocean. Their pollen had powdered my shoes and the neck of the horse beneath me.

Everything had gone off more or less as it usually did. I had gone into the box with the colt, buckled on the muzzle underneath his head collar then walked him quietly out to a soft, level spot in the field. I left a man at the head holding a long shank on the head collar and poured the first half ounce of chloroform on to the sponge, watching the colt snuffling and shaking his head at the strange scent. As the man walked him slowly round I kept adding a little more chloroform till the colt began to stagger and sway; this stage always took a few minutes and I waited confidently for Siegfried's little speech which always came about now. I was not disappointed.

43

'He isn't going to go down, you know, James. Don't you think we should tie a foreleg up?'

I adopted my usual policy of feigning deafness and a few seconds later the colt gave a final lurch and collapsed on his side. Siegfried, released from his enforced inactivity, sprang into action. 'Sit on his head!' he yelled. 'Get a rope on that upper hind leg and pull it forward! Bring me that bucket of water over here! Come on—move!'

It was a violent transition. Just moments ago, peace and silence and now men scurrying in all directions, bumping into each other, urged on by Siegfried's cries.

Thirty years later I am still dropping horses for Siegfried and he is still saying 'He isn't going to go down, James'.

These days I mostly use an intravenous injection of Thiopentone and it puts a horse out in about ten seconds. It doesn't give Siegfried much time to say his piece but he usually gets it in somewhere between the seventh and tenth seconds.

This morning's case was an injury. But it was a pretty dramatic one, justifying general anaesthetic to repair it. The colt, bred from a fine hunter mare, had been galloping round his paddock and had felt the urge to visit the outside world. He had chosen the only sharp fence post to try to jump over and had been impaled between the forelegs; in his efforts to escape he had caused so much damage in the breast region that it looked like something from a butcher's shop with the skin extensively lacerated and the big sternal muscles hanging out, chopped through as though by a cleaver.

'Roll him on his back,' said Siegfried. 'That's better.' He took a probe from the tray which lay on the grass near by and carefully explored the wound. 'No damage to the bone,' he grunted, still peering into the depths. Then he took a pair of forceps and fished out all the loose debris he could find before turning to me.

'It's just a big stitching job. You can carry on if you like.'

As we changed places it occurred to me that he was disappointed it was not something more interesting. I couldn't see him asking me to take over in a rig operation or something like that. Then, as I picked up the needle, my mind clicked back to that gastrotomy on the dog. Maybe I was on trial for my wasteful ways. This time I would be on my guard.

I threaded the needle with a minute length of gut, took a bite at the severed muscle and, with an effort, stitched it back into place. But it was a laborious business tying the little short ends—it was taking me at least three times as long as it should. However, I stuck to it doggedly. I had been warned and I didn't want another lecture.

I had put in half a dozen sutures in this way when I began to feel the waves. My employer was kneeling close to me on the horse's neck and the foaming breakers of disapproval were crashing into me from close range.

I held out for another two sutures then Siegfried exploded in a fierce whisper.

'What the hell are you playing at, James?'

'Well, just stitching. What do you mean?'

'But why are you buggering about with those little bits of gut? We'll be here all bloody day!'

I fumbled another knot into the muscle. 'For reasons of economy.' I whispered back virtuously.

Siegfried leaped from the neck as though the horse had bitten him.

'I can't stand any more of this! Here, let me have a go.'

He strode over to the tray, selected a needle and caught hold of the free end of the catgut protruding from the jar. With a scything sweep of his arm he pulled forth an enormous coil of gut, setting the bobbin inside the jar whirring wildly like a salmon reel with a big fish on the line. He returned to the horse, stumbling slightly as the gut caught round his ankles, and began to stitch. It wasn't easy because even at the full stretch of his arm he was unable to pull the suture tight and had to keep getting up and down; by the time he had tacked the muscles back into their original positions he was puffing and I could see a faint dew of perspiration on his forehead.

'Drop of blood seeping from somewhere down there.' he muttered and visited the tray again where he tore savagely at a huge roll of cotton wool. Trailing untidy white streamers over the buttercups he returned and swabbed out the wound with one corner of the mass.

Back to the tray again. 'Just a touch of powder before I stitch the skin,' he said lightly and seized a two pound carton. He poised for a moment over the wound then began to dispense the powder with extravagant jerks of the wrist. A considerable amount did go into the wound but much more floated over other parts of the horse, over me, over the buttercups, and one particularly wayward flick obscured the sweating face of the man on the foot rope. When he had finished coughing he looked very like Coco the clown.

Siegfried completed the closure of tne skin, using several yards of silk, and when he stood back and surveyed the tidy result I could see he was in excellent humour.

'Well now, that's fine. A young horse like that will heal in no time. Shouldn't be surprised if it doesn't even leave a mark.'

He came over and addressed me as I washed the instruments in the bucket. 'Sorry I pushed you out like that, James, but honestly I couldn't think what had come over you—you were like an old hen. You know it looks bad trying to work with piddling little amounts of materials. One has to operate with a certain . . . well . . . panache, if I can put it that way, and you just can't do that if you stint yourself.'

I finished washing the instruments, dried them off and laid them on the enamel tray. Then I lifted the tray and set off for the gate at the end of the field. Siegfried, walking alongside me, laid his hand on my shoulder. 'Mind you, don't think I'm blaming you, James. It's probably your Scottish upbringing. And don't misunderstand me, this same upbringing has inculcated in you so many of the qualities I admire— integrity, industry, loyalty. But I'm sure you will be the first to admit,' and here he stopped and wagged a finger at me 'that you Scots sometimes overdo the thrift.' He gave a light laugh. 'So remember, James, don't be too—er—canny when you are operating.'

I measured him up. If I dropped the tray quickly I felt sure I could fell him with a right hook.

Siegfried went on. 'But I know I don't have to ramble on at you, James. You always pay attention to what I say, don't you?'

I tucked the tray under my arm and set off again. 'Yes,' I replied. 'I do. Every single time.'

Chapter Seven

'I CAN SEE YOU LIKE PIGS,' said Mr Worley as I edged my way into the pen.

'You can?'

'Oh yes, I can always tell. As soon as you went in there nice and quiet and scratched Queenie's back and spoke to her I said "There's a young man as likes pigs".'

'Oh good. Well, as a matter of fact you're absolutely right. I do like pigs.' I had, in truth, been creeping very cautiously past Queenie, wondering just how she was going to react. She was a huge animal and sows with litters can be very hostile to strangers. When I had come into the building she had got up from where she was suckling her piglets and eyed me with a non-committal grunt, reminding me of the number of times I had left a pig pen a lot quicker than I had gone in. A big, barking, gaping-mouthed sow has always been able to make me move very smartly.

Now that I was right inside the narrow pen, Queenie seemed to have accepted me. She grunted again, but peaceably, then carefully collapsed on the straw and exposed her udder to the eager little mouths. When she was in this position I was able to examine her foot.

'Aye, that's the one,' Mr Worley said anxiously. 'She could hardly hobble when she got up this morning.'

There didn't seem to be much wrong. A flap of the horn of one claw was a bit overgrown and was rubbing on the sensitive sole, but we didn't usually get called out for little things like that. I cut away the overgrown part and dressed the sore place with our multi-purpose ointment, ung. *pini sedativum,* while all the time Mr Worley knelt by Queenie's head and patted her and sort of crooned into her ear. I couldn't make out the words he used—maybe it was pig language because the sow really seemed to be answering him with little soft grunts. Anyway, it worked better than an anaesthetic and everybody was happy including the long row of piglets working busily at the double line of teats.

'Right, Mr Worley.' I straightened up and handed him the jar of ung. *pini.* 'Keep rubbing in a little of that twice a day and I think she'll be sound in no time.'

'Thank ye, thank ye, I'm very grateful.' He shook my hand vigorously as though I had saved the animal's life. 'I'm very glad to meet you for the first time, Mr Herriot. I've known Mr Farnon for a year or two, of course, and I think a bit about him. Loves pigs does that man, loves them. And his young brother's been here once or twice—I reckon he's fond of pigs, too.'

'Devoted to them, Mr Worley.'

'Ah yes, I thought so. I can always tell.' He regarded me for a while with a moist eye, then smiled, well satisfied.

We went out into what was really the back yard of an inn. Because Mr Worley wasn't a regular farmer, he was the landlord of the Langthorpe Falls Hotel and his precious livestock were crammed into what had once been the stables and coach houses of the inn. They were all Tamworths and whichever door you opened you found yourself staring into the eyes of ginger-haired pigs; there were a few porkers and the odd one being fattened for bacon but Mr Worley's pride was his sows. He had six of them—Queenie, Princess, Ruby, Marigold, Delilah and Primrose.

For years expert farmers had been assuring Mr Worley that he'd never do any good with his sows. If you were going in for breeding, they said, you had to have proper premises; it wasn't a bit of use shoving sows into converted buildings like his. And for years Mr Worley's sows had responded by producing litters of unprecedented size and raising them with tender care. They were all good mothers and didn't savage their families or crush them clumsily under their bodies so it turned out with uncanny regularity that at the end of eight weeks Mr Worley had around twelve chunky weaners to take to market.

It must have spoiled the farmers' beer—none of them could equal that, and the pill was all the more bitter because the landlord had come from the industrial West Riding—Halifax, I think it was—a frail, short-sighted little retired newsagent with no agricultural background. By all the laws he just didn't have a chance.

Leaving the yard we came on to the quiet loop of road where my car was parked. Just beyond, the road dipped steeply into a tree-lined ravine where the Darrow hurled itself over a great broken shelf of rock in its passage to the lower Dale. I couldn't see down there from where I was standing, but I could hear the faint roar of the water and could picture the black cliff lifting sheer from the boiling river and on the other bank the gentle slope of turf where people from the towns came to sit and look in wonder.

Some of them were here now. A big, shiny car had drawn up and its occupants were disembarking. The driver, sleek, fat and impressive, strolled towards us and called out: 'We would like some tea.'

Mr Worley swung round on him. 'And you can 'ave some, maister, but when I'm ready. I have some very important business with this gentleman.' He turned his back on the man and began to ask me for final instructions about Queenie's foot.

The man was obviously taken aback and I couldn't blame him. It seemed to me that Mr Worley might have shown a little more tact—after all serving food and drink was his living—but as I came to know him better I realized that his pigs came first and everything else was an irritating intrusion.

Knowing Mr Worley better had its rewards. The time when I feel most like a glass of beer is not in the evening when the pubs are open but at around four-thirty on a hot afternoon after wrestling with young cattle in some stifling cow-shed. It was delightful to retire, sweating and weary, to the shaded sanctuary of Mr Worley's back kitchen and sip at the bitter ale, cool, frothing, straight from the cellar below.

The smooth working of the system was facilitated by the attitude of the local constable, P.C. Dalloway, a man whose benign disposition and elastic interpretation of the licensing laws had made him deeply respected in the district. Occasionally he joined us, took off his uniform jacket and, in shirt and braces, consumed a pint with a massive dignity which was peculiar to him.

But mostly Mr Worley and I were on our own and when he had brought the tall jug up from the cellar he would sit down and say 'Well now, let's have a piggy talk!' His use of this particular phrase made me wonder if perhaps he had some humorous insight into his obsessive preoccupation with the porcine species. Maybe he had but for all that our conversations seemed to give him the deepest pleasure.

We talked about erysipelas and swine fever, brine poisoning and paratyphoid, the relative merits of dry and wet mash, while pictures of his peerless sows with their show rosettes looked down at us from the walls.

On one occasion, in the middle of a particularly profound discussion on the ventilation of farrowing houses Mr Worley stopped suddenly and, blinking rapidly behind his thick spectacles, burst out:

'You know, Mr Herriot, sitting here talking like this with you, I'm 'appy as king of England!'

His devotion resulted in my being called out frequently for very trivial things and I swore freely under my breath when I heard his voice on the other end of the line at one o'clock one morning.

'Marigold pigged this afternoon, Mr Herriot, and I don't think she's got much milk. Little pigs look very hungry to me. Will you come?'

I groaned my way out of bed and downstairs and through the long garden to the yard. By the time I had got the car out into the lane I had begun to wake up and when I rolled up to the inn was able to greet Mr Worley fairly cheerfully.

But the poor man did not respond. In the light from the oil lamp his face was haggard with worry.

'I hope you can do something quick. I'm real upset about her—she's just laid there doing nothin' and it's such a lovely litter. Fourteen she's had.'

I could understand his concern as I looked into the pen. Marigold was stretched motionless on her side while the tiny piglets swarmed around her udder; they were rushing from teat to teat, squealing and falling over each other in their desperate quest for nourishment. And the little bodies had the narrow, empty look which meant they had nothing in their stomachs. I hated to see a litter die off from sheer starvation but it could happen so easily. There came a time when they stopped trying to suck and began to lie about the pen. After that it was hopeless.

Crouching behind the sow with my thermometer in her rectum I looked along the swelling flank, the hair a rich copper red in the light from the lamp. 'Did she eat anything tonight?'

'Aye, cleaned up just as usual.'

The thermometer reading was normal. I began to run my hands along the udder, pulling in turn at the teats. The ravenous piglets caught at my fingers with their sharp teeth as I pushed them to one side but my efforts failed to produce a drop of milk. The udder seemed full, even engorged, but I was unable to get even a bead down to the end of the teat.

'There's nowt there, is there?' Mr Worley whispered anxiously.

I straightened up and turned to him. 'This is simply agalactia. There's no mastitis and Marigold isn't really ill, but there's something interfering with the let-down mechanism of the milk. She's got plenty of milk and there's an injection which ought to bring it down.'

I tried to keep the triumphant look off my face as I spoke, because this was one of my favourite party tricks. There is a flavour of magic in the injection of pituitrin in these cases; it works within a minute and though no skill is required the effect is spectacular.

Marigold didn't complain as I plunged in the needle and administered 3 c.c. deep into the muscle of her thigh. She was too busy conversing with her owner—they were almost nose to nose, exchanging soft pig noises.

After I had put away the syringe and listened for a few moments to the cooing sounds from the front end I thought it might be time. Mr Worley looked up in surprise as I reached down again to the udder.

'What are you doing now?'

'Having a feel to see if the milk's come down yet.'

'Why damn, it can't be! You've only just given t'stuff and she's bone dry!'

Oh, this was going to be good. A roll of drums would be appropriate at this moment. With finger and thumb I took hold of one of the teats at the turgid back end of the udder. I suppose it is a streak of exhibitionism in me which always makes me send the jet of milk spraying against the opposite wall in these circumstances; this time I thought it would be more impressive if I directed my shot past the innkeeper's left ear, but I got my trajectory wrong and sprinkled his spectacles instead.

He took them off and wiped them slowly as if he couldn't believe what he had seen. Then he bent over and tried for himself.

'It's a miracle!' he cried as the milk spouted eagerly over his hand. 'I've never seen owt like it!'

It didn't take the little pigs long to catch on. Within a few seconds they had stopped their fighting and squealing and settled down in a long, silent row. Their utterly rapt expressions all told the same stcry—they were going to make up for lost time.

I went into the kitchen to wash my hands and was using the towel hanging behind the door when I noticed something odd; there was a subdued hum of conversation, the low rumble of many voices. It seemed unusual in a pub at 2 a.m. and I looked through the partly open door into the bar. The place was crowded. In the light of a single weak electric bulb I could see a row of men drinking at the counter while others sat behind foaming pint pots on the wooden settles against the walls.

Mr Worley grinned as I turned to him in surprise.

'Didn't expect to see this lot, did you? Well, I'll tell you, the real drinkers don't come in till after closing time. Aye, it's a rum 'un—every night I lock front door and these lads come in the back.'

I pushed my head round the door for another look. It was a kind of rogue's gallery of Darrowby. All the dubious characters in the town seemed to be gathered in that room; the names which regularly enlivened the columns of the weekly newspaper with their activities. Drunk and disorderly, non-payment of rates, wife-beating, assault and battery—I could almost see the headings as I went from face to face.

I had been spotted. Beery cries of welcome rang out and I was suddenly conscious that all eyes were fixed on me in the smoky atmosphere. Above the rest a voice said 'Are you going to have a drink?' What I wanted most was to get back to my bed, but it wouldn't look so good just to close the door and go. I went inside and over to the bar. I seemed to have plenty of friends there and within seconds was in the centre of a merry group with a pint glass in my hand.

My nearest neighbour was a well-known Darrowby worthy called Gobber Newhouse, an enormously fat man who had always seemed able to get through life without working at all. He occupied his time with drinking, brawling and gambling. At the moment he was in a mellow mood and his huge, sweating face, pushed close to mine, was twisted into a comradely leer.

'Nah then, Herriot, ow's dog trade?' he enquired courteously.

I had never heard my profession described in this way and was wondering how to answer when I noticed that the company were looking at me expectantly. Mr Worley's niece who served behind the bar was looking at me expectantly too.

'Six pints of best bitter—six shillings please,' she said. clarifying the situation.

I fumbled the money from my pocket. Obviously my first impression that somebody had invited me to have a drink with them had been mistaken. Looking round the faces, there was no way of telling who had called out, and as the beer disappeared, the group round the bar thinned out like magic; the members just drifted away as though by accident till I found myself alone. I was no longer an object of interest and nobody paid any attention as I drained my glass and left.

The glow from the pig pen showed through the darkness of the yard and as I crossed over, the soft rumble of pig and human voices told me that Mr Worley was still talking things over with his sow. He looked up as I came in and his face in the dim light was ecstatic.

'Mr Herriot,' he whispered. 'Isn't that a beautiful sight?'

He pointed to the little pigs who were lying motionless in a layered heap, sprawled over each other without plan or pattern, eyes tightly closed, stomachs bloated with Marigold's bountiful fluid.

'It is indeed,' I said, prodding the sleeping mass with my finger but getting no response beyond the lazy opening of an eye. 'You'd have to go a long way to beat it.'

And I did share his pleasure; it was one of the satisfying little jobs. Climbing into the car I felt that the nocturnal visit had been worth while even though I had been effortlessly duped into buying a round with no hope of reciprocation. Not that I wanted to drink any more—my stomach wasn't used to receiving pints of ale at 2 a.m. and a few whimpers of surprise and indignation were already coming up—but I was just a bit ruffled by the offhand, professional way those gentlemen in the tap room had handled me.

But, winding my way home through the empty, moonlit

roads, I was unaware that the hand of retribution was hovering over that happy band. This was, in fact, a fateful night, because ten minutes after I had left, Mr Worley's pub was raided. Perhaps that is a rather dramatic word, but it happened that it was the constable's annual holiday and the relief man, a young policeman who did not share Mr Dalloway's liberal views, had come up on his bicycle and pinched everybody in the place.

The account of the court proceedings in the *Darrowby and Houlton Times* made good reading. Gobber Newhouse and company were all fined £2 each and warned as to their future conduct. The magistrates, obviously a heartless lot, had remained unmoved by Gobber's passionate protestations that the beer in the glasses had all been purchased before closing time and that he and his friends had been lingering over it in light conversation for the subsequent four hours.

Mr Worley was fined £15 but I don't think he really minded; Marigold and her litter were doing well.

Chapter Eight

THIS WAS THE LAST GATE. I got out to open it since
Tristan was driving, and looked back at the farm, a long way
below us now, and at the marks our tyres had made on the
steep, grassy slopes. Strange places, some of these Dales farms;
this one had no road to it—not even a track. From down
there you just drove across the fields from gate to gate till
you got to the main road above the valley. And this was the
last one; ten minutes' driving and we'd be home.

Tristan was acting as my chauffeur, as my left hand had
been infected after a bad calving and I had my arm in a sling.
He didn't drive up through the gate but got out of the car,
leaned his back against the gate post and lit a Woodbine.

Obviously he wasn't in any rush to leave. And with the sun
warm on the back of his neck and the two bottles of Whit-
bread's nestling comfortably in his stomach I could divine
that he felt pretty good. Come to think of it, it had been all
right back there. He had taken some warts off a heifer's teats
and the farmer had said he shaped well for a young 'un,
('Aye, you really framed at t'job, lad') and asked us in for a
bottle of beer since it was so hot. Impressed by the ecstatic
speed with which Tristan had consumed his, he had given
him another.

Yes, it had been all right, and I could see Tristan thought
so too. With a smile of utter content he took a long, deep
gulp of moorland air and Woodbine smoke and closed his
eyes.

He opened them quickly as a grinding noise came from
the car. 'Christ! She's off, Jim!' he shouted.

57

The little Austin was moving gently backwards down the slope—it must have slipped out of gear and it had no brakes to speak of. We both leaped after it. Tristan was nearest and he just managed to touch the bonnet with one finger; the speed was too much for him. We gave it up and watched.

The hillside was steep and the little car rapidly gathered momentum, bouncing crazily over the uneven ground. I glanced at Tristan; his mind invariably worked quickly and clearly in a crisis and I had a good idea what he was thinking. It was only a fortnight since he had turned the Hillman over, taking a girl home from a dance. It had been a complete write-off and the insurance people had been rather nasty about it; and of course Siegfried had gone nearly berserk and had finished by sacking him finally, once and for all—never wanted to see his face in the place again.

But he had been sacked so often; he knew he had only to keep out of his way for a bit and his brother would forget. And he had been lucky this time because Siegfried had talked his bank manager into letting him buy a beautiful new Rover and this had blotted everything else from his mind.

It was distinctly unfortunate that this should happen when he, as driver, was technically in charge of the Austin. The car appeared now to be doing about 70 m.p.h. hurtling terrifyingly down the long, green hill. One by one the doors burst open till all four flapped wildly and the car swooped downwards looking like a huge, ungainly bird.

From the open doors, bottles, instruments, bandages, cotton wool cascaded out on to the turf, leaving a long, broken trail. Now and again a packet of nux vomica and bicarb stomach powder would fly out and burst like a bomb, splashing vivid white against the green.

Tristan threw up his arms. 'Look! The bloody thing's going straight for that hut.' He drew harder on his Woodbine.

There was indeed only one obstruction on the bare hillside—a small building near the foot where the land levelled out and the Austin, as if drawn by a magnet, was thundering straight towards it.

I couldn't bear to watch. Just before the impact I turned away and focused my attention on the end of Tristan's cigarette which was glowing bright red when the crash came. When I looked back down the hill the building was no longer there. It had been completely flattened and everything I had ever heard about houses of cards surged into my mind. On top of the shattered timbers the little car lay peacefully on its side, its wheels still turning lazily.

As we galloped down the hill it was easy to guess Tristan's thoughts. He wouldn't be looking forward to telling Siegfried he had wrecked the Austin; in fact it was something the mind almost refused to contemplate. But as we neared the scene of devastation, passing on our way syringes, scalpels, bottles of vaccine, it was difficult to see any other outcome.

Arriving at the car, we made an anxious inspection. The body had been so bashed and dented before that it wasn't easy to identify any new marks. Certainly the rear end was pretty well caved in but it didn't show up very much. The only obvious damage was a smashed rear light. Our hopes rising, we set off for the farm for help.

The farmer greeted us amiably. 'Now then, you lads, hasta come back for more beer?'

'It wouldn't come amiss,' Tristan replied. 'We've had a bit of an accident.'

We went into the house and the hospitable man opened some more bottles. He didn't seem disturbed when he heard of the demolition of the hut. 'Nay, that's not mine. Belongs to t'golf club—it's t'club house.'

Tristan's eyebrows shot up. 'Oh no! Don't say we've flattened the headquarters of the Darrowby Golf Club!'

'Aye, lad, you must have. It's t'only wooden building in them fields. I rent that part of my land to the club and they've made a little nine hole course. Don't worry, hardly anybody plays on it—mainly t'bank manager and ah don't like that feller.'

Mr Prescott got a horse out of the stable and we went back to the car and pulled it upright again. Trembling a little, Tristan climbed in and pressed the starter. The sturdy little engine burst into a confident roar immediately and he drove carefully over the prostrate wooden walls on to the grass.

'Well thanks a lot, Mr Prescott,' he shouted. 'We seem to have got away with it.'

'Champion, lad, champion. You're as good as new.' Then the farmer winked and held up a finger. 'Now you say nowt about this job and I'll say nowt. Right?'

'Right! Come on, Jim, get in.' Tristan put his foot down and we chugged thankfully up the hill once more.

He seemed thoughtful on the way and didn't speak till we got on to the road.

Then he turned to me.

'You know, Jim, it's all very well, but I've still got to confess to Siegfried about that rear light. And of course I'll get the lash again. Don't you think it's just a bit hard the way I get blamed for everything that happens to his cars? You've seen it over and over again—he gives me a lot of bloody old wrecks to drive and when they start to fall to bits it's always my fault. The bloody tyres are all down to the canvas but if I get a puncture there's hell to pay. It isn't fair.'

'Well Siegfried isn't the man to suffer in silence, you know,' I said. 'He's got to lash out and you're nearest.'

Tristan was silent for a moment then he took a deeper drag at his Woodbine, blew out his cheeks and assumed a judicial expression. 'Mind you, I'm not saying I was entirely blameless with regard to the Hillman—I was taking that sharp turn in Dringley at sixty with my arm round a little nurse— but all in all I've just had sheer bad luck. In fact, Jim, I'm a helpless victim of prejudice.'

Siegfried was out of sorts when we met in the surgery. He was starting a summer cold and was sniffly and listless, but he still managed to raise a burst of energy at the news.

'You bloody young maniac! It's the rear light now, is it? God help me, I think all I work for is to pay for the repair bills you run up. You'll ruin me before you're finished. Go on, get to hell out of it. I'm finished with you.'

Tristan retired with dignity and followed his usual policy of lying low. He didn't see his brother until the following morning. Siegfried's condition had deteriorated; the cold had settled in his throat, always his weak spot, and he was down with laryngitis. His neck was swathed in vinegar-soaked Thermogene and when Tristan and I came into the bedroom he was feebly turning over the pages of the *Darrowby and Houlton Times*.

He spoke in a tortured whisper. 'Have you seen this? It says here that the golf clubhouse was knocked down yesterday and there's no clue as to how it happened. Damn funny thing. On Prescott's land, isn't it?' His head jerked suddenly from the pillow and he glared at his brother. 'You were there yesterday!' he croaked, then he fell back, muttering. 'Oh no, no, I'm sorry, it's too ridiculous—and it's wrong of me to blame you for everything.'

Tristan stared. He had never heard this kind of talk from Siegfried before. I too felt a pang of anxiety; could my boss be delirious?

Siegfried swallowed painfully. 'I've just had an urgent call from Armitage of Sorton. He's got a cow down with milk fever and I want you to drive James out there straight away. Go on, now—get moving.'

'Afraid I can't, Tristan shrugged. 'Jim's car is in Hammond's garage. They're fixing that light—it'll take them about an hour.'

'Oh God, yes, and they said they couldn't let us have a spare. Well, Armitage is in a bit of a panic—that cow could be dead in an hour. What the hell can we do?'

'There's the Rover,' Tristan said quietly.

Siegfried's form stiffened suddenly under the blankets and wild terror flickered in his eyes. For a few moments his head rolled about on the pillow and his long, bony fingers picked nervously at the quilt, then with an effort he heaved himself on to his side and stared into his brother's eyes. He spoke slowly and the agonized hissing of his voice lent menace to his words.

'Right, so you'll have to take the Rover. I never thought I'd see the day when I'd let a wrecker like you drive it, but just let me tell you this. If you put a scratch on that car I'll kill you. I'll kill you with my own two hands.'

The old pattern was asserting itself. Siegfried's eyes had begun to bulge, a dark flush was creeping over his cheeks while Tristan's face had lost all expression.

Using the last remnants of his strength, Siegfried hoisted himself even higher. 'Now do you really think you are capable of driving that car five miles to Sorton and back without smashing it up? All right then, get on with it and just remember what I've said.'

Tristan withdrew in offended silence and as I followed him I took a last look at the figure in the bed. Siegfried had fallen back and was staring at the ceiling with feverish eyes. His lips moved feebly as though he were praying.

Outside the room, Tristan rubbed his hands delightedly. 'What a break, Jim! A chance in a lifetime! You know I never thought I'd get behind the wheel of that Rover in a hundred years.' He dropped his voice to a whisper. 'Just shows you—everything happens for the best.'

Five minutes later he was backing carefully out of the yard and into the lane and once on the Sorton road I saw he was beginning to enjoy himself. For two miles the way ahead stretched straight and clear except for a milk lorry approaching in the far distance; a perfect place to see what the Rover could do. He nestled down in the rich leather upholstery and pressed his foot hard on the accelerator.

We were doing an effortless eighty when I saw a car beginning to overtake the milk lorry; it was an ancient, square-topped, high-built vehicle like a biscuit tin on wheels and it had no business trying to overtake anything. I waited for it to pull back but it still came on. And the lorry, perhaps with a sporting driver, seemed to be spurting to make a race of it.

With increasing alarm I saw the two vehicles abreast and

bearing down on us only a few hundred yards away and not a foot of space on either side of them. Of course the old car would pull in behind the lorry—it had to, there was no other way—but it was taking a long time about it. Tristan jammed on his brakes. If the lorry did the same, the other car would just be able to dodge between. But within seconds I realized nothing like that was going to happen and as they thundered towards us I resigned myself with dumb horror to a head-on collision.

Just before I closed my eyes I had a fleeting glimpse of a large, alarmed face behind the wheel of the old car, then something hit the left side of the Rover with a rending crash.

When I opened my eyes we were stationary. There was just Tristan and myself staring straight ahead at the road, empty and quiet, curving ahead of us into the peaceful green of the hills.

I sat motionless, listening to my thumping heart then I looked over my shoulder and saw the lorry disappearing at high speed round a distant bend; in passing I studied Tristan's face with interest—I had never seen a completely green face before.

After quite a long time, feeling a draught from the left, I looked carefully round in that direction. There were no doors on that side—one was lying by the roadside a few yards back and the other hung from a single broken hinge; as I watched, this one too, clattered on to the tarmac with a note of flat finality. Slowly, as in a dream, I got out and surveyed the damage; the left side of the Rover was a desert of twisted metal where the old car, diving for the verge at the last split second, had ploughed its way.

Tristan had flopped down on to the grass, his face blank. A nasty scratch on the paintwork might have sent him into a panic but this wholesale destruction seemed to have numbed his senses. But this state didn't last long; he began to blink, then his eyes narrowed and he felt for his Wood-bines. His agile mind was back at work and it wasn't dif-ficult to read his thoughts. What was he going to do now?

It seemed to me after a short appraisal of the situation that he had three possible courses of action. First, and most attractive, he could get out of Darrowby permanently—emigrate if necessary. Second, he could go straight to the railway station and board a train for Brawton where he could live quietly with his mother till this had blown over. Third, and it didn't bear thinking about, he could go back to Skeldale House and tell Siegfried he had smashed up his new Rover.

As I weighed up the possibilities I spotted the old car which had hit us; it was lying upside down in a ditch about fifty yards down the road. Hurrying towards it, I could hear a loud cackling coming from the interior and I remembered it was market day and many of the farmers would be bringing in crates of hens and maybe twenty or thirty dozen eggs to sell. We peered in through a window and Tristan gasped. A fat man, obviously unhurt, was lying in a great pool of smashed eggs. His face wore a wide, reassuring smile—in fact, his whole expression was ingratiating as far as it could be seen through the mask of egg which covered his features. The rest of the interior was filled with frantic hens which had escaped from their crates in the crash and were hunting for a way out.

The fat man, smiling up happily from his bed of eggs, was shouting something, but it was difficult to hear him above the wild cackling. I managed to pick up odd phrases: 'Very sorry indeed—entirely my fault—I'll make good the damage.' The words floated up cheerfully while the hens scampered across the man's beaming face and yolks coursed sluggishly down his clothes.

With an effort, Tristan managed to wrench open a door and was driven back immediately by a rush of hens. Some of them galloped off in various directions till they were lost to sight, while their less adventurous companions began to peck about philosophically by the roadside.

'Are you all right?' Tristan shouted.

'Yes, yes, young man. I'm not hurt. Please don't worry

about me.' The fat man struggled vainly to rise from the squelching mass. 'Ee, I am sorry about this, but I'll see you right, you can be sure.'

He held up a dripping hand and we helped him out on to the road. Despite his saturated clothes and the pieces of shell sticking to his hair and moustache he hadn't lost his poise. In fact he radiated confidence, the same confidence, I thought, which made him think his old car could overtake that speeding lorry.

He laid his hand on Tristan's shoulder. 'There's a simple explanation, you know. The sun got in my eyes.'

It was twelve noon and the fat man had been driving due north, but there didn't seem much point in arguing.

We lifted the shattered doors from the road, put them inside the Rover, drove to Sorton, treated the milk fever cow and returned to Darrowby. Tristan gave me a single despairing look then squared his shoulders and marched straight to his brother's room. I followed close on his heels.

Siegfried was worse. His face was red with fever and his eyes burned deeply in their sockets. He didn't move when Tristan walked over to the foot of the bed.

'Well, how did you get on?' The whisper was barely audible.

'Oh fine, the cow was on her feet when we left. But there's just one thing—I had a bit of a bump with the car.'

Siegfried had been wheezing stertorously and staring at the ceiling but the breathing stopped as if it had been switched off. There was an eerie silence then from the completely motionless figure two strangled words escaped. 'What happened?'

'Wasn't my fault. Chap tried to overtake a lorry and didn't make it. Caught one side of the Rover.'

Again the silence and again the whisper.

'Much damage?'

'Front and rear wings pretty well mangled, I'm afraid— and both doors torn off the left side.'

As if operated by a powerful spring, Siegfried came bolt

upright in the bed. It was startlingly like a corpse coming to life and the effect was heightened by the coils of Thermogene which had burst loose and trailed in shroud-like garlands from the haggard head. The mouth opened wide in a completely soundless scream.

'You bloody fool! You're sacked!'

He crashed back on to the pillow as though the mechanism had gone into reverse and lay very still. We watched him for a few moments in some anxiety, but when we heard the breathing restart we tiptoed from the room.

On the landing Tristan blew out his cheeks and drew a Woodbine from its packet. 'A tricky little situation, Jim, but you know what I always say.' He struck a match and pulled the smoke down blissfully. 'Things usually turn out better than you expect.'

Chapter Nine

A LOT OF THE DALES FARMS were anonymous and it was a help to find this one so plainly identified. 'Heston Grange' it said on the gate in bold black capitals.

I got out of the car and undid the latch. It was a good gate, too, and swung easily on its hinges instead of having to be dragged round with a shoulder under the top spar. The farmhouse lay below me, massive, grey-stoned, with a pair of bow windows which some prosperous Victorian had added to the original structure.

It stood on a flat, green neck of land in a loop of the river and the lushness of the grass and the quiet fertility of the surrounding fields contrasted sharply with the stark hill behind. Towering oaks and beeches sheltered the house and a thick pine wood covered the lower slopes of the fell.

I walked round the buildings shouting as I always did, because some people considered it a subtle insult to go to the house and ask if the farmer was in. Good farmers are indoors only at meal times. But my shouts drew no reply, so I went over and knocked at the door set deep among the weathered stones.

A voice answered 'Come in,' and I opened the door into a huge, stone-flagged kitchen with hams and sides of bacon hanging from hooks in the ceiling. A dark girl in a check blouse and green linen slacks was kneading dough in a bowl. She looked up and smiled.

'Sorry I couldn't let you in. I've got my hands full.' She held up her arms, floury-white to the elbow.

'That's all right. My name is Herriot. I've come to see a calf. It's lame, I understand.'

'Yes, we think he's broken his leg. Probably got his foot in a hole when he was running about. If you don't mind waiting a minute, I'll come with you. My father and the men are in the fields. I'm Helen Alderson, by the way.'

She washed and dried her arms and pulled on a pair of short wellingtons. 'Take over this bread will you, Meg,' she said to an old woman who came through from an inner room. 'I have to show Mr Herriot the calf.'

Outside, she turned to me and laughed. 'We've got a bit of a walk, I'm afraid. He's in one of the top buildings. Look, you can just see it up there.' She pointed to a squat, stone barn, high on the fell-side. I knew all about these top buildings; they were scattered all over the high country and I got a lot of healthy exercise going round them. They were used for storing hay and other things and as shelters for the animals on the hill pastures.

I looked at the girl for a few seconds. 'Oh, that's all right, I don't mind. I don't mind in the least.'

We went over the field to a narrow bridge spanning the river, and, following her across, I was struck by a thought; this new fashion of women wearing slacks might be a bit revolutionary but there was a lot to be said for it. The path led upward through the pine wood and here the sunshine was broken up into islands of brightness among the dark trunks, the sound of the river grew faint and we walked softly on a thick carpet of pine needles. It was cool in the wood and silent except when a bird call echoed through the trees.

Ten minutes of hard walking brought us out into the hot sun on the open moor and the path curved steeper still round a series of rocky outcrops. I was beginning to puff, but the girl kept up a brisk pace, swinging along with easy strides. I was glad when we reached the level ground cn the top and the barn came in sight again.

When I opened the half door I could hardly see my patient in the dark interior which was heavy with the fragrance of hay piled nearly to the roof. He looked very small and sorry for himself with his dangling foreleg which trailed uselessly along the strawed floor as he tried to walk.

'Will you hold his head while I examine him, please?' I said.

The girl caught the calf expertly, one hand under its chin, the other holding an ear. As I felt my way over the leg the little creature stood trembling, his face a picture of woe.

'Well, your diagnosis was correct. Clean fracture of the radius and ulna, but there's very little displacement so it should do well with a plaster on it.' I opened my bag, took out some plaster bandages then filled a bucket with water from a nearby spring. I soaked one of the bandages and applied it to the leg, following it with a second and a third till the limb was encased in a rapidly hardening white sheath from elbow to foot.

'We'll just wait a couple of minutes till it hardens, then we can let him go.' I kept tapping the plaster till I was satisfied it was set like stone. 'All right,' I said finally. 'He can go now.'

The girl released the head and the little animal trotted away. 'Look,' she cried. 'He's putting his weight on it already! And doesn't he look a lot happier!' I smiled. I felt I had really done something. The calf felt no pain now that the broken ends of the bone were immobilized; and the fear which always demoralizes a hurt animal had vanished.

'Yes,' I said. 'He certainly has perked up quickly.' My words were almost drowned by a tremendous bellow and the patch of blue above the half door was suddenly obscured by a large shaggy head. Two great liquid eyes stared down anxiously at the little calf and it answered with a high-pitched bawl. Soon a deafening duet was in progress.

'That's his mother,' the girl shouted above the din. 'Poor old thing, she's been hanging about here all morning wondering what we've done with her calf. She hates being separated from him.'

I straightened up and drew the bolt on the door. 'Well she can come in now.'

The big cow almost knocked me down as she rushed past me. Then she started a careful, sniffing inspection of her calf, pushing him around with her muzzle and making muffled lowing noises deep in her throat.

The little creature submitted happily to all the fuss and when it was over and his mother was finally satisfied, he limped round to her udder and began to suck heartily.

'Soon got his appetite back,' I said and we both laughed.

I threw the empty tins into my bag and closed it. 'He'll have to keep the plaster on for a month, so if you'll give me a ring then I'll come back and take it off. Just keep an eye on him and make sure his leg doesn't get sore round the top of the bandage.'

As we left the barn the sunshine and the sweet warm air met us like a high wave. I turned and looked across the valley to the soaring green heights, smooth, enormous, hazy in the noon heat. Beneath my feet the grassy slopes fell away steeply to where the river glimmered among the trees.

'It's wonderful up here,' I said. 'Just look at that gorge over there. And that great hill—I suppose you could call it a mountain.' I pointed at a giant which heaved its heather-mottled shoulders high above the others.

'That's Heskit Fell—nearly two and a half thousand feet. And that's Eddleton just beyond, and Wedder Fell on the other side and Colver and Sennor.' The names with their wild, Nordic ring fell easily from her tongue; she spoke of them like old friends and I sensed the affection in her voice.

We sat down on the warm grass of the hillside, a soft breeze pulled at the heads of the moorland flowers, somewhere a curlew cried. Darrowby and Skeldale House and veterinary practice seemed a thousand miles away.

'You're lucky to live here,' I said. 'But I don't think you need me to tell you that.'

'No, I love this country. There's nowhere else quite like it.' She paused and looked slowly around her. 'I'm glad it appeals to you too—a lot of people find it too bare and wild. It almost seems to frighten them.'

I laughed. 'Yes, I know, but as far as I'm concerned I can't help feeling sorry for all the thousands of vets who don't work in the Yorkshire Dales.'

I began to talk about my work, then almost without knowing, I was going back over my student days, telling her of the good times, the friends I had made and our hopes and aspirations.

I surprised myself with my flow of talk—I wasn't much of a chatterbox usually—and I felt I must be boring my companion. But she sat quietly looking over the valley, her arms around her green-clad legs, nodding at times as though she understood. And she laughed in all the right places.

I wondered, too, at the silly feeling that I would like to forget all about the rest of the day's duty and stay up here on this sunny hillside. It came to me that it had been a long time since I had sat down and talked to a girl of my own age. I had almost forgotten what it was like.

I didn't hurry back down the path and through the scented pine wood but it seemed no time at all before we were walking across the wooden bridge and over the field to the farm.

I turned with my hand on the car door. 'Well, I'll see you in a month.' It sounded like an awful long time.

The girl smiled. 'Thank you for what you've done.' As I started the engine she waved and went into the house.

'Helen Alderson?' Siegfried said later over lunch. 'Of course I know her. Lovely girl.'

Tristan, across the table, made no comment, but he laid down his knife and fork, raised his eyes reverently to the ceiling and gave a long, low whistle. Then he started to eat again.

Siegfried went on. 'Oh yes, I know her very well. And I admire her. Her mother died a few years ago and she runs the whole place. Cooks and looks after her father and a younger brother and sister.' He spooned some mashed potatoes on to his plate. 'Any men friends? Oh, half the young bloods in the district are chasing her but she doesn't seem to be going steady with any of them. Choosy sort, I think.'

71

Chapter Ten

IT WAS WHEN I was plodding up Mr Kay's field for the ninth time that it began to occur to me that this wasn't going to be my day. For some time now I had been an L.V.I., the important owner of a little certificate informing whosover it may concern that James Herriot M.R.C.V.S., was a Local Veterinary Inspector of the Ministry of Agriculture and Fisheries. It meant that I was involved in a lot of routine work like clinical examinations and tuberculin testing. It also highlighted something which I had been suspecting for some time —the Dales farmers' attitude to time was different from my own.

It had been all right when I was calling on them to see a sick animal; they were usually around waiting for me and the beast would be confined in some building when I arrived. It was very different, however, when I sent them a card saying I was coming to inspect their dairy cows or test their herd. It stated quite clearly on the card that the animals must be assembled indoors and that I would be there at a certain time and I planned my day accordingly; fifteen minutes or so for a clinical and anything up to several hours for a test depending on the size of the herd. If I was kept waiting for ten minutes at every clinical while they got the cows in from the field it meant simply that after six visits I was running an hour late.

So when I drove up to Mr Kay's farm for a tuberculin test and found his cows tied up in their stalls I breathed a sigh of relief. We were through them in no time at all and I thought I was having a wonderful start to the day when the farmer said he had only half a dozen young heifers to do to complete the job. It was when I left the buildings and saw the group of shaggy roans and reds grazing contentedly at the far end of a large field that I felt the old foreboding.

'I thought you'd have them inside, Mr Kay,' I said apprehensively.

Mr Kay tapped out his pipe on to his palm, mixed the sodden dottle with a few strands of villainous looking twist and crammed it back into the bowl. 'Nay, nay,' he said, puffing appreciatively, 'Ah didn't like to put them in on a grand 'ot day like this. We'll drive them up to that little house.' He pointed to a tumble-down grey-stone barn at the summit of the long, steeply sloping pasture and blew out a cloud of choking smoke. 'Won't take many minutes.'

At his last sentence a cold hand clutched at me. I'd heard these dreadful words so many times before. But maybe it would be all right this time. We made our way to the bottom of the field and got behind the heifers.

'Cush, cush!' cried Mr Kay.

'Cush, cush!' I added encouragingly, slapping my hands against my thighs.

The heifers stopped pulling the grass and regarded us with mild interest, their jaws moving lazily, then in response to further cries they began to meander casually up the hill. We managed to coax them up to the door of the barn but there they stopped. The leader put her head inside for a moment then turned suddenly and made a dash down the hill. The others followed suit immediately and though we danced about and waved our arms they ran past us as if we weren't there. I looked thoughtfully at the young beasts thundering down the slope, their tails high, kicking up their heels like mustangs; they were enjoying this new game.

Down the hill once more and again the slow wheedling up to the door and again the sudden breakaway. This time one of them tried it on her own and as I galloped vainly to and fro trying to turn her the others charged with glee through the gap and down the slope again.

It was a long, steep hill, and as I trudged up for the third time with the sun blazing on my back I began to regret being so conscientious about my clothes; in the instructions to the new L.V.I.'s the Ministry had been explicit that they expected us to be properly attired to carry out our duties. I had taken it to heart and rigged myself out in the required uniform but I realized now that a long oilskin coat and wellingtons was not an ideal outfit for the job in hand. The sweat was trickling into my eyes and my shirt was beginning to cling to me.

When, for the third time, I saw the retreating backs careering joyously down the hill, I thought it was time to do something about it.

'Just a minute,' I called to the farmer, 'I'm getting a bit warm.'

I took off the coat, rolled it up and placed it on the grass well away from the barn. And as I made a neat pile of my syringe, the box of tuberculin, my calipers, scissors, notebook and pencil, the thought kept intruding that I was being cheated in some way. After all, Ministry work was easy—any practitioner would tell you that. You didn't have to get up in the middle of the night, you had nice set hours and you never really had to exert yourself. In fact it was money for old rope—a pleasant relaxation from the real thing. I wiped my streaming brow and stood for a few seconds panting gently—this just wasn't fair.

We started again and at the fourth visit to the barn I thought we had won because all but one of the heifers strolled casually inside. But that last one just wouldn't have it. We cushed imploringly, waved and even got near enough to poke at its rump but it stood in the entrance regarding the interior with deep suspicion. Then the heads of its mates began to reappear in the doorway and I knew we had lost again; despite my frantic dancing and shouting they wandered out one by one before joining again in their happy downhill dash. This time I found myself galloping down after them in an agony of frustration.

We had another few tries during which the heifers introduced touches of variation by sometimes breaking away half way up the hill or occasionally trotting round the back of the barn and peeping at us coyly from behind the old stones before frisking to the bottom again.

After the eighth descent I looked appealingly at Mr Kay who was relighting his pipe calmly and didn't appear to be troubled in any way. My time schedule was in tatters but I don't think he had noticed that we had been going on like this for about forty minutes.

'Look, we're getting nowhere,' I said. 'I've got a lot of other work waiting for me. Isn't there anything more we can do?'

The farmer stamped down the twist with his thumb, drew deeply and pleasurably a few times then looked at me with mild surprise.

'Well, let's see. We could bring dog out but I don't know as he'll be much good. He's nobbut a young 'un.'

He sauntered back to the farmhouse and opened a door. A shaggy cur catapulted out, barking in delight, and Mr Kay brought him over to the field. 'Get away by!' he cried gesturing towards the cattle who had resumed their grazing and the dog streaked behind them. I really began to hope as we went up the hill with the hairy little figure darting in, nipping at the heels, but at the barn the rot set in again. I could see the heifers beginning to sense the inexperience of the dog and one of them managed to kick him briskly under the chin as he came in. The little animal yelped and his tail went down. He stood uncertainly, looking at the beasts, advancing on him now, shaking their horns threateningly, then he seemed to come to a decision and slunk away. The young cattle went after him at increasing speed and in a moment I was looking at the extraordinary spectacle of the dog going flat out down the hill with the heifers drumming close behind him. At the foot he disappeared under a gate and we saw him no more.

Something seemed to give way in my head. 'Oh God,' I yelled, 'we're never going to get these damn things tested!

75

I'll just have to leave them. I don't know what the Ministry is going to say, but I've had enough!'

The farmer looked at me ruminatively. He seemed to recognize that I was at breaking point. 'Aye, it's no good,' he said, tapping his pipe out on his heel. 'We'll have to get Sam.'

'Sam?'

'Aye, Sam Broadbent. Works for me neighbour. He'll get 'em in all right.'

'How's he going to do that?'

'Oh, he can imitate a fly.'

For a moment my mind reeled. 'Did you say imitate a fly?'

'That's right. A warble fly, tha knows. He's a bit slow is t'lad but by gaw he can imitate a fly. I'll go and get him—he's only two fields down the road.'

I watched the farmer's retreating back in disbelief then threw myself down on the ground. At any other time I would have enjoyed lying there on the slope with the sun on my face and the grass cool against my sweating back; the air was still and heavy with the fragrance of clover and when I opened my eyes the gentle curve of the valley floor was a vision of peace. But my mind was a turmoil. I had a full day's Ministry work waiting for me and I was an hour behind time already. I could picture the long succession of farmers waiting for me and cursing me heartily. The tension built in me till I could stand it no longer; I jumped to my feet and ran down to the gate at the foot. I could see along the road from there and was relieved to find that Mr Kay was on his way back.

Just behind him a large, fat man was riding slowly on a very small bicycle, his heels on the pedals, his feet and knees sticking out at right angles. Tufts of greasy black hair stuck out at random from under a kind of skull cap which looked like an old bowler without the brim.

'Sam's come to give us a hand,' said Mr Kay with an air of quiet triumph.

'Good morning,' I said and the big man turned slowly and nodded. The eyes in the round, unshaven face were vacant

76

and incurious and I decided that Sam did indeed look a bit slow. I found it difficult to imagine how he could possibly be of any help.

The heifers, standing near by, watched with languid interest as we came through the gate. They had obviously enjoyed every minute of the morning's entertainment and it seemed they were game for a little more fun if we so desired; but it was up to us, of course—they weren't worried either way.

Sam propped his bicycle against the wall and paced solemnly forward. He made a circle of his thumb and forefinger and placed it to his lips. His cheeks worked as though he was getting everything into place then he took a deep breath. And, from nowhere it seemed came a sudden swelling of angry sound, a vicious humming and buzzing which made me look round in alarm for the enraged insect zooming in for the kill.

The effect on the heifers was electric. Their superior air vanished and was replaced by rigid anxiety; then, as the noise increased in volume, they turned and charged up the hill. But it wasn't the carefree frolic of before—no tossing heads, waving tails and kicking heels; this time they kept shoulder to shoulder in a frightened block.

Mr Kay and I, trotting on either side, directed them yet again up to the building where they formed a group, looking nervously around them.

We had to wait for a short while for Sam to arrive. He was clearly a one-pace man and ascended the slope unhurriedly. At the top he paused to regain his breath, fixed the animals with a blank gaze and carefully adjusted his fingers against his mouth. A moment's tense silence then the humming broke out again, even more furious and insistent than before.

The heifers knew when they were beaten. With a chorus of startled bellows they turned and rushed into the building and I crashed the half door behind them; I stood leaning against it unable to believe my troubles were over. Sam joined me and looked into the dark interior. As if to finally establish his mastery he gave a sudden sharp blast, this time without his fingers, and his victims huddled still closer against the far wall.

A few minutes later, after Sam had left us, I was happily clipping and injecting the necks. I looked up at the farmer. 'You know, I can still hardly believe what I saw there. It was like magic. That chap has a wonderful gift.'

Mr Kay looked over the half door and I followed his gaze down the grassy slope to the road. Sam was riding away and the strange black headwear was just visible, bobbing along the top of the wall.

'Aye, he can imitate a fly all right. Poor awd lad, it's t'only thing he's good at.'

Chapter Eleven

HURRYING AWAY from Mr Kay's to my second test I reflected that if I had to be more than an hour late for an appointment it was a lucky thing that my next call was at the Hugills. The four brothers and their families ran a herd which, with cows, followers and calves must have amounted to nearly two hundred and I had to test the lot of them; but I knew that my lateness wouldn't bring any querulous remarks on my head because the Hugills had developed the Dales tradition of courtesy to an extraordinary degree. The stranger within their gates was treated like royalty.

As I drove into the yard I could see everybody leaving their immediate tasks and advancing on me with beaming faces. The brothers were in the lead and they stopped opposite me as I got out of the car, and I thought as I always did that I had never seen such healthy-looking men. Their ages ranged from Walter, who was about sixty, down through Thomas and Fenwick to William, the youngest, who would be in his late forties, and I should say their average weight would be about fifteen stones. They weren't fat, either, just huge, solid men with bright red, shining faces and clear eyes.

William stepped forward from the group and I knew what was coming; this was always his job. He leaned forward, suddenly solemn, and looked into my face.

'How are you today, sorr?' he asked.

'Very well, thank you, Mr Hugill,' I replied.

'Good!' said William fervently, and the other brothers all repeated 'Good, good, good,' with deep satisfaction.

William took a deep breath. 'And how is Mr Farnon?'

'Oh, he's very fit, thanks.'

'Good!' Then the rapid fire of the responses from behind him: 'Good, good, good.'

William hadn't finished yet. He cleared his throat. 'And how is young Mr Farnon?'

'In really top form.'

'Good!' But this time William allowed himself a gentle smile and from behind him came a few dignified ho-ho's. Walter closed his eyes and his great shoulders shook silently. They all knew Tristan.

William stepped back into line, his appointed task done and we all went into the byre. I braced myself as I looked at the long row of backs, the tails swishing at the flies. There was some work ahead here.

'Sorry I'm so late,' I said, as I drew the tuberculin into the syringe. 'I was held up at the last place. It's difficult to forecast how long these tests will take.'

All four brothers replied eagerly. 'Aye, you're right, sorr. It's difficult. It IS difficult. You're right, you're right, it's difficult.'

They went on till they had thrashed the last ounce out of the statement.

I finished filling the syringe, got out my scissors and began to push my way between the first two cows. It was a tight squeeze and I puffed slightly in the stifling atmosphere.

'It's a bit warm in here,' I said.

Again the volley of agreement. 'You're right, sorr. Aye, it's warm. It IS warm. You're right. It's warm. It's warm. Aye, you're right.' This was all delivered with immense conviction and vigorous nodding of heads as though I had made some incredible discovery; and as I looked at the grave, intent faces still pondering over my brilliant remark, I could feel my tensions beginning to dissolve. I was lucky to work here. Where else but in the high country of Yorkshire would I meet people like these?

I pushed along the cow and got hold of its ear, but Walter stopped me with a gentle cough.

'Nay, Mr Herriot, you won't have to look in the ears. I have all t'numbers wrote down.'

'Oh, that's fine. It'll save us a lot of time.' I had always found scratching the wax away to find ear tattoos an over-rated pastime. And it was good to hear that the Hugills were attending to the clerical side; there was a section in the Ministry form which said: 'Are the herd records in good order?' I always wrote 'Yes', keeping my fingers crossed as I thought of the scrawled figures on the backs of old bills, milk recording sheets, anything.

'Aye,' said Walter. 'I have 'em all set down proper in a book.'

'Great! Can you go and get it, then?'

'No need, sorr, I have it 'ere.' Walter was the boss, there was no doubt about it. They all seemed to live in perfect harmony but when the chips were down Walter took over automatically. He was the organizer, the acknowledged brains of the outfit. The battered trilby which he always wore in contrast with the others' caps gave him an extra air of authority.

Everybody watched respectfully as he slowly and deliber-ately extracted a spectacle case from an inside pocket. He opened it and took out an old pair of steel-rimmed spectacles, blowing away fragments of the hay and corn chaff with which the interior of the case was thickly powdered. There was a quiet dignity and importance in the way he unhur-riedly threaded the side pieces over his ears and stood grimacing slightly to work everything into place. Then he put his hand into his waistcoat pocket.

When he took it out he was holding some object but it was difficult to identify, being almost obscured by his enor-mous thumb. Then I saw that it was a tiny, black-covered miniature diary about two inches square—the sort of novelty people give each other at Christmas.

'Is that the herd record?' I asked.

'Yes, this is it. It's all set down in here.' Walter daintily flicked over the pages with a horny forefinger and squinted

81

through his spectacles. 'Now that fust cow—she's number eighty-fower.'

'Splendid!' I said. 'I'll just check this one and then we can go by the book.' I peered into the ear. 'That's funny, I make it twenty-six.'

The brothers had a look. 'You're right, sorr, you're right. It IS twenty-six.'

Walter pursed his lips. 'Why, that's Bluebell's calf, isn't it?'

'Nay,' said Fenwick, 'she's out of awd Buttercup.'

'Can't be,' mumbled Thomas. 'Awd Buttercup was sold to Jim Jefferson afore this 'un was born. This is Brenda's calf.'

William shook his head. 'Ah'm sure we got her as a heifer at Bob Ashby's sale.'

'All right,' I said, holding up a hand. 'We'll put in twenty-six.' I had to cut in. It was in no way an argument, just a leisurely discussion but it looked as if it could go on for some time. I wrote the number in my notebook and injected the cow. 'Now how about this next one?'

'Well ah DO know that 'un,' said Walter confidently, stabbing at an entry in the diary. 'Can't make no mistake, she's number five.'

I looked in the ear. 'Says a hundred and thirty-seven here.'

It started again. 'She was bought in, wasn't she?' 'Nay, nay, she's out of awd Dribbler.' 'Don't think so—Dribbler had nowt but bulls . . .'

I raised my hand again. 'You know, I really think it might be quicker to look in all the ears. Time's getting on.'

'Aye, you're right, sorr, it IS getting on.' Walter returned the herd book to his waistcoat pocket philosophically and we started the laborious business of clipping, measuring and injecting every animal, plus rubbing the inside of the ears with a cloth soaked in spirit to identify the numbers which had often faded to a few unrelated dots. Occasionally Walter referred to his tiny book. 'Ah, that's right, ninety-two. I thowt so. It's all set down here.'

Fighting with the loose animals in the boxes round the fold yard was like having a dirty Turkish bath while wearing oilskins. The brothers caught the big beasts effortlessly and even the strongest bullock grew quickly discouraged when it tried to struggle against those mighty arms. But I noticed one strange phenomenon: the men's fingers were so thick and huge that they often slipped out of the animals' noses through sheer immobility.

It took an awful long time but we finally got through. The last little calf had a space clipped in his shaggy neck and bawled heartily as he felt the needle, then I was out in the sweet air throwing my coat in the car boot. I looked at my watch—three o'clock I was nearly two hours behind my schedule now and already I was hot and weary, with skinned toes on my right foot where a cow had trodden and a bruised left instep caused by the sudden descent of Fenwick's size thirteen hobnails during a particularly violent mêlée. As I closed the boot and limped round to the car door I began to wonder a little about this easy Ministry work.

Walter loomed over me and inclined his head graciously. 'Come in and sit down and have a drink o' tea.'

'It's very kind of you and I wish I could, Mr Hugill. But I've got a long string of inspections waiting and I don't know when I'll get round them. I've fixed up far too many and I completely underestimated the time needed for your test. I really am an absolute fool.'

And the brothers intoned sincerely. 'Aye, you're right, sorr, you're right, you're right.'

Well, there was no more testing today, but ten inspections still to do and I should have been at the first one two hours ago. I roared off, feeling that little ball tightening in my stomach as it always did when I was fighting the clock. Gripping the wheel with one hand and exploring my lunch packet with the other, I pulled out a piece of Mrs Hall's ham and egg pie and began to gnaw it as I went along.

But I had gone only a short way when reason asserted itself. This was no good. It was an excellent pie and I might as well enjoy it. I pulled off the unfenced road on to the grass, switched off the engine and opened the windows wide. The farm back there was like an island of activity in the quiet landscape and now that I was away from the noise and the stuffiness of the buildings the silence and the emptiness enveloped me like a soothing blanket. I leaned my head against the back of the seat and looked out at the checkered greens of the little fields along the flanks of the hills; thrusting upwards between their walls till they gave way to the jutting rocks and the harsh brown of the heather which flooded the wild country above.

I felt better when I drove away and didn't particularly mind when the farmer at the first inspection greeted me with a scowl.

'This isn't one o'clock, Maister!' he snapped. 'My cows have been in all afternoon and look at the bloody mess they've made. Ah'll never get the place clean again!'

I had to agree with him when I saw the muck piled up behind the cows; it was one of the snags about housing animals in grass time. And the farmer's expression grew blacker as most of them cocked their tails as though in welcome and added further layers to the heaps.

'I won't keep you much longer,' I said briskly, and began to work my way down the row. Before the tuberculin testing scheme came into being, these clinical examinations were the only means of detecting tuberculous cows and I moved from animal to animal palpating the udders for any unusual induration. The routine examinations were known jocularly in the profession as 'bag-snatching' or 'cow-punching' and it was a job that soon got tedious.

I found the only way to stop myself going nearly mad with boredom was to keep reminding myself what I was there for. So when I came to a gaunt red cow with a pendulous udder I straightened up and turned to the farmer.

'I'm going to take a milk sample from this one. She's a bit hard in that left hind quarter.'

The farmer sniffed. 'Please yourself. There's nowt wrong with her but I suppose it'll make a job for somebody.'

Squirting milk from the quarter into a two ounce bottle, I thought about Siegfried's veterinary friend who always took a pint sample from the healthiest udder he could find to go with his lunchtime sandwiches.

I labelled the bottle and put it into the car. We had a little electric centrifuge at Skeldale House and tonight I would spin this milk and examine the sediment on a slide after staining by Ziehl-Neelsen. Probably I would find nothing but at times there was the strange excitement of peering down the microscope at a clump of bright red, iridescent T.B. bacilli. When that happened the cow was immediately slaughtered and there was always the thought that I might have lifted the death sentence from some child—the meningitis, the spinal and lung infections which were so common in those days.

Returning to the byre I finished the inspection by examining the wall in front of each cow.

The farmer watched me dourly. 'What you on with now?'

'Well, if a cow has a cough you can often find some spit on the wall.' I had, in truth, found more tuberculous cows this way than any other—by scraping a little sputum on to a glass slide and then staining it as for the milk.

The modern young vet just about never sees a T.B. cow, thank heavens, but 'screws' were all too common thirty years ago. There were very few in the high Pennines but in the low country on the plain you found them; the cows that 'weren't doing right', the ones with the soft, careful cough and slightly accelerated breathing. Often they were good milkers and ate well, but they were killers and I was learning to spot them. And there were the others, the big, fat, sleek animals which could still be riddled with the disease. They were killers of a more insidious kind and nobody could pick them out. It took the tuberculin test to do that.

At the next four places I visited, the farmers had got tired of waiting for me and had turned their cows out. They had all to be brought in from the field and they came slowly and reluctantly; there was nothing like the rodeo I had had with

Mr Kay's heifers but a lot more time was lost. The animals kept trying to turn back to the field while I sped around their flanks like a demented sheep dog; and as I panted to and fro each farmer told me the same thing—that cows only liked to come in at milking time.

Milking time did eventually come and I caught three of my herds while they were being milked, but it was after six when I came tired and hungry to my second last inspection. A hush hung over the place and after shouting my way round the buildings without finding anybody I walked over to the house.

'Is your husband in, Mrs Bell?' I asked.

'No, he's had to go into t'village to get the horse shod but he won't be long before he's back. He's left cows in for you,' the farmer's wife replied.

That was fine. I'd soon get through this lot. I almost ran into the byre and started the old routine, feeling sick to death of the sight and smell of cows and fed up with pawing at their udders. I was working along almost automatically when I came to a thin, rangy cow with a narrow red and white face; she could be a crossed Shorthorn-Ayrshire. I had barely touched her udder when she lashed out with the speed of light and caught me just above the kneecap.

I hopped round the byre on one leg, groaning and swearing in my agony. It was some time before I was able to limp back to have another try and this time I scratched her back and cush-cushed her in a wheedling tone before sliding my hand gingerly between her legs. The same thing happened again only this time the sharp-edged cloven foot smacked slightly higher up my leg.

Crashing back against the wall, I huddled there, almost weeping with pain and rage. After a few minutes I reached a decision. To hell with her. If she didn't want to be examined she could take her luck. I had had enough for one day—I was in no mood for heroics.

Ignoring her, I proceeded down the byre till I had inspected the others. But I had to pass her on my way back and paused to have another look; and whether it was sheer stubbornness or whether I imagined she was laughing at me, I don't know, but I decided to have just one more go. Maybe she didn't like me coming from behind. Perhaps if I worked from the side she wouldn't mind so much.

Carefully I squeezed my way between her and her neighbour, gasping as the craggy pelvic bones dug into my ribs. Once in the space beyond, I thought, I would be free to do my job; and that was my big mistake. Because as soon as I had got there the cow went to work on me in earnest. Switching her back end round quickly to cut off my way of escape, she began to kick me systematically from head to foot. She kicked forward, reaching at times high on my chest as I strained back against the wall.

Since then I have been kicked by an endless variety of cows in all sorts of situations but never by such an expert as this one. There must be very few really venomous bovines and when one of them uses her feet it is usually an instinctive reaction to being hurt or frightened; and they kick blindly. But this cow measured me up before each blow and her judgement of distance was beautiful. And as she drove me further towards her head she was able to hook me in the back with her horns by way of variety. I am convinced she hated the human race.

My plight was desperate. I was completely trapped and it didn't help when the apparently docile cow next door began to get into the act by prodding me off with her horns as I pressed against her.

I don't know what made me look up, but there, in the thick wall of the byre was a hole about two feet square where some of the crumbling stone had fallen out. I pulled myself up with an agility that amazed me and as I crawled through head first a sweet fragrance came up to me. I was looking into a hay barn and, seeing a deep bed of finest clover just below, I launched myself into space and did a very creditable roll in the air before landing safely on my back.

Lying there, bruised and breathless, with the front of my

coat thickly patterned with claw marks I finally abandoned any lingering illusions I had had that Ministry work was a soft touch.

I was rising painfully to my feet when Mr Bell strolled in. 'Sorry ah had to go out,' he said, looking me over with interest, 'But I'd just about given you up. You're 'ellish late.'

I dusted myself down and picked a few strands of hay from my hair.

'Yes, sorry about that. But never mind, I managed to get the job done.'

'But . . . were you havin' a bit of a kip, then?'

'No, not exactly. I had some trouble with one of your cows.' There wasn't much point in standing on my dignity. I told him the story.

Even the friendliest farmer seems to derive pleasure from a vet's discomfiture and Mr Bell listened with an ever-widening grin of delight. By the time I had finished he was doubled up, beating his breeches knees with his hands.

'I can just imagine it. That Ayrshire cross! She's a right bitch. Picked her up cheap at market last spring and thought ah'd got a bargain, but ah soon found out. Took us a fort-night to get bugger tied up!'

'Well, I just wish I'd known,' I said, rather tight-lipped.

The farmer looked up at the hole in the wall. 'And you crawled through . . .' he went into another convulsion which lasted some time, then he took off his cap and wiped his eyes with the lining.

'Oh dear, oh dear,' he murmured weakly. 'By gaw, I wish I'd been here.'

My last call was just outside Darrowby and I could hear the church clock striking a quarter past seven as I got stiffly out of the car. After my easy day in the service of the government I felt broken in mind and body; I had to suppress a scream when I saw yet another long line of cows' backsides awaiting me. The sun was low, and dark thunderclouds piling up in the west had thrown the countryside into an eerie darkness; and in the old-fashioned, slit-windowed byre the animals looked shapeless and ill-defined in the gloom.

Right, no messing about. I was going to make a quick job of this and get off home; home to some food and an armchair. I had no further ambitions. So left hand on the root of the tail, right hand between the hind legs, a quick feel around and on to the next one. Eyes half closed, my mind numb, I moved from cow to cow going through the motions like a robot with the far end of the byre seeming like the promised land.

And finally here it was, the very last one up against the wall. Left hand on tail, right hand between legs . . . At first my tired brain didn't take in the fact that there was something different here, but there was . . . something vastly different. A lot of space and instead of the udder a deeply cleft, pendulous something with no teats anywhere.

I came awake suddenly and looked along the animal's side. A huge woolly head was turned towards me and two wide-set eyes regarded me enquiringly. In the dull light I could just see the gleam of the copper ring in the nose.

The farmer who had watched me in silence, spoke up.

'You're wasting your time there, young man. There's nowt wrong wi' HIS bag.'

Chapter Twelve

THE CARD DANGLED above the old lady's bed. It read 'God is Near' but it wasn't like the usual religious text. It didn't have a frame or ornate printing. It was just a strip of cardboard about eight inches long with plain lettering which might have said 'No smoking' or 'Exit' and it was looped carelessly over an old gas bracket so that Miss Stubbs from where she lay could look up at it and read 'God is Near' in square black capitals.

There wasn't much more Miss Stubbs could see; perhaps a few feet of privet hedge through the frayed curtains but mainly it was just the cluttered little room which had been her world for so many years.

The room was on the ground floor and in the front of the cottage, and as I came up through the wilderness which had once been a garden I could see the dogs watching me from where they had jumped on to the old lady's bed. And when I knocked on the door the place almost erupted with their barking. It was always like this. I had been visiting regularly for over a year and the pattern never changed; the furious barking, then Mrs Broadwith who looked after Miss Stubbs would push all the animals but my patient into the back kitchen and open the door and I would go in and see Miss Stubbs in the corner in her bed with the card hanging over it.

She had been there for a long time and would never get up again. But she never mentioned her illness and pain to me; all her concern was for her three dogs and two cats.

Today it was old Prince and I was worried about him. It

was his heart—just about the most spectacular valvular incompetence I had ever heard. He was waiting for me as I came in, pleased as ever to see me, his long, fringed tail waving gently.

The sight of that tail used to make me think there must be a lot of Irish Setter in Prince but I was inclined to change my mind as I worked my way forward over the bulging black and white body to the shaggy head and upstanding Alsatian ears. Miss Stubbs often used to call him 'Mr Heinz' and though he may not have had 57 varieties in him his hybrid vigour had stood him in good stead. With his heart he should have been dead long ago.

'I thought I'd best give you a ring, Mr Herriot,' Mrs Broadwith said. She was a comfortable, elderly widow with a square, ruddy face contrasting sharply with the pinched features on the pillow. 'He's been coughing right bad this week and this morning he was a bit staggery. Still eats well, though.'

'I bet he does.' I ran my hands over the rolls of fat on the ribs. 'It would take something really drastic to put old Prince off his grub.'

Miss Stubbs laughed from the bed and the old dog, his mouth wide, eyes dancing, seemed to be joining in the joke. I put my stethoscope over his heart and listened, knowing well what I was going to hear. They say the heart is supposed to go 'Lub-dup, lub-dup', but Prince's went 'swish-swoosh, swish-swoosh'. There seemed to be nearly as much blood leaking back as was being pumped into the circulatory system. And another thing, the 'swish-swoosh' was a good bit faster than last time; he was on oral digitalis but it wasn't quite doing its job.

Gloomily I moved the stethoscope over the rest of the chest. Like all old dogs with a chronic heart weakness he had an ever-present bronchitis and I listened without enthusiasm to the symphony of whistles, rales, squeaks and bubbles which signalled the workings of Prince's lungs. The old dog stood very erect and proud, his tail still waving slowly. He

91

always took it as a tremendous compliment when I examined him and there was no doubt he was enjoying himself now. Fortunately his was not a very painful ailment.

Straightening up, I patted his head and he responded immediately by trying to put his paws on my chest. He didn't quite make it and even that slight exertion started his ribs heaving and his tongue lolling. I gave him an intramuscular injection of digitalin and another of morphine hydrochloride which he accepted with apparent pleasure as part of the game.

'I hope that will steady his heart and breathing, Miss Stubbs. You'll find he'll be a bit dopey for the rest of the day and that will help, too. Carry on with the tablets, and I'm going to leave you some more medicine for his bronchitis.'

I handed over a bottle of my old standby mixture of ipecacuanha and ammonium acetate.

The next stage of the visit began now as Mrs Broadwith brought in a cup of tea and the rest of the animals were let out of the kitchen. There was Ben, a Sealyham, and Sally, a Cocker Spaniel, and they started a deafening barking contest with Prince. They were closely followed by the cats, Arthur and Susie, who stalked in gracefully and began to rub themselves against my trouser legs.

It was the usual scenario for the many cups of tea I had drunk with Miss Stubbs under the little card which dangled above her bed.

'How are you today?' I asked.

'Oh, much better,' she replied and immediately, as always, changed the subject.

Mostly she liked to talk about her pets and the ones she had known right back to her girlhood. She spoke a lot, too, about the days when her family were alive. She loved to describe the escapades of her three brothers and today she showed me a photograph which Mrs Broadwith had found at the bottom of a drawer.

I took it from her and three young men in the knee breeches and little round caps of the nineties smiled up at me from the yellowed old print; they all held long church-warden pipes and the impish humour in their expressions came down undimmed over the years.

'My word, they look really bright lads, Miss Stubbs,' I said.

'Oh, they were young rips!' she exclaimed. She threw back her head and laughed and for a moment her face was radiant, transfigured by her memories.

The things I had heard in the village came back to me; about the prosperous father and his family who lived in the big house many years ago. Then the foreign investments which crashed and the sudden change in circumstances. 'When t'owd feller died he was about skint,' one old man had said. 'There's not much brass there now.'

Probably just enough brass to keep Miss Stubbs and her animals alive and to pay Mrs Broadwith. Not enough to keep the garden dug or the house painted or for any of the normal little luxuries.

And, sitting there, drinking my tea, with the dogs in a row by the bedside and the cats making themselves comfortable on the bed itself, I felt as I had often felt before—a bit afraid of the responsibility I had. The one thing which brought some light into the life of the brave old woman was the transparent devotion of this shaggy bunch whose eyes were never far from her face. And the snag was that they were all elderly.

There had, in fact, been four dogs originally, but one of them, a truly ancient golden Labrador, had died a few months previously. And now I had the rest of them to look after and none of them less than ten years old.

They were perky enough but all showing some of the signs of old age; Prince with his heart, Sally beginning to drink a lot of water which made me wonder if she was starting with a pyometra. Ben growing steadily thinner with his nephritis. I couldn't give him new kidneys and I hadn't much faith in the hexamine tablets I had prescribed. Another peculiar thing about Ben was that I was always having to clip his claws; they grew at an extraordinary rate.

The cats were better, though Susie was a bit scraggy and I

kept up a morbid kneading of her furry abdomen for signs of lymphosarcoma. Arthur was the best of the bunch; he never seemed to ail anything beyond a tendency for his teeth to tartar up.

This must have been in Miss Stubbs's mind because, when I had finished my tea, she asked me to look at him. I hauled him across the bedspread and opened his mouth.

'Yes, there's a bit of the old trouble there. Might as well fix it while I'm here.'

Arthur was a huge, grey, neutered Tom, living denial of all those theories that cats are cold-natured, selfish and the rest. His fine eyes, framed in the widest cat face I have ever seen, looked out on the world with an all-embracing benevolence and tolerance. His every movement was marked by immense dignity.

As I started to scrape his teeth his chest echoed with a booming purr like a distant outboard motor. There was no need for anybody to hold him; he sat there placidly and moved only once—when I was using forceps to crack off a tough piece of tartar from a back tooth and accidentally nicked his gum. He casually raised a massive paw as if to say 'Have a care, chum', but his claws were sheathed.

My next visit was less than a month later and was in response to an urgent summons from Mrs Broadwith at six o'clock in the evening. Ben had collapsed. I jumped straight into my car and in less than ten minutes was threading my way through the overgrown grass in the front garden with the animals watching from their window. The barking broke out as I knocked, but Ben's was absent. As I went into the little room I saw the old dog lying on his side, very still, by the bed.

D.O.A. is what we write in the day book. Dead on arrival. Just three words but they covered all kinds of situations— the end of milk fever cows, bloated bullocks, calves in fits. And tonight they meant that I wouldn't be clipping old Ben's claws any more.

It wasn't often these nephritis cases went off so suddenly

but his urine albumen had been building up dangerously lately.

'Well, it was quick, Miss Stubbs. I'm sure the old chap didn't suffer at all.' My words sounded lame and ineffectual.

The old lady was in full command of herself. No tears, only a fixity of expression as she looked down from the bed at her companion for so many years. My idea was to get him out of the place as quickly as possible and I pulled a banket under him and lifted him up. As I was moving away, Miss Stubbs said, 'Wait a moment.' With an effort she turned on to her side and gazed at Ben. Still without changing expression, she reached out and touched his head lightly. Then she lay back calmly as I hurried from the room.

In the back kitchen I had a whispered conference with Mrs Broadwith. 'I'll run down t'village and get Fred Manners to come and bury him,' she said. 'And if you've got time could you stay with the old lady while I'm gone. Talk to her, like, it'll do her good.'

I went back and sat down by the bed. Miss Stubbs looked out of the window for a few moments then turned to me. 'You know, Mr Herriot,' she said casually. 'It will be my turn next.'

'What do you mean?'

'Well, tonight Ben has gone and I'm going to be the next one. I just know it.'

'Oh, nonsense! You're feeling a bit low, that's all. We all do when something like this happens.' But I was disturbed. I had never heard her even hint at such a thing before.

'I'm not afraid,' she said. 'I know there's something better waiting for me. I've never had any doubts.' There was silence between us as she lay calmly looking up at the card on the gas bracket.

Then the head on the pillow turned to me again. 'I have only one fear.' Her expression changed with startling suddenness as if a mask had dropped. The brave face was almost unrecognizable. A kind of terror flickered in her eyes and she quickly grasped my hand.

95

'It's my dogs and cats, Mr Herriot. I'm afraid I might never see them when I'm gone and it worries me so. You see, I know I'll be reunited with my parents and my brothers, but . . .'

'Well, why not with your animals?'

'That's just it.' She rocked her head on the pillow and for the first time I saw tears on her cheeks. 'They say animals have no souls.'

'Who says?'

'Oh, I've read it and I know a lot of religious people believe it.'

'Well I don't believe it.' I patted the hand which still grasped mine. 'If having a soul means being able to feel love and loyalty and gratitude, then animals are better off than a lot of humans. You've nothing to worry about there.'

'Oh, I hope you're right. Sometimes I lie at night thinking about it.'

'I know I'm right, Miss Stubbs, and don't you argue with me. They teach us vets all about animals' souls.'

The tension left her face and she laughed with a return of her old spirit. 'I'm sorry to bore you with this and I'm not going to talk about it again. But before you go, I want you to be absolutely honest with me. I don't want reassurance from you—just the truth. I know you are very young but please tell me—what are your beliefs? Will my animals go with me?'

She stared intently into my eyes. I shifted in my chair and swallowed once or twice.

'Miss Stubbs, I'm afraid I'm a bit foggy about all this,' I said. 'But I'm absolutely certain of one thing. Wherever you are going, they are going too.'

She still stared at me but her face was calm again. 'Thank you, Mr Herriot, I know you are being honest with me. That is what you really believe, isn't it?'

'I do believe it,' I said. 'With all my heart I believe it.'

It must have been about a month later and it was entirely by accident that I learned I had seen Miss Stubbs for the last time. When a lonely, penniless old woman dies people don't rush up to you in the street to tell you. I was on my rounds and a farmer happened to mention that the cottage in Corby village was up for sale.

'But what about Miss Stubbs?' I asked.

'Oh, went off sudden about three weeks ago. House is in a bad state, they say—nowt been done at it for years.'

'Mrs Broadwith isn't staying on, then?'

'Nay, I hear she's staying at t'other end of village.'

'Do you know what's happened to the dogs and cats?'

'What dogs and cats?'

I cut my visit short. And I didn't go straight home though it was nearly lunch time. Instead I urged my complaining little car at top speed to Corby and asked the first person I saw where Mrs Broadwith was living. It was a tiny house but attractive and Mrs Broadwith answered my knock herself.

'Oh, come in, Mr Herriot. It's right good of you to call.' I went inside and we sat facing each other across a scrubbed table top.

'Well, it was sad about the old lady,' she said.

'Yes, I've only just heard.'

'Any road, she had a peaceful end. Just slept away at finish.'

'I'm glad to hear that.'

Mrs Broadwith looked round the room. 'I was real lucky to get this place—it's just what I've always wanted.'

I could contain myself no longer. 'What's happened to the animals?' I blurted out.

'Oh, they're in t'garden,' she said calmly. 'I've got a grand big stretch at back.' She got up and opened the door and with a surge of relief I watched my old friends pour in.

Arthur was on my knee in a flash, arching himself ecstatically against my arm while his outboard motor roared softly above the barking of the dogs. Prince, wheezy as ever, tail fanning the air, laughed up at me delightedly between barks.

'They look great, Mrs Broadwith. How long are they going to be here?'

'They're here for good. I think just as much about them as t'old lady ever did and I couldn't be parted from them. They'll have a good home with me as long as they live.'

I looked at the typical Yorkshire country face, at the heavy cheeks with their grim lines belied by the kindly eyes. 'This is wonderful,' I said. 'But won't you find it just a bit ... er ... expensive to feed them?'

'Nay, you don't have to worry about that. I 'ave a bit put away.'

'Well fine, fine, and I'll be looking in now and then to see how they are. I'm through the village every few days.' I got up and started for the door.

Mrs. Broadwith held up her hand. 'There's just one thing I'd like you to do before they start selling off the things at the cottage. Would you please pop in and collect what's left of your medicines. They're in t'front room.'

I took the key and drove along to the other end of the village. As I pushed open the rickety gate and began to walk through the tangled grass, the front of the cottage looked strangely lifeless without the faces of the dogs at the window; and when the door creaked open and I went inside, the silence was like a heavy pall.

Nothing had been moved. The bed with its rumpled blankets was still in the corner. I moved around, picking up half empty bottles, a jar of ointment, the cardboard box with old Ben's tablets—a lot of good they had done him.

When I had got everything I looked slowly round the little room. I wouldn't be coming here any more and at the door I paused and read for the last time the card which hung over the empty bed.

Chapter Thirteen

I WAS SPENDING Tuesday evening as I spent all the Tuesday evenings—staring at the back of Helen Alderson's head at the Darrowby Music Society. It was a slow way of getting to know her better but I had been unable to think of a better idea.

Since the morning on the high moor when I had set the calf's leg, I had scanned the day book regularly in the hope of getting another visit to the farm. But the Aldersons seemed to have lamentably healthy stock. I had to be content with the thought that there was the visit at the month end to take off the plaster. The really crushing blow came when Helen's father rang up to say that, since the calf was going sound he had removed the plaster himself. He was pleased to say that the fracture had knitted perfectly and there was no sign of lameness.

I had come to admire the self-reliance and initiative of the Dalesmen but I cursed it now at great length; and I joined the Music Society. I had seen Helen going into the school-room where the meetings were held and, with the courage of desperation, had followed her inside.

That was weeks ago and, I reflected miserably, I had made no progress at all. I couldn't remember how many tenors, sopranos and male voice choirs had come and gone, and on one occasion the local brass band had packed themselves into the little room and almost burst my ear drums; but I was no further forward.

Tonight a string quartet was scraping away industriously, but I hardly heard them. My eyes, as usual, were focused on

Helen, several rows in front of me, sitting between the two old ladies she always seemed to bring with her. That was part of the trouble; those two old girls were always there, cutting out any chance of private conversation, even at the half-time break for tea.

And there was the general atmosphere of the place; the members were nearly all elderly, and over everything hung the powerful schoolroom scent of ink and exercise books and chalk and lead pencils. It was the sort of place where you just couldn't say without warning 'Are you doing anything on Saturday night?'

The scraping stopped and everybody clapped. The vicar got up from the front row and beamed on the company. 'And now, ladies and gentlemen, I think we might stop for fifteen minutes as I see our willing helpers have prepared tea. The price, as usual is threepence.' There was laughter and a general pushing back of chairs.

I went to the back of the hall with the others, put my threepence on the plate and collected a cup of tea and a biscuit. This was when I tried to get near Helen in the blind hope that something might happen. It wasn't always easy, because I was often buttonholed by the school headmaster and others who regarded a vet who liked music as an interesting curiosity, but tonight I managed to edge myself as if by accident into her group.

She looked at me over the top of her cup.

'Good evening, Mr Herriot, are you enjoying it?'

Oh God, she always said that. And Mr Herriot! But what could I do? 'Call me Jim', would sound great.

I replied, as always, 'Good evening, Miss Alderson. Yes, it's very nice, isn't it.' Things were going with a bang again.

I munched my biscuit while the old ladies talked about Mozart. It was going to be the same as all the other Tuesdays. It was about time I gave up the whole thing. I felt beaten.

The vicar approached our group, still beaming.

'I'm afraid I have to call on somebody for the washing-up rota. Perhaps our two young friends would take it on tonight.' His friendly gaze twinkled from Helen to me and back again.

The idea of washing up teacups had never held much attraction for me but suddenly it was like sighting the promised land.

'Yes, certainly, delighted—that is if it's all right with Miss Alderson.'

Helen smiled. 'Of course it's all right. We all have to take a turn, don't we?'

I wheeled the trolley of cups and saucers into the scullery. It was a cramped, narrow place with a sink and a few shelves and there was just about room for the two of us to get inside.

'Would you like to wash or dry?' Helen asked.

'I'll wash,' I replied and began to run the hot water into the sink. It shouldn't be too difficult now, I thought, to work the conversation round to where I wanted it. I'd never have a better chance than now, jammed into this little room with Helen.

But it was surprising how the time went by. Five whole minutes and we hadn't talked about anything but music. With mounting frustration I saw that we had nearly got through the pile of crockery and I had achieved nothing.

The feeling changed to near panic when I lifted the last cup from the soapy water.

It had to be now. I held out the cup to Helen and she tried to take it from me; but I kept a grip on the handle while I waited for inspiration. She pulled gently but I clung to it tenaciously. It was developing into a tug of war. Then I heard a hoarse croak which I only just recognized as my own voice.

'Can I see you some time?'

For a moment she didn't answer and I tried to read her face. Was she surprised, annoyed, even shocked?

She flushed and replied, 'If you like.'

I heard the croak again. 'Saturday evening?'

She nodded, dried the cup and was gone.

I went back to my seat with my heart thudding. The

strains of mangled Haydn from the quartet went unheeded. I had done it at last. But did she really want to come out? Had she been hustled into it against her will? My toes curled with embarrassment at the thought, but I consoled myself with the knowledge that for better or for worse it was a step forward. Yes, I had done it at last.

Chapter Fourteen

AS I SAT AT BREAKFAST I looked out at the autumn mist dissolving in the early sunshine. It was going to be another fine day but there was a chill in the old house this morning, a shiveriness as though a cold hand had reached out to remind us that summer had gone and the hard months lay just ahead.

'It says here,' Siegfried said, adjusting his copy of the *Darrowby and Houlton Times* with care against the coffee-pot, 'that farmers have no feeling for their animals.'

I buttered a piece of toast and looked across at him.

'Cruel, you mean?'

'Well, not exactly, but this chap maintains that to a farmer, livestock are purely commercial—there's no sentiment in his attitude towards them, no affection.'

'Well, it wouldn't do if they were all like poor Kit Bilton, would it? They'd all go mad.'

Kit was a lorry driver who, like so many of the working men of Darrowby, kept a pig at the bottom of his garden for family consumption. The snag was that when killing time came, Kit wept for three days. I happened to go into his house on one of these occasions and found his wife and daughter hard at it cutting up the meat for pies and brawn while Kit huddled miserably by the kitchen fire, his eyes swimming with tears. He was a huge man who could throw a twelve stone sack of meal on to his wagon with a jerk of his arms, but he seized my hand in his and sobbed at me 'I can't bear it, Mr Herriot. He was like a Christian was that pig, just like a Christian.'

'No, I agree.' Siegfried leaned over and sawed off a slice of Mrs Hall's home-baked bread. 'But Kit isn't a real farmer. This article is about people who own large numbers of animals. The question is, is it possible for such men to become emotionally involved? Can the dairy farmer milking maybe fifty cows become really fond of any of them or are they just milk-producing units?'

'It's an interesting point,' I said, 'And I think you've put your finger on it with the numbers. You know there are a lot of our farmers up in the high country who have only a few stock. They always have names for their cows—Daisy, Mabel, I even came across one called Kipperlugs the other day. I do think these small farmers have an affection for their animals but I don't see how the big men can possibly have.'

Siegfried rose from the table and stretched luxuriously. 'You're probably right. Anyway, I'm sending you to see a really big man this morning. John Skipton of Dennaby Close —he's got some tooth rasping to do. Couple of old horses losing condition. You'd better take all the instruments, it might be anything.'

I went through to the little room down the passage and surveyed the tooth instruments. I always felt at my most mediaeval when I was caught up in large animal dentistry and in the days of the draught horse it was a regular task. One of the commonest jobs was knocking the wolf teeth out of young horses. I have no idea how it got its name but you found the little wolf tooth just in front of the molars and if a young horse was doing badly it always got the blame.

It was no good the vets protesting that such a minute, vestigial object couldn't possibly have any effect on a horse's health and that the trouble was probably due to worms. The farmers were adamant; the tooth had to be removed.

We did this by having the horse backed into a corner, placing the forked end of a metal rod against the tooth and giving a sharp tap with an absurdly large wooden mallet. Since the tooth had no proper root the operation was not particularly painful, but the horse still didn't like it. We usually had a couple of fore-feet waving around our ears at each tap.

And the annoying part was that after we had done the job and pointed out to the farmer that we had only performed this bit of black magic to humour him, the horse would take an immediate turn for the better and thrive consistently from then on. Farmers are normally reticent about our successful efforts for fear we might put a bit more on the bill but in these cases they cast aside all caution. They would shout at us across the market place: 'Hey, remember that 'oss you knocked wolf teeth out of? Well, he never looked back. It capped him.'

I looked again with distaste at the tooth instruments; the vicious forceps with two-feet-long arms, sharp-jawed shears, mouth gags, hammers and chisels, files and rasps; it was rather like a quiet corner of the Spanish Inquisition. We kept a long wooden box with a handle for carrying the things and I staggered out to the car with a fair selection.

Dennaby Close was not just a substantial farm, it was a monument to a man's endurance and skill. The fine old house, the extensive buildings, the great sweep of lush grassland along the lower slopes of the fell were all proof that old John Skipton had achieved the impossible; he had started as an uneducated farm labourer and he was now a wealthy landowner.

The miracle hadn't happened easily; old John had a lifetime of grinding toil behind him that would have killed most men, a lifetime with no room for a wife or family or creature comforts, but there was more to it than that; there was a brilliant acumen in agricultural matters that had made the old man a legend in the district. 'When all t'world goes one road, I go t'other' was one of his quoted sayings and it is true that the Skipton farms had made money in the hard times when others were going bankrupt. Dennaby was only one of John's farms; he had two large arable places of about four hundred acres each lower down the Dale.

He had conquered, but to some people it seemed that he

had himself been conquered in the process. He had battled against the odds for so many years and driven himself so fiercely that he couldn't stop. He could be enjoying all kinds of luxuries now but he just hadn't the time; they said that the poorest of his workers lived in better style than he did.

I paused as I got out of the car and stood gazing at the house as though I had never seen it before; and I marvelled again at the elegance which had withstood over three hundred years of the harsh climate. People came a long way to see Dennaby Close and take photographs of the graceful manor with its tall, leaded windows, the massive chimneys towering over the old moss-grown tiles; or to wander through the neglected garden and climb up the sweep of steps to the entrance with its wide stone arch over the great studded door.

There should have been a beautiful woman in one of those pointed hats peeping out from that mullioned casement or a cavalier in ruffles and hose pacing beneath the high wall with its pointed copings. But there was just old John stumping impatiently towards me, his tattered, buttonless coat secured only by a length of binder twine round his middle.

'Come in a minute, young man,' he cried. 'I've got a little bill to pay you.' He led the way round to the back of the house and I followed, pondering on the odd fact that it was always a 'little bill' in Yorkshire. We went in through a flagged kitchen to a room which was graceful and spacious but furnished only with a table, a few wooden chairs and a collapsed sofa.

The old man bustled over to the mantelpiece and fished out a bundle of papers from behind the clock. He leafed through them, threw an envelope on to the table then produced a cheque book and slapped it down in front of me. I did the usual—took out the bill, made out the amount on the cheque and pushed it over for him to sign. He wrote with a careful concentration, the small-featured, weathered face bent low, the peak of the old cloth cap almost touching the pen. His trousers had ridden up his legs as he sat down showing the skinny calves and bare ankles. There were no socks underneath the heavy boots.

When I had pocketed the cheque, John jumped to his feet. 'We'll have to walk down to t'river; 'osses are down there.' He left the house almost at a trot.

I eased my box of instruments from the car boot. It was a funny thing but whenever I had heavy equipment to lug about, my patients were always a long way away. This box seemed to be filled with lead and it wasn't going to get any lighter on the journey down through the walled pastures.

The old man seized a pitchfork, stabbed it into a bale of hay and hoisted it effortlessly over his shoulder. He set off again at the same brisk pace. We made our way down from one gateway to another, often walking diagonally across the fields. John didn't reduce speed and I stumbled after him, puffing a little and trying to put away the thought that he was at least fifty years older than me.

About half way down we came across a group of men at the age-old task of 'walling'—repairing a gap in one of the dry stone walls which trace their patterns everywhere on the green slopes of the Dales.

One of the men looked up. 'Nice mornin', Mr Skipton,' he sang out cheerfully.

'Bugger t'mornin'. Get on wi' some work,' grunted old John in reply and the man smiled contentedly as though he had received a compliment.

I was glad when we reached the flat land at the bottom. My arms seemed to have been stretched by several inches and I could feel a trickle of sweat on my brow. Old John appeared unaffected; he flicked the fork from his shoulder and the bale thudded on to the grass.

The two horses turned towards us at the sound. They were standing fetlock deep in the pebbly shallows just beyond a little beach which merged into the green carpet of turf; nose to tail, they had been rubbing their chins gently along each other's backs, unconscious of our approach. A high cliff over-hanging the far bank made a perfect wind-break while on either side of us clumps of oak and beech blazed in the autumn sunshine.

'They're in a nice spot, Mr Skipton,' I said.

'Aye, they can keep cool in the hot weather and they've got the barn when winter comes.' John pointed to a low, thick-walled building with a single door. 'They can come and go as they please.'

The sound of his voice brought the horses out of the river at a stiff trot and as they came near you could see they really were old. The mare was a chestnut and the gelding was a light bay but their coats were so flecked with grey that they almost looked like roans. This was most pronounced on their faces where the sprinkling of white hairs, the sunken eyes and the deep cavity above the eyes gave them a truly venerable appearance.

For all that, they capered around John with a fair attempt at skittishness, stamping their feet, throwing their heads about, pushing his cap over his eyes with their muzzles.

'Get by, leave off!' he shouted. 'Daft awd beggars.' But he tugged absently at the mare's forelock and ran his hands briefly along the neck of the gelding.

'When did they last do any work?' I asked.

'Oh, about twelve years ago, I reckon.'

I stared at John. 'Twelve years! And have they been down here all that time?'

'Aye, just lazin' about down here, retired like. They've earned it an' all.' For a few moments he stood silent, shoulders hunched, hands deep in the pockets of his coat, then he spoke quietly as if to himself. 'They were two slaves when I was a slave.' He turned and looked at me and for a revealing moment I read in the pale blue eyes something of the agony and struggle he had shared with the animals.

'But twelve years! How old are they, anyway?'

John's mouth twisted up at one corner. 'Well you're t'vet. You tell me.'

I stepped forward confidently, my mind buzzing with Galvayne's groove, shape of marks, degree of slope and the rest;

I grasped the unprotesting upper lip of the mare and looked at her teeth.

'Good God!' I gasped, 'I've never seen anything like this.' The incisors were immensely long and projecting forward till they met at an angle of about forty-five degrees. There were no marks at all—they had long since gone.

I laughed and turned back to the old man. 'It's no good, I'd only be guessing. You'll have to tell me.'

'Well she's about thirty and gelding's a year or two younger. She's had fifteen grand foals and never ailed owt except a bit of teeth trouble. We've had them rasped a time or two and it's time they were done again, I reckon. They're both losing ground and dropping bits of half chewed hay from their mouths. Gelding's the worst—has a right job champin' his grub.'

I put my hand into the mare's mouth, grasped her tongue and pulled it out to one side. A quick exploration of the molars with my other hand revealed what I suspected; the outside edges of the upper teeth were overgrown and jagged and were irritating the cheeks while the inside edges of the lower molars were in a similar state and were slightly excoriating the tongue.

'I'll soon make her more comfortable, Mr Skipton. With those sharp edges rubbed off she'll be as good as new.' I got the rasp out of my vast box, held the tongue in one hand and worked the rough surface along the teeth, checking occasionally with my fingers till the points had been sufficiently reduced.

'That's about right,' I said after a few minutes. 'I don't want to make them too smooth or she won't be able to grind her food.'

John grunted. 'Good enough. Now have a look at t'other. There's summat far wrong with him.'

I had a feel at the gelding's teeth. 'Just the same as the mare. Soon put him right, too.'

But pushing at the rasp, I had an uncomfortable feeling that something was not quite right. The thing wouldn't go fully to the back of the mouth, something was stopping it. I stopped rasping and explored again, reaching with my fingers as far as I could. And I came upon something very strange, something which shouldn't have been there at all. It was like a great chunk of bone projecting down from the roof of the mouth.

It was time I had a proper look. I got out my pocket torch and shone it over the back of the tongue. It was easy to see the trouble now; the last upper molar was overlapping the lower one resulting in a gross overgrowth of the posterior border. The result was a sabre-like barb about three inches long stabbing down into the tender tissue of the gum.

That would have to come off—right now. My jauntiness vanished and I suppressed a shudder; it meant using the horrible shears—those great long-handled things with the screw operated by a cross bar. They gave me the willies because I am one of those people who can't bear to watch anybody blowing up a balloon and this was the same sort of thing only worse. You fastened the sharp blades of the shears on to the tooth and began to turn the bar slowly, slowly. Soon the tooth began to groan and creak under the tremendous leverage and you knew that any second it would break off and when it did it was like somebody letting off a rifle in your ear. That was when all hell usually broke loose but mercifully this was a quiet old horse and I wouldn't expect him to start dancing around on his hind legs. There was no pain for the horse because the overgrown part had no nerve supply—it was the noise that caused the trouble.

Returning to my crate I produced the dreadful instrument and with it a Haussman's gag which I inserted on the incisors and opened on its ratchet till the mouth gaped wide. Everything was easy to see then and, of course, there it was—a great prong at the other side of the mouth exactly like the first. Great, great, now I had two to chop off.

The old horse stood patiently, eyes almost closed, as though he had seen it all and nothing in the world was going to bother him. I went through the motions with my toes curling and when the sharp crack came, the white-bordered eyes opened wide, but only in mild surprise. He never even moved. When I did the other side he paid no attention at all; in fact, with the gag prising his jaws apart he looked exactly as though he was yawning with boredom.

As I bundled the tools away, John picked up the bony spicules from the grass and studied them with interest. 'Well, poor awd beggar. Good job I got you along, young man. Reckon he'll feel a lot better now.'

On the way back, old John, relieved of his bale, was able to go twice as fast and he stumped his way up the hill at a furous pace, using the fork as a staff. I panted along in the rear, changing the box from hand to hand every few minutes.

About half way up, the thing slipped out of my grasp and it gave me a chance to stop for a breather. As the old man muttered impatiently I looked back and could just see the two horses; they had returned to the shallows and were playing together, chasing each other jerkily, their feet splashing in the water. The cliff made a dark backcloth to the picture —the shining river, the trees glowing bronze and gold and the sweet green of the grass.

Back in the farmyard, John paused awkwardly. He nodded once or twice, said 'Thank ye, young man,' then turned abruptly and walked away.

I was dumping the box thankfully into the boot when I saw the man who had spoken to us on the way down. He was sitting, cheerful as ever, in a sunny corner, back against a pile of sacks, pulling his dinner packet from an old army satchel.

'You've been down to see t'pensioners, then? By gaw, awd John should know the way.'

'Regular visitor, is he?'

'Regular? Every day God sends you'll see t'awd feller plod-din' down there. Rain, snow or blow, never misses. And allus has summat with him—bag o' corn, straw for their bedding,'

'And he's done that for twelve years?'

The man unscrewed his thermos flask and poured himself a cup of black tea. 'Aye, them 'osses haven't done a stroke o' work all that time and he could've got good money for them from the horse flesh merchants. Rum 'un, isn't it?'

'You're right,' I said, 'it is a rum 'un.'

Just how rum it was occupied my thoughts on the way back to the surgery. I went back to my conversation with Siegfried that morning; we had just about decided that the man with a lot of animals couldn't be expected to feel affection for individuals among them. But those buildings back there were full of John Skipton's animals—he must have hundreds.

Yet what made him trail down that hillside every day in all weathers? Why had he filled the last years of those two old horses with peace and beauty? Why had he given them a final ease and comfort which he had withheld from himself?

It could only be love.

Chapter Fifteen

THE LONGER I WORKED in Darrowby the more the charms of the Dales beguiled me. And there was one solid advantage of which I became more aware every day—the Dales farmers were all stocksmen. They really knew how to handle animals, and to a vet whose patients are constantly trying to thwart him or injure him it was a particular blessing.

So this morning I looked with satisfaction at the two men holding the cow. It wasn't a difficult job—just an intravenous injection of magnesium lactate—but still it was reassuring to have two such sturdy fellows to help me. Maurice Bennison, medium sized but as tough as one of his own hill beasts, had a horn in his right hand while the fingers of his left gripped the nose; I had the comfortable impression that the cow wouldn't jump very far when I pushed the needle in. His brother George whose job it was to raise the vein, held the choke rope limply in enormous hands like bunches of carrots. He grinned down at me amiably from his six feet four inches.

'Right, George,' I said. 'Tighten up that rope and lean against the cow to stop her coming round on me.' I pushed my way between the cow and her neighbour, past George's unyielding bulk and bent over the jugular vein. It was standing out very nicely. I poised the needle, feeling the big man's elbow on me as he peered over my shoulder, and thrust quickly into the vein.

'Lovely!' I cried as the dark blood fountained out and spattered thickly on the straw bedding beneath. 'Slacken your rope, George.' I fumbled in my pocket for the flutter valve. 'And for God's sake, get your weight off me!'

Because George had apparently decided to rest his full fourteen stones on me instead of the cow, and as I tried desperately to connect the tube to the needle I felt my knees giving way. I shouted again, despairingly, but he was inert, his chin resting on my shoulder, his breathing stertorous in my ear.

There could only be one end to it. I fell flat on my face and lay there writhing under the motionless body. My cries went unheeded; George was unconscious.

Mr Bennison, attracted by the commotion, came in to the byre just in time to see me crawling out from beneath his eldest son. 'Get him out, quick!' I gasped, 'Before the cows trample on him.' Wordlessly, Maurice and his father took an ankle apiece and hauled away in unison. George shot out from under the cows, his head beating a brisk tattoo on the cobbles, traversed the dung channel, then resumed his sleep on the byre floor.

Mr. Bennison moved back to the cow and waited for me to continue with my injection but I found the presence of the sprawled body distracting. 'Look, couldn't we sit him up against the wall and put his head between his legs?' I suggested apologizing. The others glanced at each other then, as though deciding to humour me, grabbed George's shoulders and trundled him over the floor with the expertise of men used to throwing around bags of fertiliser and potatoes. But even propped against the rough stones, his head slumped forward and his great long arms hanging loosely, the poor fellow still didn't look so good.

I couldn't help feeling a bit responsible. 'Don't you think we might give him a drink?'

But Mr Bennison had had enough. 'Nay, nay, he'll be right,' he muttered testily. 'Let's get on with t'job.' Evidently he felt he had pampered George too much already.

The incident started me thinking about this question of people's reactions to the sight of blood and other disturbing realities. Even though it was only my second year of practice I had already formulated certain rules about this, and one

114

was that it was always the biggest men who went down. (I had, by this time, worked out a few other, perhaps unscientific theories, e.g. big dogs were kept by people who lived in little houses and vice versa. Clients who said 'spare no expense' never paid their bills, ever. When I asked my way in the Dales and was told 'you can't miss it', I knew I'd soon be hopelessly lost.)

I had begun to wonder if perhaps country folk, despite their closer contact with fundamental things, were perhaps more susceptible than city people. Ever since Sid Blenkhorn had staggered into Skeldale House one evening. His face was ghastly white and he had obviously passed through a shattering experience. 'Have you got a drop o' whisky handy, Jim?' he quavered, and when I had guided him to a chair and Siegfried had put a glass in his hand he told us he had been at a first aid lecture given by Dr Allinson, a few doors down the street. 'He was talking about veins and arteries and things,' groaned Sid, passing a hand across his forehead. 'God, it was awful!' Apparently Fred Ellison the fishmonger had been carried out unconscious after only ten minutes and Sid himself had only just made it to the door. It had been a shambles.

I was interested because this sort of thing, I had found, was always just round the corner. I suppose we must have more trouble in this way than the doctors because in most cases when our medical colleagues have any cutting or carving to do they send their patients to hospital while the vets just have to get their jackets off and operate on the spot. It means that the owners and attendants of the animals are pulled in as helpers and are subjected to some unusual sights.

So, even in my short experience, I had become a fair authority on the various manifestations of 'coming over queer'. I suppose it was a bit early to start compiling statistics but I had never seen a woman or a little man pass out even though they might exhibit various shadings of the squeamish spectrum. The big chap was the best bet every time, especially the boisterous, super-confident type.

I have a vivid recollection of a summer evening when I had to carry out a rumenotomy on a cow. As a rule I was inclined to play for time when I suspected a foreign body—there were so many other conditions with similar symptoms that I was never in a hurry to make a hole in the animal's side. But this time diagnosis was easy; the sudden fall in milk yield, loss of cudding; grunting, and the rigid, sunken-eyed appearance of the cow. And to clinch it the farmer told me he had been repairing a hen house in the cow pasture—nailing up loose boards. I knew where one of the nails had gone.

The farm, right on the main street of the village, was a favourite meeting place for the local lads. As I laid out my instruments on a clean towel draped over a straw bale a row of grinning faces watched from above the half door of the box; not only watched but encouraged me with ribald shouts. When I was about ready to start it occurred to me that an extra pair of hands would be helpful and I turned to the door. 'How would one of you lads like to be my assistant?' There was even more shouting for a minute or two, then the door was opened and a huge young man with a shock of red hair ambled into the box; he was a magnificent sight with his vast shoulders and the column of sunburned neck rising from the open shirt. It needed only the bright blue eyes and the ruddy, high-cheekboned face to remind me that the Norsemen had been around the Dales a thousand years ago. This was a Viking.

I had him roll up his sleeves and scrub his hands in a bucket of warm water and antiseptic while I infiltrated the cow's flank with local anaesthetic. When I gave him artery forceps and scissors to hold he pranced around, making stabbing motions at the cow and roaring with laughter.

'Maybe you'd like to do the job yourself?' I asked. The Viking squared his great shoulders. 'Aye, I'll 'ave a go,' and the heads above the door cheered lustily.

As I finally poised my Bard Parker scalpel with its new razor-sharp blade over the cow, the air was thick with earthy witticisms. I had decided that this time I really would make the bold incision recommended in the surgery books; it was about time I advanced beyond the stage of pecking nervously at the skin. 'A veritable blow,' was how one learned author had described it. Well, that was how it was going to be.

I touched the blade down on the clipped area of the flank and with a quick motion of the wrist laid open a ten-inch wound. I stood back for a few seconds admiring the clean-cut edges of the skin with only a few capillaries spurting on to the glistening, twitching abdominal muscles. At the same time I noticed that the laughter and shouting from the heads had been switched off and was replaced by an eerie silence broken only by a heavy, thudding sound from behind me.

'Forceps, please,' I said, extending my hand back. But nothing happened. I looked round; the top of the half door was bare—not a head in sight. There was only the Viking spreadeagled in the middle of the floor, arms and legs flung wide, chin pointing to the roof. The attitude was so theatrical that I thought he was still acting the fool, but a closer examination erased all doubts: the Viking was out cold. He must have gone straight over backwards like a stricken oak.

The farmer, a bent little man who couldn't have scaled much more than eight stones, had been steadying the cow's head. He looked at me with the faintest flicker of amusement in his eyes. 'Looks like you and me for it, then, guvnor.' He tied the halter to a ring on the wall, washed his hands methodically and took up his place at my side. Throughout the operation, he passed me my instruments, swabbed away the seeping blood and clipped the sutures, whistling tunelessly through his teeth in a bored manner; the only time he showed any real emotion was when I produced the offending nail from the depths of the reticulum. He raised his eyebrows slightly, said ' 'ello, 'ello,' then started whistling again.

We were too busy to do anything for the Viking. Halfway through, he sat up, shook himself a few times, then got to

117

his feet and strolled with elaborate nonchalance out of the box. The poor fellow seemed to be hoping that perhaps we had noticed nothing unusual.

I don't suppose we could have done much to bring him round anyway. There was only one time I discovered a means of immediate resuscitation and that was by accident.

It was when Henry Dickson asked me to show him how to castrate a ruptured pig without leaving a swelling. Henry was going in for pigs in a big way and had a burning ambition to equip himself with veterinary skills.

When he showed me the young pig with the gross scrotal swelling I demurred. 'I really think this is a vet's job, Henry. Castrate your normal pigs by all means, but I don't think you could make a proper job of this sort of thing.'

'How's that, then?'

'Well, there's the local anaesthetic, danger of infection— and you really need a knowledge of anatomy to know what you're doing.'

All the frustrated surgeon in Henry showed in his eyes. 'Gaw, I'd like to know how to do it.'

'I'll tell you what,' I said. 'How about if I do this one as a demonstration and you can make up your own mind. I'll give him a general anaesthetic so you don't have to hold him.'

'Right, that's a good idea.' Henry thought for a moment. 'What'll you charge me to do 'im?'

'Seven and six.'

'Well, I suppose you have to have your pound of flesh. Get on.'

I injected a few c.c.s of Nembutal into the little pig's peritoneum and after some staggering he rolled over in the straw and lay still. Henry had rigged up a table in the yard and we laid the sleeping animal on it. I was preparing to start when Henry pulled out a ten-shilling note.

'Better pay you now before I forget.'

'All right, but my hands are clean now—push it into my pocket and I'll give you the change when we finish.'

118

I rather fancy myself as a teacher and soon warmed to my task. I carefully incised the skin over the inguinal canal and pulled out the testicle, intact in its tunics. 'See there, Henry, the bowels have come down the canal and are lying in with the testicle.' I pointed to the loops of intestine, pale pink through the translucent membranes. 'Now if I do this, I can push them right back into the abdomen, and if I press here, out they pop again. You see how it works? There, they've gone; now they're out again. Once more I make them disappear and whoops, there they are back with us! Now in order to retain them permanently in the abdomen I take the spermatic cord and wind it in its coverings tightly down to the . . .'

But my audience was no longer with me. Henry had sunk down on an upturned oil drum and lay slumped across the table, his head cradled on his arms. My disappointment was acute, and finishing off the job and inserting the sutures was a sad anticlimax with my student slumbering at the end of the table.

I put the pig back in his pen and gathered up my gear; then I remembered I hadn't given Henry his change. I don't know why I did it but instead of half-a-crown, I slapped down a shilling and sixpence on the wood a few inches from his face. The noise made him open his eyes and he gazed dully at the coins for a few seconds, then with almost frightening suddenness he snapped upright, ashen-faced but alert and glaring.

'Hey!' he shouted. 'I want another shillin'!'

Chapter Sixteen

VETS ARE USELESS CREATURES, parasites on the agricultural community, expensive layabouts who really know nothing about animals or their diseases. You might as well get Jeff Mallock the knacker man as send for a vet.

At least that was the opinion, frequently expressed, of the Sidlow family. In fact, when you came right down to it, just about the only person for miles around who knew how to treat sick beasts was Mr Sidlow himself. If any of their cows or horses fell ill it was Mr Sidlow who stepped forward with his armoury of sovereign remedies. He enjoyed a God-like prestige with his wife and large family and it was an article of their faith that father was infallible in these matters; the only other being who had ever approached his skill was long-dead Grandpa Sidlow from whom father had learned so many of his cures.

Mind you, Mr Sidlow was a just and humane man. After maybe five or six days of dedicated nursing during which he would perhaps push half-a-pound of lard and raisins down the cow's throat three times a day, rub its udder vigorously with turpentine or maybe cut a bit off the end of the tail to let the bad out, he always in the end called the vet. Not that it would do any good, but he liked to give the animal every chance. When the vet arrived he invariably found a sunken-eyed, dying creature and the despairing treatment he gave was like a figurative administration of the last rites. The animal always died so the Sidlows were repeatedly confirmed in their opinion—vets were useless.

The farm was situated outside the normal area of the practice and we were the third firm Mr Sidlow had dealt with. He had been a client of Grier of Brawton but had found him wanting and moved to Wallace away over in Mansley. Wallace had disappointed him grievously so he had decided to try Darrowby. He had been with us for over a year but it was an uncomfortable relationship because Siegfried had offended him deeply on his very first visit. It was to a moribund horse, and Mr Sidlow, describing the treatment to date, announced that he had been pushing raw onions up the horse's rectum; he couldn't understand why it was so uneasy on its legs. Siegfried had pointed out that if he were to insert a raw onion in Mr Sidlow's rectum, he, Mr Sidlow, would undoubtedly be uneasy on his legs.

It was a bad start but there were really no other available vets left. He was stuck with us.

I had been really lucky in that I had been at Darrowby for more than a year and had never had to visit this farm. Mr Sidlow rarely called us up during normal working hours as, after wrestling with his conscience for a few days, he always seemed to lose the battle around eleven o'clock at night (he made exceptions in the case of the occasional Sunday afternoon) and it had always landed on Siegfried's duty nights. It was Siegfried who had trailed out, swearing quietly, and returned, slightly pop-eyed, in the small hours.

So when it did finally come round to my turn I didn't rush out with any great enthusiasm, even though the case was just a choking bullock and should present no difficulties. (This was when a beast got a piece of turnip or a potato stuck in its gullet, preventing regurgitation of gases and causing bloating which can be fatal. We usually either relieved the bloat by puncturing the stomach or we carefully pushed the obstruction down into the stomach by means of a long flexible leather instrument called a probang.) Anyway, they had realized they couldn't wait for days this time and by way of a change it was only four o'clock in the afternoon.

The farm was nearer Brawton than Darrowby and lay in the low country down on the Plain of York. I didn't like the look of the place; there was something depressing about the dilapidated brick buildings in the dreary setting of ploughing land with only the occasional mound of a potato clamp to relieve the flatness.

My first sight of Mr Sidlow reminded me that he and his family were members of a fanatically narrow religious sect. I had seen that gaunt, blue-jowled face with the tortured eyes staring at me from the pages of history books long ago. I had the feeling that Mr Sidlow would have burnt me at the stake without a qualm.

The bullock was in a gloomy box off the fold yard. Several of the family had filed in with us; two young men in their twenties and three teenage girls, all good-looking in a dark gipsy way, but all with the same taut, unsmiling look as their father. As I moved around, examining the animal, I noticed another peculiarity—they all looked at me, the bullock, each other, with quick sideways glances without any head movement. Nobody said anything.

I would have liked to break the silence but couldn't think of anything cheerful to say. This beast didn't have the look of an ordinary choke. I could feel the potato quite distinctly from the outside, half-way down the oesophagus but all around was an oedematous mass extending up and down the left side of the neck. Not only that, but there was a bloody foam dripping from the mouth. There was something funny here.

A thought struck me. 'Have you been trying to push the potato down with something?

I could almost feel the battery of flitting glances, and the muscles of Mr Sidlow's clenched jaw stood out in a twitching ridge. He swallowed carefully. 'Aye, we've tried a bit.'

'What did you use?'

Again the rippling jaw muscles under the dark skin. 'Broom handle and a bit of hose pipe. Same as usual.'

That was enough; a sense of doom enveloped me. It would have been nice to be the first vet to make a good impression here but it wasn't to be. I turned to the farmer. 'I'm afraid you've ruptured the gullet. It's a very delicate tube, you know, and you only have to push a bit too hard and you're through. You can see the fluid collection round the rupture.'

A quivering silence answered me. I ploughed on. 'I've seen this happen before. It's a pretty black outlook.'

'All right,' Mr Sidlow ground out. 'What are you going to do about it?'

Well, we were at it now. What was I going to do about it? Maybe now, thirty years later, I might have tried to repair the gullet, packed the wound with antibiotic powder and given a course of penicillin injections. But there, in that cheerless place, looking at the patient animal gulping painfully, coughing up the gouts of blood, I knew I was whacked. A ruptured oesophagus was as near hopeless as anything could be. I searched my mind for a suitable speech.

'I'm sorry, Mr Sidlow, but I can't do anything about it.' The glances crackled around me and the farmer breathed in sharply through his nose. I didn't need to be told what they were all thinking—another no-good, useless vet. I took a deep breath and continued. 'Even if I shifted the potato the wound would get contaminated when the beast tried to eat. He'd have gangrene in no time and that means a painful death. He's in pretty good condition—if I were you I'd have him slaughtered immediately.'

The only reply was a virtuoso display from the jaw muscles. I tried another tack. 'I'll give you a certificate. I'm sure the meat will pass for the butcher.'

No cries of joy greeted this remark. If anything, Mr Sidlow's expression became still more bleak.

'That beast isn't ready for killin' yet,' he whispered.

'No, but you'd be sending him in before long—another month, maybe. I'm sure you won't lose much. I tell you what,' with a ghastly attempt at heartiness, 'if I can come into the house I'll write you this chit now and we'll get the job over. There's really nothing else for it.'

I turned and headed across the fold yard for the farm kitchen. Mr Sidlow followed wordlessly with the family. I wrote the certificate quickly, waves of disapproval washing around me in the silent room. As I folded the paper I had the sudden conviction that Mr Sidlow wasn't going to pay the slightest attention to my advice. He was going to wait a day or two to see how things turned out. The picture of the big, uncomprehending animal trying vainly to swallow as his hunger and thirst increased was too strong for me. I walked over to the phone on the window sill.

'I'll just give Harry Norman a ring at the abattoir. I know he'll come straight up if I ask him.' I made the arrangements, hung up the receiver and started for the door, addressing Mr Sidlow's profile as I left. 'It's fixed. Harry will be along within half-an-hour. Much better to get it done immediately.'

Going across the yard, I had to fight the impulse to break into a gallop. As I got into the car I recalled Siegfried's advice: 'In sticky situations always get your car backed round before you examine the animal. Leave the engine running if necessary. The quick getaway is essential.' He was right, it took a long time reversing and manœuvring under the battery of unseen eyes. I don't blush easily but my face was burning as I finally left the farm.

That was my first visit to the Sidlows and I prayed that it might be my last. But my luck had run out. From then on, every time they sent for us it just happened to be me on duty. I would rather not say anything about the cases I treated there except to record that something went wrong every time. The very name Sidlow became like a jinx. Try as I might I couldn't do a thing right on that farm so that within a short time I was firmly established with the family as the greatest menace to the animal population they had ever encountered. They didn't think much of vets as a whole and they'd met some real beauties in their time, but I was by far the worst. My position as the biggest nincompoop of them all was unassailable.

It got so bad that if I saw any Sidlows in the town I would dive down an alley to avoid them and one day in the market place I had the unnerving experience of seeing the entire family, somehow jammed into a large old car, passing within a few feet of me. Every face looked rigidly to the front but every eye, I knew, was trained balefully on me. Fortunately I was just outside the Drovers' Arms, so I was able to reel inside and steady myself with a half-pint of Younger's Special Heavy.

However, the Sidlows were far from my mind on the Saturday morning when Siegfried asked me if I would go through and officiate at Brawton races.

'They've asked me to do it as Grier is on holiday,' he said. 'But I'd already promised to go through to Casborough to help Dick Henley with a big operation. I can't let him down. There's nothing much to the race job: the regular course vet will be there and he'll keep you right.'

He hadn't been gone more than a few minutes when there was a call from the racecourse. One of the horses had fallen while being unloaded from its box and had injured its knee. Would I come right away.

Even now I am no expert on racehorses; they form a little branch of practice all by itself, with its own stresses, its own mystique. In my short spell in Darrowby I had had very little to do with them as Siegfried was fascinated by anything equine and usually gobbled up anything in that line which came along. So my practical experience was negligible.

I wasn't at all reassured when I saw my patient. The knee was a terrible mess. He had tripped at the bottom of the ramp and come down with his full weight on the stony ground. The lacerated skin hung down in bloody ribbons exposing the joint capsule over an area of about six inches and the extensor tendons gleamed through a tattered layer of fascia. The beautiful three-year-old held the limb up, trembling, with the toe just touching the ground; the ravaged knee made a violent contrast with the sleek, carefully groomed coat.

Examining the wound, gently feeling round the joint, I was immediately thankful for one thing—it was a quiet animal. Some light horses are so highly strung that the slightest touch sends them up in the air, but this one hardly moved as I tried to piece together the jigsaw of skin pieces. Another lucky break—there was nothing missing.

I turned to the stable head lad, small, square, hands deep in his coat pockets, who was standing watching. 'I'll clean up the wound and stitch it but he'll need some expert care when you get him home. Can you tell me who will be treating him?'

'Yes sir, Mr Brayley-Reynolds. He'll have charge of 'im.'

I came bolt upright from my crouching position. The name was like a trumpet call echoing down from my student days. When you talked about horses you usually talked about Brayley-Reynolds sooner or later. I could imagine the great man inspecting my handiwork. 'And who did you say treated this? Herriot . . . ? Herriot . . . ?'

I got down to the job again with my heart beating faster. Mercifully the joint capsule and tendon sheaths were undamaged—no escape of synovia. Using a solution of Chinosol, I swabbed out every last cranny of the wound till the ground around me was white with cotton wool pledgets, then I puffed in some iodoform powder and tacked down the loose shreds of fascia. Now the thing was to make a really good job of the skin to avoid disfigurement if possible. I chose some fine silk and a very small suture needle and squatted down again.

I must have stayed there for nearly an hour, pulling the flaps of skin carefully into position and fastening them down with innumerable tiny sutures. There is a fascination in repairing a ragged wound and I always took pains over it even without an imaginary Brayley-Reynolds peering over my shoulder. When I finally straightened up I did so slowly, like an old man, easing the kinks from my neck and back. With shaking knees I looked down at the head lad almost without recognition. He was smiling.

'You've made a proper job of that,' he said. 'It looks nearly as good as new. I want to thank you, sir—he's one of my

favourites, not just because he's a good 'orse, but he's kind.'
He patted the three-year-old's flank.

'Well, I hope he does all right.' I got out a packet of
gauze and a bandage. 'I'm just going to cover up the knee
with this and then you can put on a stable bandage. I'll give
him a shot against tetanus and that's it.'

I was packing my gear away in the car when the head lad
hovered again at my side. 'Do you back 'orses?'

I laughed. 'No, hardly ever. Don't know much about it.'

'Well never mind.' The little man looked around him and
lowered his voice. 'But I'll tell you something to back this
afternoon. Kemal in the first race. He's one of ours and he's
going to win. You'll get a nice price about him.'

'Well, thanks, it'll give me something to do. I'll have half-
a-crown on him.'

The tough little face screwed up in disgust. 'No, no, put a
fiver on him. This is the goods, I mean it. Keep it to yourself
but get a fiver on him.' He walked rapidly away.

I don't know what madness took hold of me, but by the
time I had got back to Darrowby I had decided to take his
advice. There had been something compelling about that
last hoarse whisper and the utter confidence in the black
pebble eyes. The little chap was trying to do me a good turn.
I had noticed him glancing at my old jacket and rumpled
flannels, so different from the natty outfit of the typical horse
vet; maybe he thought I needed the money.

I dropped in at the Midland Bank and drew out five
pounds which at the time represented approximately half
my available capital. I hurried round the remaining visits,
had a quick lunch and got into my best suit. There was
plenty of time to get to the course, meet the officials and get
my fiver on Kemal before the first race at 2.30.

The phone rang just as I was about to leave the house. It
was Mr Sidlow. He had a scouring cow which needed attention immediately. It was fitting, I thought dully, that in my
moment of eager anticipation it should be my old jinx who
should stretch out his cold hand and grasp me. And it was

Saturday afternoon; that was fitting too. But I shook myself —the farm was near Brawton and it shouldn't take long to deal with a scouring cow; I could still make it.

When I arrived, my immaculate appearance set up an immediate flurry of oblique glances among the assembled family while Mr Sidlow's rigid lips and squared shoulders bore witness that he was prepared to endure another visit from me with courage.

A numbness filled me as we went into the byre. It continued as Mr Sidlow described how he had battled against this cow's recurring bouts of diarrhoea for several months; how he had started quietly with ground eggshells in gruel and worked up to his most powerful remedy, blue vitriol and dandelion tea, but all to no avail. I hardly heard him because it was fairly obvious at a glance that the cow had Jöhne's disease.

Nobody could be quite sure, of course, but the animal's advanced emaciation, especially in the hind end, and the stream of bubbly, foetid scour which she had ejected as I walked in were almost diagnostic. Instinctively I grasped her tail and thrust my thermometer into the rectum: I wasn't much interested in her temperature but it gave me a couple of minutes to think.

However, in this instance I got only about five seconds because, without warning, the thermometer disappeared from my fingers. Some sudden suction had drawn it inside the cow. I ran my fingers round just inside the rectum— nothing; I pushed my hand inside without success; with a feeling of rising panic I rolled up my sleeve and groped about in vain.

There was nothing else for it—I had to ask for a bucket of hot water, soap and a towel and strip off as though preparing for some large undertaking. Over my thirty-odd years in practice I can recall many occasions when I looked a complete fool, but there is a peculiarly piercing quality about the memory of myself, bare to the waist, the centre of a ring of hostile stares, guddling frantically inside that cow. At the time, all I could think of was that this was the Sidlow place; anything could happen here. In my mental turmoil I had discarded all my knowledge of pathology and anatomy and could visualize the little glass tube working its way rapidly along the intestinal tract until it finally pierced some vital organ. There was another hideous image of myself carrying out a major operation, a full-scale laparotomy on the cow to recover my thermometer.

It is difficult to describe the glorious relief which flooded through me when at last I felt the thing between my fingers; I pulled it out, filthy and dripping and stared down stupidly at the graduations on the tube.

Mr Sidlow cleared his throat. 'Well, wot does it say? Has she got a temperature?'

I whipped round and gave him a piercing look. Was it possible that this man could be making a joke? But the dark, tight-shut face was expressionless.

'No,' I mumbled in reply. 'No temperature.'

The rest of that visit has always been mercifully blurred in my mind. I know I got myself cleaned up and dressed and told Mr Sidlow that I thought his cow had Jöhne's disease which was incurable but I would take away a faeces sample to try to make sure. The details are cloudy but I do know that at no point was there the slightest gleam of light or hope.

I left the farm, bowed down by an ever greater sense of disgrace than usual and drove with my foot on the boards all the way to Brawton. I roared into the special car park at the racecourse, galloped through the owners' and trainers' entrance and seized the arm of the gatekeeper.

'Has the first race been run?' I gasped.

'Aye, just finished,' he replied cheerfully. 'Kemel won it—ten to one.'

I turned and walked slowly towards the paddock. Fifty pounds! A fortune snatched from my grasp by cruel fate. And hanging over the whole tragedy was the grim spectre of Mr Sidlow.

I could forgive Mr Sidlow, I thought bitterly, for dragging me out at all sorts of ungodly hours; I could forgive him for presenting me with a long succession of hopeless cases which had lowered my self-esteem to rock bottom; I could forgive him for thinking I was the biggest idiot in Yorkshire and for proclaiming his opinion far and wide. But I'd never forgive him for losing me that fifty pounds.

Chapter Seventeen

'THE RENISTON, EH?' I fidgeted uneasily. 'Bit grand, isn't it?'

Tristan lay rather than sat in his favourite chair and peered up through a cloud of cigarette smoke. 'Of course it's grand. It's the most luxurious hotel in the country outside of London, but for your purpose it's the only possible place. Look, tonight is your big chance isn't it? You want to impress this girl, don't you? Well, ring her up and tell her you're taking her to the Reniston. The food is wonderful and there's a dinner dance every Saturday night. And today is Saturday.' He sat up suddenly and his eyes widened. 'Can't you see it, Jim? The music oozing out of Benny Thornton's trombone and you, full of lobster thermidor, floating round the floor with Helen snuggling up to you. The only snag is that it will cost you a packet, but if you are prepared to spend about a fortnight's wages you can have a really good night.'

I hardly heard the last part. I was concentrating on the blinding vision of Helen snuggling up to me. It was an image which blotted out things like money and I stood with my mouth half open listening to the trombone. I could hear it quite clearly.

Tristan broke in. 'There's one thing—have you got a dinner-jacket? You'll need one.'

'Well, I'm not very well off for evening-dress. In fact, when I went to Mrs Pumphrey's party I hired a suit from Brawton, but I wouldn't have time for that now.' I paused and thought for a moment. 'I do have my first and only dinner-suit but

I got it when I was about seventeen and I don't know whether I'd be able to get into it.'

Tristan waved this aside. He dragged the Woodbine smoke into the far depths of his lungs and released it reluctantly in little wisps and trickles as he spoke. 'Doesn't matter in the least, Jim. As long as you're wearing the proper gear they'll let you in, and with a big, good-looking chap like you the fit of the suit is unimportant.'

We went upstairs and extracted the garment from the bottom of my trunk. I had cut quite a dash in this suit at the college dances and though it had got very tight towards the end of the course it had still been a genuine evening-dress outfit and as such had commanded a certain amount of respect.

But now it had a pathetic, lost look. The fashion had changed and the trend was towards comfortable jackets and soft, unstarched shirts. This one was rigidly of the old school and included an absurd little waistcoat with lapels and a stiff, shiny-fronted shirt with a tall, winged collar.

My problems really started when I got the suit on. Hard work, Pennine air and Mrs Hall's good food had filled me out and the jacket failed to meet across my stomach by six inches. I seemed to have got taller, too, because there was a generous space between the bottom of the waistcoat and the top of the trousers. The trousers themselves were skin tight over the buttocks, yet seemed foolishly baggy lower down.

Tristan's confidence evaporated as I paraded before him and he decided to call on Mrs Hall for advice. She was an unemotional woman and endured the irregular life at Skeldale House without noticeable reaction, but when she came into the bedroom and looked at me her facial muscles went into a long, twitching spasm. She finally overcame the weakness, however, and became very businesslike.

' A little gusset at the back of your trousers will work wonders, Mr Herriot, and I think if I put a bit of silk cord across the front of your jacket it'll hold it nicely. Mind you, there'll be a bit of a space, like, but I shouldn't think that'll worry you. And I'll give the whole suit a good press—makes all the difference in the world.'

I had never gone in much for intensive grooming, but that night I really went to work on myself, scrubbing and anointing and trying a whole series of different partings in my hair before I was satisfied. Tristan seemed to have appointed himself master of the wardrobe and carried the suit tenderly upstairs, still warm from Mrs Hall's ironing board. Then, like a professional valet, he assisted in every step of the robing. The high collar gave most trouble and he drew strangled oaths from me as he trapped the flesh of my neck under the stud.

When I was finally arrayed he walked around me several times, pulling and patting the material and making delicate adjustments here and there.

Eventually he stopped his circling and surveyed me from the front. I had never seen him look so serious. 'Fine, Jim, fine—you look great. Distinguished, you know. It's not everybody who can wear a dinner-jacket—so many people look like conjurers, but not you. Hang on a minute and I'll get your overcoat.'

I had arranged to pick up Helen at seven o'clock and as I climbed from the car in the darkness outside her house a strange unease crept over me. This was different. When I had come here before it had been as a veterinary surgeon— the man who knew, who was wanted, who came to render assistance in time of need. It had never occurred to me how much this affected my outlook every time I walked on to a farm. This wasn't the same thing at all. I had come to take this man's daughter out. He might not like it, might positively resent it.

Standing outside the farmhouse door I took a deep breath. The night was very dark and still. No sound came from the great trees nearby and only the distant roar of the Darrow disturbed the silence. The recent heavy rains had transformed the leisurely, wandering river into a rushing torrent which in places overflowed its banks and flooded the surrounding pastures.

I was shown into the large kitchen by Helen's young brother. The boy had a hand over his mouth in an attempt to hide a wide grin. He seemed to find the situation funny. His little sister sitting at a table doing her homework was pretending to concentrate on her writing but she, too, wore a fixed smirk as she looked down at her book.

Mr Alderson was reading the *Farmer and Stockbreeder*, his breeches unlaced, his stockinged feet stretched towards a blazing pile of logs. He looked up over his spectacles.

'Come in, young man, and sit by the fire,' he said absently. I had the uncomfortable impression that it was a frequent and boring experience for him to have young men calling for his eldest daughter.

I sat down at the other side of the fire and Mr Alderson resumed his study of the *Farmer and Stockbreeder*. The ponderous tick-tock of a large wall clock boomed out into the silence. I stared into the red depths of the fire till my eyes began to ache, then I looked up at a big oil painting in a gilt frame hanging above the mantelpiece. It depicted shaggy cattle standing knee-deep in a lake of an extra-ordinary bright blue; behind them loomed a backcloth of fearsome, improbable mountains, their jagged summits wreathed in a sulphurous mist.

Averting my eyes from this, I examined, one by one, the sides of bacon and the hams hanging from the rows of hooks in the ceiling. Mr Alderson turned over a page. The clock ticked on. Over by the table, spluttering noises came from the children.

After about a year I heard footsteps on the stairs, then Helen came into the room. She was wearing a blue dress—the kind, without shoulder straps, that seems to stay up by magic. Her dark hair shone under the single pressure lamp which lit the kitchen, shadowing the soft curves of her neck and shoulders. Over one white arm she held a camel-hair coat.

I felt stunned. She was like a rare jewel in the rough setting of stone flags and whitewashed walls. She gave me her quiet, friendly smile and walked towards me. 'Hello, I hope I haven't kept you waiting too long.'

I muttered something in reply and helped her on with her coat. She went over and kissed her father who didn't look up but waved his hand vaguely. There was another outburst of giggling from the table. We went out.

In the car I felt unusually tense and for the first mile or two had to depend on some inane remarks about the weather to keep a conversation going. I was beginning to relax when I drove over a little hump-backed bridge into a dip in the road. Then the car suddenly stopped. The engine coughed gently and then we were sitting silent and motionless in the darkness. And there was something else; my feet and ankles were freezing cold.

'My God!' I shouted. 'We've run into a bit of flooded road. The water's right into the car.' I looked round at Helen. 'I'm terribly sorry about this—your feet must be soaked.'

But Helen was laughing. She had her feet tucked up on the seat, her knees under her chin. 'Yes, I am a bit wet, but it's no good sitting about like this. Hadn't we better start pushing?'

Wading out into the black icy waters was a nightmare but there was no escape. Mercifully it was a little car and between us we managed to push it beyond the flooded patch. Then by torchlight I dried the plugs and got the engine going again.

Helen shivered as we squelched back into the car. 'I'm afraid I'll have to go back and change my shoes and stockings. And so will you. There's another road back through Fensley. You take the first turn on the left.'

Back at the farm, Mr Alderson was still reading the *Farmer and Stockbreeder* and kept his finger on the list of pig prices while he gave me a baleful glance over his spectacles. When he learned that I had come to borrow a pair of his shoes and socks he threw the paper down in exasperation and rose, groaning, from his chair. He shuffled out of the room and I could hear him muttering to himself as he mounted the stairs.

Helen followed him and I was left alone with the two young children. They studied my sodden trousers with undisguised delight. I had wrung most of the surplus water out of them but the final result was remarkable. Mrs Hall's knife-edge crease reached to just below the knee, but then there was chaos. The trousers flared out at that point in a crumpled, shapeless mass and as I stood by the fire to dry them a gentle steam rose about me. The children stared at me, wide-eyed and happy. This was a big night for them.

Mr Alderson reappeared at length and dropped some shoes and rough socks at my feet. I pulled on the socks quickly but shrank back when I saw the shoes. They were a pair of dancing slippers from the early days of the century and their cracked patent leather was topped by wide, black silk bows.

I opened my mouth to protest but Mr Alderson had dug himself deep into his chair and had found his place again among the pig prices. I had the feeling that if I asked for another pair of shoes Mr Alderson would attack me with the poker. I put the slippers on.

We had to take a roundabout road to avoid the floods but I kept my foot down and within half-an-hour we had left the steep sides of the Dale behind us and were heading out on to the rolling plain. I began to feel better. We were making good time and the little car, shuddering and creaking, was going well. I was just thinking that we wouldn't be all that late when the steering-wheel began to drag to one side.

I had a puncture most days and recognised the symptoms immediately. I had become an expert at changing wheels and with a word of apology to Helen was out of the car like a flash. With my rapid manipulation of the rusty jack and brace the wheel was off within three minutes. The surface of the crumpled tyre was quite smooth except for the lighter, frayed parts where the canvas showed through. Working like a demon, I screwed on the spare, cringing inwardly as I saw that this tyre was in exactly the same condition as the other. I steadfastly refused to think of what I would do if its frail fibres should give up the struggle.

By day, the Reniston dominated Brawton like a vast mediaeval fortress, bright flags fluttering arrogantly from its four turrets, but tonight it was like a dark cliff with a glowing cavern at street level where the Bentleys discharged their expensive cargoes. I didn't take my vehicle to the front entrance but tucked it away quietly at the back of the car park. A magnificent commissionaire opened the door for us and we trod noiselessly over the rich carpeting of the entrance hall.

We parted there to get rid of our coats, and in the men's cloakroom I scrubbed frantically at my oily hands. It didn't do much good; changing that wheel had given my finger nails a border of deep black which defied ordinary soap and water. And Helen was waiting for me.

I looked up in the mirror at the white-jacketed attendant hovering behind me with a towel. The man, clearly fascinated by my ensemble, was staring down at the wide-bowed pierrot shoes and the rumpled trouser bottoms. As he handed over the towel he smiled broadly as if in gratitude for this little bit of extra colour in his life.

I met Helen in the reception hall and we went over to the desk. 'What time does the dinner dance start?' I asked.

The girl at the desk looked surprised. 'I'm sorry, sir, there's no dance tonight. We only have them once a fortnight.'

I turned to Helen in dismay but she smiled encouragingly. 'It doesn't matter,' she said. 'I don't really care what we do.'

'We can have dinner, anyway,' I said. I tried to speak cheerfully but a little black cloud seemed to be forming just above my head. Was anything going to go right tonight? I could feel my morale slumping as I padded over the lush carpet and my first sight of the dining-room didn't help.

It looked as big as a football field with great marble pillars supporting a carved, painted ceiling. The Reniston had been built in the late Victorian period and all the opulence and ornate splendour of those days had been retained in this tremendous room. Most of the tables were occupied by the usual clientele, a mixture of the county aristocracy and industrialists from the West Riding. I had never seen so many beautiful women and masterful-looking men under one roof and I noticed with a twinge of alarm that, though the men were wearing everything from dark lounge suits to hairy tweeds, there wasn't another dinner jacket in sight.

A majestic figure in white tie and tails bore down on us. With his mane of white hair falling back from the lofty brow, the bulging waistline, the hooked nose and imperious expression he looked exactly like a Roman emperor. His eyes flickered expertly over me and he spoke tonelessly.

'You want a table, sir?'

'Yes please,' I mumbled, only just stopping myself saying 'sir' to the man in return. 'A table for two.'

'Are you staying, sir?'

This question baffled me. How could I possibly have dinner here if I wasn't staying.

'Yes, I am staying.'

The emperor made a note on a pad. 'This way, sir.'

He began to make his way with great dignity among the tables while I followed abjectly in his wake with Helen. It was a long way to the table and I tried to ignore the heads which turned to have a second look at me as I passed. It was Mrs Hall's gusset that worried me most and I imagined it standing out like a beacon below the short jacket. It was literally burning my buttocks by the time we arrived.

The table was nicely situated and a swarm of waiters descended on us, pulling out our chairs and settling us into them, shaking out our napkins and spreading them on our laps. When they had dispersed, the emperor took charge again. He poised a pencil over his pad.

'May I have your room number, sir?'

138

I swallowed hard and stared up at him over my dangerously billowing shirt front. 'Room number? Oh, I'm not
living in the hotel.'

'Ah, NOT staying.' He fixed me for a moment with an icy
look before crossing out something on the pad with unnecessary violence. He muttered something to one of the waiters
and strode away.

It was about then that the feeling of doom entered into
me. The black cloud over my head spread and descended,
enveloping me in a dense cloud of misery. The whole evening had been a disaster and would probably get worse. I must
have been mad to come to this sumptuous place dressed up
like a knockabout comedian. I was as hot as hell inside this
ghastly suit and the stud was biting viciously into my neck.

I took a menu card from a waiter and tried to hold it with
my fingers curled inwards to hide my dirty nails. Everything
was in French and in my numbed state the words were
largely meaningless, but somehow I ordered the meal and,
as we ate, I tried desperately to keep a conversation going.
But long deserts of silence began to stretch between us; it
seemed that only Helen and I were quiet among all the
surrounding laughter and chatter.

Worst of all was the little voice which kept telling me that
Helen had never really wanted to come out with me anyway.
She had done it out of politeness and was getting through a
boring evening as best she could.

The journey home was a fitting climax. We stared straight
ahead as the headlights picked out the winding road back
into the Dales. We made stumbling remarks then the
strained silence took over again. By the time we drew up
outside the farm my head had begun to ache.

We shook hands and Helen thanked me for a lovely evening. There was a tremor in her voice and in the moonlight
her face was anxious and withdrawn. I said goodnight, got
into the car and drove away.

Chapter Eighteen

IF ONLY MY CAR had had any brakes I would certainly have enjoyed looking down on Worton village from the high moor. The old stone houses straggling unevenly along the near bank of the river made a pleasant splash of grey on the green floor of the valley and the little gardens with their clipped lawns gave a touch of softness to the bare, rising sweep of the fellside on the other side of the Dale.

But the whole scene was clouded by the thought that I had to get down that road with its 1 in 4 gradient and those two villainous S bends. It was like a malevolent snake coiling almost headlong from where I sat. And, as I said, I had no brakes.

Of course the vehicle had originally been fitted with the means of bringing it to a halt, and during most of the year I had ridden in it a violent pressure on the pedal would have the desired effect even though it caused a certain amount of veering about on the road. But lately the response had been growing weaker and now it was nil.

During the gradual deterioration I had brought the matter up with Siegfried now and then and he had expressed sympathy and concern.

'That won't do at all, James. I'll have a word with Hammond about it. Leave it with me.'

And then a few days later when I made a further appeal.

'Oh Lord, yes. I've been meaning to fix it up with Hammond. Don't worry, James, I'll see to it.'

Finally I had to tell him that when I put my foot on the pedal there was nothing at all and the only way I had of stopping the car was to crash it into bottom gear.

'Oh bad luck, James. Must be a nuisance for you. But never mind, I'll arrange everything.'

Some time later I asked Mr Hammond down at the garage if he had heard anything from Siegfried, but he hadn't. The motor man did, however, hop into the car and drive it slowly down the street.

He came to a jerking, shuddering halt about fifty yards away and then got out. He made no attempt to back up but walked thoughtfully towards me. Normally an imperturbable man, he had gone rather pale and he looked at me wonderingly.

'And you mean to tell me, lad, that you do all your rounds in that car?'

'Well, yes, I do.'

'You ought to have a medal, then. I dursn't drive across market place in that bloody thing.'

There wasn't much I could do. The car was Siegfried's property and I'd have to await his pleasure. Of course I had had experience of this sort of thing before in the shape of the movable passenger seat he had in his own vehicle when I first came to Darrowby. He never seemed to notice when I went over backwards every time I sat in it and I don't suppose he would ever have done anything about it but for an incident one market day when he noticed an old lady with a large basket of vegetables walking into Darrowby and courteously offered her a lift.

'Poor old girl's feet went straight up in the air and she just disappeared into the back. Had a hell of a job getting her out—thought we'd have to get a block and tackle. Cabbages and cauliflowers rolling all over the place.'

I looked again down the steep track. The sensible thing, of course, would be to go back into Darrowby and take the low road into Worton. No danger that way. But it meant a round trip of nearly ten miles and I could actually see the small-holding I wanted to visit just a thousand feet below. The calf with joint ill was in that shed with the green door—in fact there was old Mr Robinson coming out of the house now and pottering across the yard with a bucket. I could almost reach out and touch him.

I thought, not for the first time, that if you had to drive a car with no brakes one of the last places in England you'd want to be was the Yorksire Dales. Even on the flat it was bad enough but I got used to it after a week or two and often forgot all about it. As when one day I was busy with a cow and the farmer jumped into my car to move it so that one of his men could get past with a tractor. I never said a word as the unsuspecting man backed round quickly and confidently and hit the wall of the barn with a sickening crash. With typical Yorkshire understatement, all he said was; 'Your brakes aren't ower savage, mister.'

Anyway, I had to make up my mind. Was it to be back to Darrowby or straight over the top? It had become a common situation and every day I had the experience of sitting wrestling with myself on the edge of a hill with my heart thumping as it was now. There must have been scores of these unwitnessed dramas played out in the green silence of the fells.

At last, I started the engine and did what I always did—took the quick way down.

But this hill really was a beauty, a notorious road even in this country, and as I nosed gingerly on to it, the whole world seemed to drop away from me. With the gear lever in bottom and my hand jammed against it I headed, dry-mouthed, down the strip of tarmac which now looked to be almost vertical.

It is surprising what speed you can attain in bottom gear if you have nothing else to hold you back and as the first bend rushed up at me the little engine started a rising scream of protest. When I hit the curve, I hauled the wheel round desperately to the right, the tyres spun for a second in the stones and loose soil of the verge, then we were off again.

This was a longer stretch and even steeper and it was like being on the big dipper with the same feeling of lack of control over one's fate. Hurtling into the bend, the idea of turning at this speed was preposterous but it was that or straight over the edge.

Terror-stricken, I closed my eyes and dragged the wheel to the left. This time, one side of the car lifted and I was sure we were over, then it rocked back on to the other side and for a horrible second or two kept this up till it finally decided to stay upright and I was once more on my way.

Again a yawning gradient. But as the car sped downwards, engine howling, I was aware of a curious numbness. I seemed to have reached the ultimate limits of fear and hardly noticed as we shot round the third bend. One more to go and at last the road was levelling out; my speed dropped rapidly and at the last bend I couldn't have been doing more than twenty. I had made it.

It wasn't till I was right on to the final straight that I saw the sheep. Hundreds of them, filling the road. A river of woolly backs lapping from wall to wall. They were only yards from me and I was still going downhill. Without hesitation I turned and drove straight into the wall.

There didn't seem to be much damage. A few stones slithered down as the engine stalled and fell silent.

Slowly I sank back in my seat, relaxing my clenched jaws, releasing, finger by finger, the fierce grip on the wheel. The sheep continued to flow past and I took a sideways glance at the man who was shepherding them. He was a stranger to me and I prayed he didn't recognize me either because at that moment the role of unknown madman seemed to be the ideal one. Best not to say anything; appearing round a corner and driving deliberately into a wall is no basis for a rewarding conversation.

The sheep were still passing by and I could hear the man calling to his dogs. 'Get by, Jess. Come by, Nell.' But I kept up a steady stare at the layered stones in front of me, even though he passed within a few feet.

I suppose some people would have asked me what the hell I was playing at, but not a Dales shepherd. He went quietly by without invading my privacy, but when I looked in the mirror after a few moments I could see him in the middle of the road staring back at me, his sheep temporarily forgotten.

My brakeless period has always been easy to recall. There is a piercing clarity about the memory which has kept it fresh over the years. I suppose it lasted only a few weeks but it could have gone on indefinitely if Siegfried himself hadn't become involved.

It was when we were going to a case together. For some reason he decided to take my car and settled in the driver's seat. I huddled apprehensively next to him as he set off at his usual brisk pace.

Hinchcliffe's farm lies about a mile on the main road outside Darrowby. It is a massive place with a wide straight drive leading down to the house. We weren't going there, but as Siegfried spurted to full speed I could see Mr Hinchcliffe in his big Buick ahead of us proceeding in a leisurely way along the middle of the road. As Siegfried pulled out to overtake, the farmer suddenly stuck out his hand and began to turn right towards his farm—directly across our path. Siegfried's foot went hard down on the brake pedal and his eyebrows shot right up as nothing happened. We were going straight for the side of the Buick and there was no room to go round on the left.

Siegfried didn't panic. At the last moment he turned right with the Buick and the two cars roared side by side down the drive, Mr Hinchcliffe staring at me with bulging eyes from close range. The farmer stopped in the yard, but we continued round the back of the house because we had to.

Fortunately, it was one of those places where you could drive right round and we rattled through the stackyard and back to the front of the house behind Mr Hinchcliffe who had got out and was looking round the corner to see where we had gone. The farmer whipped round in astonishment and, open-mouthed watched us as we passed, but Siegfried, retaining his aplomb to the end, inclined his head and gave a little wave before we shot back up the drive.

Before we returned to the main road I had a look back at Mr Hinchcliffe. He was still watching us and there was a certain rigidity in his pose which reminded me of the shepherd.

Once on the road, Siegfried steered carefully into a layby and stopped. For a few moments he stared straight ahead without speaking and I realized he was having a little difficulty in getting his patient look properly adjusted; but when he finally turned to me his face was transfigured, almost saintly.

I dug my nails into my palms as he smiled at me with kindly eyes.

'Really, James,' he said, 'I can't understand why you keep things to yourself. Heaven knows how long your car has been in this condition, yet never a word from you.' He raised a forefinger and his patient look was replaced by one of sorrowing gravity. 'Don't you realize we might have been killed back there? You really ought to have told me.'

Chapter Nineteen

THERE DIDN'T seem much point in a millionaire filling up
football pools coupons but it was one of the motive forces in
old Harold Denham's life. It made a tremendous bond between us because, despite his devotion to the pools, Harold
knew nothing about football, had never seen a match and
was unable to name a single player in league football; and
when he found that I could discourse knowledgeably not
only about Everton and Preston North End but even about
Arbroath and Cowdenbeath, the respect with which he had
always treated me deepened into a wide-eyed deference.

Of course we had first met over his animals. He had an
assortment of dogs, cats, rabbits, budgies and goldfish which
made me a frequent visitor to the dusty mansion whose Victorian turrets peeping above their sheltering woods could be
seen for miles around Darrowby. When I first knew him, the
circumstances of my visits were entirely normal—his fox
terrier had cut its pad or the old grey tabby was having
trouble with its sinusitis, but later on I began to wonder. He
called me out so often on a Wednesday and the excuse was
at times so trivial that I began seriously to suspect that there
was nothing wrong with the animal but that Harold was in
difficulties with his Nine Results or the Easy Six.

I could never be quite sure, but it was funny how he
always received me with the same words. 'Ah, Mr Herriot,
how are your pools?' He used to say the word in a long-
drawn, loving way—pools. This inquiry had been unvarying
ever since I had won sixteen shillings one week on the Three
Draws. I can never forget the awe with which he fingered the

little slip from Littlewoods, looking unbelievingly from it to the postal order. That was the only time I was a winner but it made no difference—I was still the oracle unchallenged, supreme. Harold never won anything, ever.

The Denhams were a family of note in North Yorkshire. The immensely wealthy industrialists of the last century had become leaders in the world of agriculture. They were 'gentlemen farmers' who used their money to build up pedigree herds of dairy cows or pigs; they ploughed out the high, stony moorland and fertilized it and made it grow crops, they drained sour bogs and made them yield potatoes and turnips; they were the chairmen of committees, masters of foxhounds, leaders of the county society.

But Harold had opted out of all that at an early age. He had refuted the age-old dictum that you can't be happy doing absolutely nothing; all day and every day he pottered around his house and his few untidy acres, uninterested in the world outside, not entirely aware of what was going on in his immediate vicinity, but utterly content. I don't think he ever gave a thought to other people's opinions which was just as well because they were often unkind; his brother, the eminent Basil Denham, referred to him invariably as 'that bloody fool' and with the country people it was often 'nob-but ninepence in t'shillin'.'

Personally I always found something appealing in him. He was kind, friendly, with a sense of fun and I enjoyed going to his house. He and his wife ate all their meals in the kitchen and in fact seemed to spend most of their time there, so I usually went round the back of the house.

On this particular day it was to see his Great Dane bitch which had just had pups and seemed unwell; since it wasn't Wednesday I felt that there really might be something amiss with her and hurried round. Harold gave me his usual greeting; he had the most attractive voice—round, fruity, mellow, like a bishop's, and for the hundredth time I thought how odd it was to hear those organ-like vocal cords intoning such incongruities as Mansfield Town or Bradford City.

'I wonder if you could advise me, Mr Herriot,' he said as we left the kitchen and entered a long, ill-lit passage. 'I'm searching for an away winner and I wondered about Sunderland at Aston Villa?'

I stopped and fell into an attitude of deep thought while Harold regarded me anxiously. 'Well, I'm not sure, Mr Denham,' I replied. 'Sunderland are a good side but I happen to know that Raich Carter's auntie isn't too well at present and it could easily affect his game this Saturday.'

Harold looked crestfallen and he nodded his head gravely a few times; then he looked closely at me for a few seconds and broke into a shout of laughter. 'Ah, Mr Herriot, you're pulling my leg again.' He seized my arm, gave it a squeeze and shuffled off along the passage, chuckling deeply.

We traversed a labyrinth of gloomy, cobwebbed passages before he led the way into a little gun room. My patient was lying on a raised wooden dog bed and I recognized her as the enormous Dane I had seen leaping around at previous visits. I had never treated her, but my first sight of her had dealt a blow at one of my new-found theories—that you didn't find big dogs in big houses. Times without number I had critically observed Bull Mastiffs, Alsatians and Old English Sheep Dogs catapulting out of tiny, back street dwellings of Darrowby, pulling their helpless owners on the end of a lead, while in the spacious rooms and wide acres of the stately homes I saw nothing but Border Terriers and Jack Russells. But Harold would have to be different.

He patted the bitch's head. 'She had the puppies yesterday and she's got a nasty dark discharge. She's eating well, but I'd like you to look her over.'

Great Danes, like most of the big breeds, are usually placid animals and the bitch didn't move as I took her temperature. She lay on her side, listening contentedly to the squeals of her family as the little blind creatures climbed over each other to get at the engorged teats.

'Yes, she's got a slight fever and you're right about the discharge.' I gently palpated the long hollow of the flank. 'I don't think there's another pup there but I'd better have a feel inside her to make sure. Could you bring me some warm water, soap and towel, please?'

As the door closed behind Harold I looked idly around the gun room. It wasn't much bigger than a cupboard and, since another of Harold's idiosyncrasies was that he never killed anything, was devoid of guns. The glass cases contained only musty bound volumes of *Blackwood's Magazine* and *Country Life*. I stood there for maybe ten minutes, wondering why the old chap was taking so long, then I turned to look at an old print on the wall; it was the usual hunting scene and I was peering through the grimy glass and wondering why they always drew those horses flying over the stream with such impossible long legs when I heard a sound behind me.

It was a faint growl, a deep rumble, soft but menacing. I turned and saw the bitch rising very slowly from her bed. She wasn't getting to her feet in the normal way of dogs, it was as though she were being lifted up by strings somewhere in the ceiling, the legs straightening almost imperceptibly, the body rigid, every hair bristling. All the time she glared at me unblinkingly and for the first time in my life I realized the meaning of blazing eyes. I had only once seen anything like this before and it was on the cover of an old copy of *The Hound of the Baskervilles*. At the time I had thought the artist ridiculously fanciful but here were two eyes filled with the same yellow fire and fixed unwaveringly on mine.

She thought I was after her pups, of course. After all, her master had gone and there was only this stranger standing motionless and silent in the corner of the room, obviously up to no good. One thing was sure—she was going to come at me any second, and I blessed the luck that had made me stand right by the door. Carefully I inched my left hand towards the handle as the bitch still rose with terrifying slowness, still rumbling deep in her chest. I had almost reached the handle when I made the mistake of making a quick grab for it.

Just as I touched the metal the bitch came out of the bed like a rocket and sank her teeth into my wrist.

I thumped her over the head with my right fist and she let go and seized me high up on the inside of the left thigh. This really made me yell out and I don't know just what my immediate future would have been if I hadn't bumped up against the only chair in the room; it was old and flimsy but it saved me. As the bitch, apparently tiring of gnawing my leg, made a sudden leap at my face I snatched the chair up and fended her off.

The rest of my spell in the gun room was a sort of parody of a lion-taming act and would have been richly funny to an impartial observer. In fact, in later years I have often wished I could have had a cine film of the episode; but at the time, with that great animal stalking me round those few cramped yards of space, the blood trickling down my leg and only a rickety chair to protect me I didn't feel a bit like laughing. There was a dreadful dedication in the way she followed me and those maddened eyes never left my face for an instant.

The pups, furious at the unceremonious removal of their delightful source of warmth and nourishment, were crawling blindly across the bed and bawling, all nine of them, at the top of their voices. The din acted as a spur to the bitch and the louder it became the more she pressed home her attack. Every few seconds she would launch herself at me and I would prance about, stabbing at her with my chair in best circus fashion. Once she bore me back against the wall, chair and all; on her hind legs she was about as tall as me and I had a disturbing close-up of the snarling gaping jaws.

My biggest worry was that my chair was beginning to show signs of wear; the bitch had already crunched two of the spars effortlessly away and I tried not to think of what would happen if the whole thing finally disintegrated. But I was working my way back to the door and when I felt the handle at my back I knew I had to do something about it. I gave a final, intimidating shout, threw the remains of the chair at the bitch and dived out into the corridor. As I slammed the door behind me and leaned against it I could feel the panels quiver as the big animal threw herself against the wood.

I was sitting on the floor with my back against the passage wall, pants round my ankles, examining my wounds when I saw Harold pass across the far end, pottering vaguely along with a basin of steaming water held in front of him and a towel over his shoulder. I could understand now why he had been so long—he had been wandering around like that all the time; being Harold it was just possible he had been lost in his own house. Or maybe he was just worrying about his Four Aways.

Back at Skeldale House I had to endure some unkind remarks about my straddling gait, but later, in my bedroom, the smile left Siegfried's face as he examined my leg.

'Right up there, by God.' He gave a low, awed whistle. 'You know, James, we've often made jokes about what a savage dog might do to us one day. Well, I tell you boy, it damn nearly happened to you.'

Chapter Twenty

THIS WAS MY SECOND WINTER in Darrowby so I didn't feel the same sense of shock when it started to be really rough in November. When they were getting a drizzle of rain down there on the plain the high country was covered in a few hours by a white blanket which filled in the road, smoothed out familiar landmarks, transformed our world into something strange and new. This was what they meant on the radio when they talked about 'snow on high ground'.

When the snow started in earnest it had a strangling effect on the whole district. Traffic crawled laboriously between the mounds thrown up by the snow ploughs. Herne Fell hung over Darrowby like a great gleaming whale and in the town the people dug deep paths to their garden gates and cleared the drifts from their front doors. They did it without fuss, with the calm of long use and in the knowledge that they would probably have to do it again tomorrow.

Every new fall struck a fresh blow at the vets. We managed to get to most of our cases but we lost a lot of sweat in the process. Sometimes we were lucky and were able to bump along in the wake of a council plough but more often we drove as far as we could and walked the rest of the way.

On the morning when Mr Clayton of Pike House rang up we had had a night of continuous snow.

'Young beast with a touch o' cold,' he said. 'Will you come?'

To get to his place you had to cross over Pike Edge and then drop down into a little valley. It was a lovely drive in the summer, but I wondered.

'What's the road like?' I asked.

'Road? Road?' Mr Clayton's reaction was typically airy. Farmers in the less accessible places always brushed aside such queries. 'Road's right enough. Just tek a bit o' care and you'll get here without any trouble.'

Siegfried wasn't so sure. 'You'll certainly have to walk over the top and it's doubtful whether the ploughs will have cleared the lower road. It's up to you.'

'Oh, I'll have a go. There's not much doing this morning and I feel like a bit of exercise.'

In the yard I found that old Boardman had done a tremendous job in his quiet way; he had dug open the big double doors and cleared a way for the cars to get out. I put what I thought I would need into a small rucksack—some expectorant mixture, a tub of electuary, a syringe and a few ampoules of pneumonia serum. Then I threw the most important item of my winter equipment, a broad-bladed shovel, into the back and left.

The bigger roads had already been cleared by the council ploughs which had been clanking past Skeldale House since before dawn, but the surface was rough and I had a slow, bumpy ride. It was more than ten miles to the Clayton farm and it was one of those iron days when the frost piled thickly on the windscreen blotting out everything within minutes. But this morning I was triumphant. I had just bought a wonderful new invention—a couple of strands of wire mounted on a strip of bakelite and fastened to the windscreen with rubber suckers. It worked from the car batteries and cleared a small space of vision.

No more did I have to climb out wearily and scrub and scratch at the frozen glass every half mile or so. I sat peering delightedly through a flawlessly clear semicircle about eight inches wide at the countryside unwinding before me like a film show; the grey stone villages, silent and withdrawn under their smothering white cloak; the low, burdened branches of the roadside trees.

I was enjoying it so much that I hardly noticed the ache

153

in my toes. Freezing feet were the rule in those days before car heaters, especially when you could see the road flashing past through the holes in the floor boards. On long journeys I really began to suffer towards the end. It was like that today when I got out of the car at the foot of the Pike Edge road; my fingers too, throbbed painfully as I stamped around and swung my arms.

The ploughs hadn't even attempted to clear the little side road which wound its way upwards and into the valley beyond. Its solid, creamy, wall-to-wall filling said, 'No, you can't come up here', with that detached finality I had come to know so well. But as always, even in my disappointment, I looked with wonder at the shapes the wind had sculpted in the night; flowing folds of the most perfect smoothness tapering to the finest of points, deep hollows with knife-edge rims, soaring cliffs with overhanging margins almost transparent in their delicacy.

Hitching the rucksack on my shoulder I felt a kind of sub-dued elation. With a leather golf jacket buttoned up to my neck and an extra pair of thick socks under my wellingtons I felt ready for anything. No doubt I considered there was something just a bit dashing and gallant in the picture of the dedicated young vet with his magic potions on his back battling against the odds to succour a helpless animal.

I stood for a moment gazing at the fell, curving clean and cold into the sullen sky. An expectant hush lay on the fields, the frozen river and the still trees as I started off.

I kept up a good pace. First over a bridge with the river white and silent beneath, then up and up, picking my way over the drifts till the road twisted, almost invisible, under some low cliffs.

Despite the cold, the sweat was beginning to prick on my back when I got to the top.

I looked around me. I had been up here several times in June and July and I could remember the sunshine, the smell of the warm grass, and the scent of flowers and pines that came up the hill from the valley below. But it was hard to relate the smiling landscape of last summer with this desolation.

The flat moorland on the fell top was a white immensity rolling away to the horizon with the sky pressing down like a dark blanket. I could see the farm down there in its hollow and it, too, looked different; small, remote, like a charcoal drawing against the hills bulking smooth and white beyond. A pine wood made a dark smudge on the slopes but the scene had been wiped clean of most of its familiar features.

I could see the road only in places—the walls were covered over most of their length, but the farm was visible all the way. I had gone about half a mile towards it when a sudden gust of wind blew up the surface snow into a cloud of fine particles. Just for a few seconds I found myself completely alone. The farm, the surrounding moor, everything disappeared and I had an eerie sense of isolation till the veil cleared.

It was hard going in the deep snow and in the drifts I sank over the tops of my wellingtons. I kept at it, head down, to within a few hundred yards of the stone buildings. I was just thinking that it had all been pretty easy, really, when I looked up and saw a waving curtain of a million black dots bearing down on me. I quickened my steps and just before the blizzard hit me I marked the position of the farm. But after ten minutes' stumbling and slithering I realized I had missed the place. I was heading for a shape that didn't exist; it was etched only in my mind.

I stood for a few moments feeling again the chilling sense of isolation. I was convinced I had gone too far to the left and after a few gasping breaths, struck off to the right. It wasn't long before I knew I had gone in the wrong direction again. I began to fall into deep holes, up to the armpits in the snow reminding me that the ground was not really flat on these high moors but pitted by countless peat haggs.

As I struggled on I told myself that the whole thing was ridiculous. I couldn't be far from the warm fireside at Pike House—this wasn't the North Pole. But my mind went back to the great empty stretch of moor beyond the farm and I had to stifle a feeling of panic.

The numbing cold seemed to erase all sense of time. Soon I had no idea of how long I had been falling into the holes and crawling out. I did know that each time it was getting harder work dragging myself out. And it was becoming more and more tempting to sit down and rest, even sleep; there was something hypnotic in the way the big, soft flakes brushed noiselessly across my skin and mounted thickly on my closed eyes.

I was trying to shut out the conviction that if I fell down many more times I wouldn't get up when a dark shape hovered suddenly ahead. Then my outflung arms touched something hard and rough. Unbelievingly I felt my way over the square stone blocks till I came to a corner. Beyond that was a square of light—it was the kitchen window of the farm.

Thumping on the door, I leaned against the smooth timbers, mouth gaping, chest heaving agonizingly. My immense relief must have bordered on hysteria because it seemed to me that when the door was opened the right thing would be to fall headlong into the room. My mind played with the picture of the family crowding round the prostrate figure, plying him with brandy.

When the door did open, however, something kept me on my feet. Mr Clayton stood there for a few seconds, apparently unmoved by the sight of the distraught snowman in front of him.

'Oh, it's you, Mr Herriot. You couldn't have come better —I've just finished me dinner. Hang on a minute till I get me 'at. Beast's just across yard.'

He reached behind the door, stuck a battered trilby on his head, put his hands in his pockets and sauntered over the cobbles, whistling. He knocked up the latch of the calf house and with a profound sense of release I stepped inside; away from the relentless cold, the sucking swirling snow, into an animal warmth and the scent of hay.

As I rid myself of my rucksack, four long-haired little bullocks regarded me calmly from over a hurdle, their jaws moving rhythmically. They appeared as unconcerned at my appearance as their owner. They showed a mild interest, nothing more. Behind the shaggy heads I could see a fifth small beast with a sack tied round it and a purulent discharge coming from its nose.

It reminded me of the reason for my visit. As my numb fingers fumbled in a pocket for my thermometer a great gust of wind buffeted the door, setting the latch clicking softly and sending a faint powdering of snow into the dark interior.

Mr Clayton turned and rubbed the pane of the single small window with his sleeve. Picking his teeth with his thumb-nail he peered out at the howling blizzard.

'Aye,' he said, and belched pleasurably. 'It's a plain sort o' day.'

Chapter Twenty-One

AS I WAITED for Seigfried to give me my morning list I pulled my scarf higher till it almost covered my ears, turned up the collar of my overcoat and buttoned it tightly under my chin. Then I drew on a pair of holed woollen gloves.

A biting north wind was driving the snow savagely past the window almost parallel with the ground, obliterating the street and everything else with big, swirling flakes.

Siegfried bent over the day book. 'Now let's see what we've got. Barnett, Gill, Sunter, Dent, Cartwright . . .' He began to scribble on a pad. 'Oh, and I'd better see Scruton's calf—you've been attending to it, I know, but I'm going right past the door. Can you tell me about it?'

'Yes, it's been breathing a bit fast and running a temperature around 103—I don't think there's any pneumonia there. In fact I rather suspect it may be developing diphtheria—it has a bit of a swelling on the jaw and the throat glands are up.'

All the time I was speaking, Siegfried continued to write on the pad and only stopped once to whisper to Miss Harbottle. Then he looked up brightly. 'Pneumonia, eh? How have you been treating it?'

'No, I said I didn't think it was pneumonia. I've been injecting Prontosil and I left some liniment to rub into the throat region.'

But Siegfried was writing hard again. He said nothing till he had made out two lists. He tore one from the pad and gave it to me. 'Right, you've been applying liniment to the chest. Suppose it might do a bit of good. Which liniment?'

'Lin. methyl. sal., but they're rubbing it on the calf's throat, not the chest.' But Siegfried had turned away to tell Miss Harbottle the order of his visits and I found myself talking to the back of his head.

Finally he straightened up and came away from the desk. 'Well, that's fine. You have your list—let's get on.' But half way across the floor he hesitated and turned back. 'Why the devil are you rubbing that liniment on the calf's throat?'

'Well, I thought it might relieve the inflammation a bit.'

'But James, why should there be any inflammation there? Don't you think the liniment would do more good on the chest wall?' Siegfried was wearing his patient look again.

'No, I don't. Not in a case of calf diphtheria.'

Siegfried put his head on one side and a smile of saintly sweetness crept over his face. He laid his hand on my shoulder. 'My dear old James, perhaps it would be a good idea if you started right at the beginning. Take all the time you want—there's no hurry. Speak slowly and calmly and then you won't become confused. You told me you were treating a calf with pneumonia—now take it from there.'

I thrust my hands deep into my coat pockets and began to churn among the thermometers and scissors and little bottles which always dwelt there. 'Look, I told you right at the start that I didn't think there was any pneumonia but that I suspected early diphtheria. There was also a bit of fever—103.'

Siegfried was looking past me at the window. 'God, just look at that snow. We're going to have some fun getting round today.' He dragged his eyes back to my face. 'Don't you think that with a temperature of 103 you should be injecting some Prontosil?' He raised his arms sideways and let them fall. 'Just a suggestion, James— I wouldn't interfere for the world but I honestly think that the situation calls for a little Prontosil.'

'But hell, I am using it!' I shouted. 'I told you that, but you weren't listening. I've been doing my damnedest to get this across to you but what chance have I got . . .'

'Come come, dear boy, come come. No need to upset yourself.' Siegfried's face was transfigured by an internal radiance. Sweetness and charity, forgiveness, tolerance and affection flowed from him in an enveloping wave. I battled with an impulse to kick him swiftly on the shin.

'James, James.' The voice was caressing. 'I've not the slightest doubt you tried in your own way to tell me about this case, but we haven't all got the gift of communication. You're the most excellent fellow but must apply yourself to this. It is simply a matter of marshalling your facts and presenting them in an orderly manner. Then you wouldn't get confused and mixed up as you've done this morning; it's only a question of practice, I'm sure.' He gave an encouraging wave of the hand and was gone.

I strode quickly through to the stock room and, seeing a big, empty cardboard box on the floor, dealt it a vicious kick. I put so much venom into it that my foot went clear through the cardboard and I was trying to free myself when Tristan came in. He had been stoking the fire and had witnessed the conversation.

He watched silently as I plunged about the room swearing and trying to shake the box loose. 'What's up, Jim? Has my big brother been getting under your skin?'

I got rid of the box at last and sank down on one of the lower shelves. 'I don't know. Why should he be getting under my skin now? I've known him quite a long time and he's always been the same. He's never been any different but it hasn't bothered me before—not like this, anyway. Any other time I'd laugh that sort of thing off. What the hell's wrong with me?'

Tristan put down his coal bucket and looked at me thoughtfully. 'There's nothing much wrong with you, Jim, but I can tell you one thing—you've been just a bit edgy since you went out with the Alderson woman.'

'Oh God,' I groaned and closed my eyes. 'Don't remind me. Anyway, I've not seen her or heard from her since, so that's the end of that and I can't blame her.'

Tristan pulled out his Woodbines and squatted down by the coal bucket. 'Yes, that's all very well, but look at you. You're suffering and there's no need for it. Yes, you had a disastrous night and she's given you the old heave ho. Well, so what? Do you know how many times I've been spurned?'

'Spurned? I never even got started.'

'Very well then, but you're still going around like a bullock with bellyache. Forget it, lad, and get out into the big world. The rich tapestry of life is waiting for you out there. I've been watching you—working all hours and when you're not working you're reading up your cases in the text books —and I tell you this dedicated vet thing is all right up to a point. But you've got to live a little. Think of all the lovely little lasses in Darrowby—you can hardly move for them. And every one just waiting for a big handsome chap like you to gallop up on his white horse. Don't disappoint them.' He leaned over and slapped my knee. 'Why don't you let me fix something up? A nice little foursome—just what you need.'

'Ach I don't know. I'm not keen, really.'

'Nonsense!' Tristan said. 'I don't know why I haven't thought of it before. This monkish existence is bad for you. Leave all the details to me.'

I decided to have an early night and was awakened around eleven o'clock by a heavy weight crashing down on the bed. The room was dark but I seemed to be enveloped in beer-scented smoke. I coughed and sat up. 'Is that you, Triss?'

'It is indeed,' said the shadowy figure on the end of the bed. 'And I bring you glad tidings. You remember Brenda?'

'That little nurse I've seen you around with?'

'The very same. Well, she's got a pal, Connie, who's even more beautiful. The four of us are going dancing at the Poulton Institute on Tuesday night.' The voice was thick with beery triumph.

'You mean me, too?'

'By God I do, and you're going to have the best time you've ever had. I'll see to that.' He blew a last choking blast of smoke into my face and left, chuckling.

Chapter Twenty-Two

'WE'RE HAVING a 'ot dinner and entertainers.'

My reaction to the words surprised me. They stirred up a mixture of emotions, all of them pleasant; fulfilment, happy acceptance, almost triumph.

I know by now that there is not the slightest chance of anybody asking me to be President of the Royal College of Veterinary Surgeons, but if they had, I wonder if I'd have been more pleased than when I heard about the 'ot dinner.

The reason, I suppose, was that the words reflected the attitude of a typical Dales farmer towards myself. And this was important because, though after just over a year I was becoming accepted as a vet, I was always conscious of the gulf which was bound to exist between these hill folk and a city product like me. Much as I admired them I was aware always that we were different; it was inevitable, I knew, but it still rankled so that a sincere expression of friendship from one of them struck a deep answering chord in me.

Especially when it came from somebody like Dick Rudd. I had first met Dick last winter on the doorstep of Skeldale House at six o'clock on the kind of black morning when country vets wonder about their choice of profession. Shivering as the ever-present passage draught struck at my pyjamaed legs, I switched on the light and opened the door. I saw a small figure muffled in an old army greatcoat and balaclava leaning on a bicycle. Beyond him the light spilled on to a few feet of streaming pavement where the rain beat down in savage swathes.

'Sorry to ring your bell at this hour, guvnor,' he said. 'My name's Rudd, Birch Tree Farm, Coulston. I've got a heifer calvin' and she's not getting on with t'job. Will you come?'

I looked closer at the thin face, at the water trickling down the cheeks and dripping from the end of the nose. 'Right, I'll get dressed and come straight along. But why don't you leave your bike here and come with me in the car? Coulston's about four miles isn't it and you must be soaked through.'

'Nay, nay, it'll be right.' The face broke into the most cheerful of grins and under the sopping balaclava a pair of lively blue eyes glinted at me. 'I'd only have to come back and get it another time. I'll get off now and you won't be there long afore me.'

He mounted his bike quickly and pedalled away. People who think farming is a pleasant, easy life should have been there to see the hunched figure disappear into the blackness and the driving rain. No car, no telephone, a night up with the heifer, eight miles biking in the rain and a back-breaking day ahead of him. Whenever I thought of the existence of the small farmer it made my own occasional bursts of activity seem small stuff indeed.

I produced a nice live heifer calf for Dick that first morning and later, gratefully drinking a cup of hot tea in the farmhouse kitchen, I was surprised at the throng of young Rudds milling around me; there were seven of them and they were unexpectedly grown up. Their ages ranged from twenty odd down to about ten and I hadn't thought of Dick as middle-aged; in the dim light of the doorway at Skeldale House and later in the byre lit only by a smoke-blackened oil lamp his lively movements and perky manner had seemed those of a man in his thirties. But as I looked at him now I could see that the short, wiry hair was streaked with grey and a maze of fine wrinkles spread from around his eyes on to his cheeks.

In their early married life the Rudds, anxious like all farmers for male children, had observed with increasing chagrin the arrival of five successive daughters. 'We nearly packed up then,' Dick confided to me once; but they didn't

163

and their perseverance was rewarded at last by the appearance of two fine boys. A farmer farms for his sons and Dick
had something to work for now.

As I came to know them better I used to observe the family
with wonder. The five girls were all tall, big-limbed, handsome, and already the two chunky young boys gave promise
of massive growth. I kept looking from them to their frail
little parents—'not a pickin' on either of us', as Mrs Rudd
used to say—and wonder how the miracle had happened.

It puzzled me, too, how Mrs Rudd, armed only with the
milk cheque from Dick's few shaggy cows, had managed to
feed them all, never mind bring them to this state of physical
perfection. I gained my first clue one day when I had been
seeing some calves and I was asked to have a 'bit o' dinner'
with them. Butcher's meat was a scarce commodity on the
hill farms and I was familiar with the usual expedients for
filling up the eager stomachs before the main course—the
doughy slab of Yorkshire pudding or the heap of suet
dumplings. But Mrs Rudd had her own method—a big bowl
of rice pudding with lots of milk was her *hors d'œuvres*. It
was a new one on me and I could see the family slowing
down as they ploughed their way through. I was ravenous
when I sat down but after the rice I viewed the rest of the
meal with total detachment.

Dick believed in veterinary advice for everything so I was
a frequent visitor at Birch Tree Farm. After every visit
there was an unvarying ritual; I was asked into the house for
a cup of tea and the whole family downed tools and sat down
to watch me drink it. On weekdays the eldest girl was out
at work and the boys were at school but on Sundays the
ceremony reached its full splendour with myself sipping the
tea and all nine Rudds sitting around in what I can only call
an admiring circle. My every remark was greeted with nods
and smiles all round. There is no doubt it was good for my
ego to have an entire family literally hanging on my words,
but at the same time it made me feel curiously humble.

I suppose it was because of Dick's character. Not that he

was unique in any way—there were thousands of small farmers just like him—but he seemed to embody the best qualities of the Dalesman; the indestructibility, the tough philosophy, the unthinking generosity and hospitality. And there were the things that were Dick's own; the integrity which could be read always in his steady eyes and the humour which was never very far away. Dick was no wit but he was always trying to say ordinary things in a funny way. If I asked him to get hold of a cow's nose for me he would say solemnly 'Ah'll endeavour to do so', or I remember when I was trying to lift a square of plywood which was penning a calf in a corner he said 'Just a minute till ah raise portcullis'. When he broke into a smile a kind of radiance flooded his pinched features.

When I held my audiences in the kitchen with all the family reflecting Dick's outlook in their eager laughter I marvelled at their utter contentment with their lot. None of them had known ease or softness but it didn't matter; and they looked on me as a friend and I was proud.

Whenever I left the farm I found something on the seat of my car—a couple of home-made scones, three eggs. I don't know how Mrs Rudd spared them but she never failed.

Dick had a burning ambition—to upgrade his stock until he had a dairy herd which would live up to his ideas. Without money behind him he knew it would be a painfully slow business but he was determined. It probably wouldn't be in his own lifetime but some time, perhaps when his sons were grown up, people would come and look with admiration at the cows of Birch Tree.

I was there to see the very beginning of it. When Dick stopped me on the road one morning and asked me to come up to his place with him I knew by his air of suppressed excitement that something big had happened. He led me into the byre and stood silent. He didn't need to say anything because I was staring unbelievingly at a bovine aristocrat.

Dick's cows had been scratched together over the years

and they were a motley lot. Many of them were old animals discarded by more prosperous farmers because of their pendulous udders or because they were 'three titted 'uns'. Others had been reared by Dick from calves and tended to be rough-haired and scruffy. But half way down the byre, contrasting almost violently with her neighbours was what seemed to me a perfect Dairy Shorthorn cow.

In these days when the Friesian has surged over England in a black and white flood and inundated even the Dales which were the very home of the Shorthorn, such cows as I looked at that day at Dick Rudd's are no longer to be seen, but she represented all the glory and pride of her breed. The wide pelvis tapering to fine shoulders and a delicate head, the level udder thrusting back between the hind legs, and the glorious colour—dark roan. That was what they used to call a 'good colour' and whenever I delivered a dark roan calf the farmer would say 'It's a good-coloured 'un', and it would be more valuable accordingly. The geneticists are perfectly right, of course: the dark roaned cows gave no more milk than the reds or the whites, but we loved them and they were beautiful.

'Where did she come from, Dick?' I said, still staring.

Dick's voice was elaborately casual.

'Oh, ah went over to Weldon's of Cranby and picked her out. D'you like her?'

'She's a picture—a show cow. I've never seen one better.' Weldons were the biggest pedigree breeders in the northern Dales and I didn't ask whether Dick had cajoled his bank manager or had been saving up for years just for this.

'Aye, she's a seven galloner when she gets goin' and top butter fat, too. Reckon she'll be as good as two of my other cows and a calf out of her'll be worth a bit.' He stepped forward and ran his hand along the perfectly level, smoothly-fleshed back. 'She's got a great fancy pedigree name but missus 'as called her Strawberry.'

I knew as I stood there in the primitive, cobbled byre with its wooden partitions and rough stone walls that I was looking not just at a cow but at the foundation of the new herd, at Dick Rudd's hopes for the future.

It was about a month later that he phoned me. 'I want you to come and look at Strawberry for me,' he said. 'She's been doing grand, tipplin' the milk out, but there's summat amiss with her this morning.'

The cow didn't really look ill and, in fact, she was eating when I examined her, but I noticed that she gulped slightly when she swallowed. Her temperature was normal and her lungs clear but when I stood up by her head I could just hear a faint snoring sound.

'It's her throat, Dick,' I said. 'It may be just a bit of inflammation but there's a chance that she's starting a little abscess in there.' I spoke lightly but I wasn't happy. Postpharyngeal abscesses were, in my limited experience, nasty things. They were situated in an inaccessible place, right away behind the back of the throat and if they got very large could interfere seriously with the breathing. I had been lucky with the few I had seen; they had either been small and regressed or had ruptured spontaneously.

I gave an injection of Prontosil and turned to Dick. 'I want you to foment this area behind the angle of the jaw with hot water, then rub this salve well in. You may manage to burst it that way. Do this at least three times a day.'

I kept looking in at her over the next ten days and the picture was one of steady development of the abscess. The cow was still not acutely ill but she was eating a lot less, she was thinner and was going off her milk. Most of the time I felt rather helpless as I knew that only the rupture of the abscess would bring relief and the various injections I was giving her were largely irrelevant. But the infernal thing was taking a long time to burst.

It happened that just then Siegfried went off to an equine conference which was to last a week; for a few days I was at full stretch and hardly had time to think about Dick's cow until he biked in to see me one morning. He was cheerful as usual but he had a strained look.

'Will you come and see Strawberry? She's gone right down t'nick over the last three days. I don't like look of her.'

I dashed straight out and was in the byre at Birch Tree before Dick was half way home. The sight of Strawberry stopped me in mid-stride and I stared, dry-mouthed at what had once been a show cow. The flesh had melted from her incredibly and she was little more than a hide-covered skeleton. Her rasping breathing could be heard all over the byre and she exhaled with a curious out-puffing of the cheeks which I had never seen before. Her terrified eyes were fixed rigidly on the wall in front of her. Occasionally she gave a painful little cough which brought saliva drooling from her mouth.

I must have stood there a long time because I became aware of Dick at my shoulder.

'She's the worst screw in the place now,' he said grimly.

I winced inwardly. 'Hell, Dick, I'm sorry. I'd no idea she'd got to this state. I can't believe it.'

'Aye well it all happened sudden like. I've never seen a cow alter so fast.'

'The abscess must be right at its peak,' I said. 'She hasn't much space to breathe through now.' As I spoke the cow's limbs began to tremble and for a moment I thought she would fall. I ran out to the car and got a tin of Kaolin poultice. 'Come on, let's get this on to her throat. It just might do the trick.'

When we had finished I looked at Dick. 'I think tonight will do it. It's just got to burst.'

'And if it doesn't she'll snuff it tomorrow,' he grunted. I must have looked very woebegone because suddenly his un-defeated grin flashed out. 'Never mind, lad, you've done everything anybody could do.'

But as I walked away I wasn't so sure. Mrs Rudd met me at the car. It was her baking day and she pushed a little loaf into my hand. It made me feel worse.

Chapter Twenty-Three

THAT NIGHT I sat alone in the big room at Skeldale House and brooded. Siegfried was still away, I had nobody to turn to and I wished to God I knew what I was going to do with that cow of Dick's in the morning. By the time I went up to bed I had decided that if nothing further had happened I would have to go in behind the angle of the jaw with a knife.

I knew just where the abscess was but it was a long way in and en route there were such horrific things as the carotid artery and the jugular vein. I tried hard to keep them out of my mind but they haunted my dreams; huge, throbbing, pulsating things with their precious contents threatening to burst at any moment through their fragile walls. I was awake by six o'clock and could stand it no longer. I got up, and without washing or shaving drove out to the farm.

As I crept fearfully into the byre I saw with a sick dismay that Strawberry's stall was empty. So that was that. She was dead. After all, she had looked like it yesterday. I was turning away when Dick called to me from the doorway.

'I've got her in a box on t'other side of the yard. Thought she'd be a bit more comfortable in there.'

I almost ran across the cobbles and as we approached the door the sound of the dreadful breathing came out to us. Strawberry was off her legs now—it had cost her the last of her strength to walk to the box and she lay on her chest, her head extended straight in front of her, nostrils dilated, eyes staring, cheeks puffing in her desperate fight for breath.

But she was alive and the surge of relief I felt seemed to prick me into action, blow away my hesitations.

'Dick,' I said, 'I've just got to operate on your cow. This thing is never going to burst in time, so it's now or never. But there's one thing I want you to know—the only way I can think of doing it is to go in from behind the jaw. I've never done this before, I've never seen it before and I've never heard of anybody doing it. If I nick any of those big blood vessels in there it'll kill her within a minute.'

'She can't last much longer like this,' Dick grunted. 'There's nowt to lose—get on with it.'

In most operations in large bovines we have to pull the animal down with ropes and then use general anaesthesia, but there was no need for this with Strawberry. She was too far gone. I just pushed gently at her shoulder and she rolled on to her side and lay still.

I quickly infiltrated the area from beneath the ear to the angle of the jaw with local anaesthetic then laid out my instruments.

'Stretch her head straight out and slightly back, Dick,' I said. Kneeling in the straw I incised the skin, cut carefully through the long thin layer of the brachiocephalic muscle and held the fibres apart with retractors. Somewhere down there was my objective and I tried to picture the anatomy of the region clearly in my mind. Just there the maxillary veins ran together to form the great jugular and, deeper and more dangerous, was the branching, ramifying carotid. If I pushed my knife straight in there, behind the mandibular salivary gland, I'd just about hit the spot. But as I held the razor-sharp blade over the small space I had cleared, my hand began to tremble. I tried to steady it but I was like a man with malaria. The fact had to be faced that I was too scared to cut any farther. I put the scalpel down, lifted a pair of long artery forceps and pushed them steadily down through the hole in the muscle. It seemed that I had gone an incredibly long way when, almost unbelievingly, I saw a thin trickle of pus along the gleaming metal. I was into the abscess.

Gingerly, I opened the forceps as wide as possible to

enlarge the drainage hole, and as I did, the trickle became a creamy torrent which gushed over my hand, down the cow's neck and on to the straw. I stayed quite still till it had stopped, then withdrew the forceps.

Dick looked at me from the other side of the head. 'Now what, boss?' he said softly.

'Well, I've emptied the thing, Dick,' I said, 'and by all the laws she should soon be a lot better. Come on, let's roll her on to her chest again.'

When we had got the cow settled comfortably with a bale of straw supporting her shoulder, I looked almost entreatingly at her. Surely she would show some sign of improvement. She must feel some relief from that massive evacuation. But Strawberry looked just the same. The breathing, if anything, was worse.

I dropped the soiled instruments into a bucket of hot water and antiseptic and began to wash them. 'I know what it is. The walls of the abscess have become indurated—thickened and hardened, you know—because it's been there a long time. We'll have to wait for them to collapse.'

Next day as I hurried across the yard I felt buoyantly confident. Dick was just coming out of the loose box and I shouted across to him, 'Well, how is she this morning?'

He hesitated and my spirits plummeted to zero. I knew what this meant; he was trying to find something good to say.

'Well, I reckon she's about t'same.'

'But dammit,' I shouted, 'she should be much better! Let's have a look at her.'

The cow wasn't just the same, she was worse. And on top of all the other symptoms she had a horribly sunken eye—the sign, usually, of approaching death in the bovine.

We both stood looking at the grim wreck of the once beautiful cow, then Dick broke the silence, speaking gently. 'Well, what do you think? Is it Mallock for her?'

The sound of the knacker man's name added the final note of despair. And indeed, Strawberry looked just like any of the other broken down animals that man came to collect.

I shuffled my feet miserably. 'I don't know what to say, Dick. There's nothing more I can do.' I took another look at the gasping staring head, the mass of bubbling foam around the lips and nostrils. 'You don't want her to suffer any more and neither do I. But don't get Mallock yet—she's distressed but not actually in pain, and I want to give her another day. If she's just the same tomorrow, send her in.' The very words sounded futile—every instinct told me the thing was hopeless. I turned to go, bowed down by a sense of failure heavier than I had ever known. As I went out into the yard, Dick called after me.

'Don't worry, lad, these things happen. Thank ye for all you've done.'

The words were like a whip across my back. If he had cursed me thoroughly I'd have felt a lot better. What had he to thank me for with his cow dying back there, the only good cow he'd ever owned? This disaster would just about floor Dick Rudd and he was telling me not to worry.

When I opened the car door I saw a cabbage on the seat. Mrs Rudd, too, was still at it. I leaned my elbow on the roof of the car and the words flowed from me. It was as if the sight of the cabbage had tapped the deep well of my frustration and I directed a soliloquy at the unheeding vegetable in which I ranged far over my many inadequacies. I pointed out the injustice of a situation where kindly people like the Rudds, in dire need of skilled veterinary assistance, had called on Mr Herriot who had responded by falling flat on his face. I drew attention to the fact that the Rudds, instead of hounding me off the place as I deserved, had thanked me sincerely and started to give me cabbages.

I went on for quite a long time and when I had finally finished I felt a little better. But not much, because, as I drove home I could not detect a glimmer of hope. If the walls of that abscess had been going to collapse they would have done so by now. I should have sent her in—she would be dead in the morning anyway.

I was so convinced of this that I didn't hurry to Birch Tree next day. I took it in with the round and it was almost midday when I drove through the gates. I knew what I would find—the usual grim signs of a vet's failure; the box door open and the drag marks where Mallock had winched the carcass across the yard on to his lorry. But everything was as usual and as I walked over to the silent box I steeled myself. The knacker man hadn't arrived yet but there was nothing surer than that my patient was lying dead in there. She couldn't possibly have hung on till now. My fingers fumbled at the catch as though something in me didn't want to look inside, but with a final wrench I threw the door wide.

Strawberry was standing there, eating hay from the rack; and not just eating it but jerking it through the bars almost playfully as cows do when they are really enjoying their food. It looked as though she couldn't get it down fast enough, pulling down great fragrant tufts and dragging them into her mouth with her rasp-like tongue. As I stared at her an organ began to play somewhere in the back of my mind; not just a little organ but a mighty instrument with gleaming pipes climbing high into the shadows of the cathedral roof. I went into the box, closed the door behind me and sat down in the straw in a corner. I had waited a long time for this. I was going to enjoy it.

The cow was almost a walking skeleton with her beautiful dark roan skin stretched tightly over the jutting bones. The once proud udder was a shrivelled purse dangling uselessly above her hocks. As she stood, she trembled from sheer weakness, but there was a light in her eye, a calm intensity in the way she ate which made me certain she would soon fight her way back to her old glory.

There were just the two of us in the box and occasionally Strawberry would turn her head towards me and regard me steadily, her jaws moving rhythmically. It seemed like a friendly look to me—in fact I wouldn't have been surprised if she had winked at me.

I don't know just how long I sat there but I savoured every minute. It took some time for it to sink in that what I was watching was really happening; the swallowing was effortless, there was no salivation, no noise from her breathing. When I finally went out and closed the door behind me the cathedral organ was really blasting with all stops out, the exultant peals echoing back from the vaulted roof.

The cow made an amazing recovery. I saw her three weeks later and her bones were magically clothed with flesh, her skin shone and, most important, the magnificent udder bulged turgid beneath her, a neat little teat proudly erect at each corner.

I was pretty pleased with myself but of course a cold assessment of the case would show only one thing—that I had done hardly anything right from start to finish. At the very beginning I should have been down that cow's throat with a knife, but at that time I just didn't know how. In later years I have opened many a score of these abscesses by going in through a mouth gag with a scalpel tied to my fingers. It was a fairly heroic undertaking as the cow or bullock didn't enjoy it and was inclined to throw itself down with me inside it almost to the shoulder. It was simply asking for a broken arm.

When I talk about this to the present-day young vets they are inclined to look at me blankly because most of these abscesses undoubtedly had a tuberculous origin and since attestation they are rarely seen. But I can imagine it might bring a wry smile to the faces of my contemporaries as their memories are stirred.

The post-pharyngeal operation had the attraction that recovery was spectacular and rapid and I have had my own share of these little triumphs. But none of them gave me as much satisfaction as the one I did the wrong way.

It was a few weeks after the Strawberry episode and I was back in my old position in the Rudds' kitchen with the family around me. This time I was in no position to drop my usual pearls of wisdom because I was trying to cope with a piece of Mrs Rudd's apple tart. Mrs Rudd, I knew, could make delicious apple tarts but this was a special kind she produced for 'lowance' time—for taking out to Dick and the family when they were working in the fields. I had chewed at the two-inch pastry till my mouth had dried out. Somewhere inside there was no doubt a sliver of apple but as yet I had been unable to find it. I didn't dare try to speak in case I blew out a shower of crumbs and in the silence which followed I wondered if anybody would help me out. It was Mrs Rudd who spoke up.

'Mr Herriot,' she said in her quiet matter-of-fact way, 'Dick has something to say to you.'

Dick cleared his throat and sat up straighter in his chair. I turned towards him expectantly, my cheeks still distended by the obdurate mass. He looked unusually serious and I felt a twinge of apprehension.

'What I want to say is this,' he said. 'It'll soon be our silver wedding anniversary and we're going to 'ave a bit of a do. We want you to be our guest.'

I almost choked. 'Dick, Mrs Rudd, that's very kind of you. I'd love that—I'd be honoured to come.'

Dick inclined his head gravely. He still looked portentous as though there was something big to follow. 'Good, I think you'll enjoy it, because it's goin' to be a right do. We've got a room booked at t'King's Head at Carsley.'

'Gosh, sounds great!'

'Aye, t'missus and me have worked it all out.' He squared his thin shoulders and lifted his chin proudly.

'We're having a 'ot dinner and entertainers.'

Chapter Twenty-Four

AS TIME PASSED and I painfully clothed the bare bones of
my theoretical knowledge with practical experience I began
to realize there was another side to veterinary practice they
didn't mention in the books. It had to do with money. Money
has always formed a barrier between the farmer and the vet.
I think this is because there is a deeply embedded, maybe
subconscious conviction in many farmers' minds that they
know more about their stock than any outsider and it is an
admission of defeat to pay somebody else to doctor them.

The wall was bad enough in those early days when they
had to pay the medical practitioners for treating their own
ailments and when there was no free agricultural advisory
service. But it is worse now when there is the Health Service
and N.A.A.S. and the veterinary surgeon stands pitilessly
exposed as the only man who has to be paid.

Most farmers, of course, swallow the pill and get out their
cheque books, but there is a proportion—maybe about ten
per cent—who do their best to opt out of the whole business.

We had our own ten per cent in Darrowby and it was a
small but constant irritation. As an assistant I was not finan-
cially involved and it didn't seem to bother Siegfried unduly
except when the quarterly bills were sent out. Then it really
got through to him.

Miss Harbottle used to type out the accounts and present
them to him in a neat pile and that was when it started. He
would go through them one by one and it was a harrowing
experience to watch his blood pressure gradually rising.

I found him crouched over his desk one night. It was

about eleven o'clock and he had had a hard day. His resistance was right down. He was scrutinizing each bill before placing it face down on a pile to his left. On his right there was a smaller pile and whenever he placed one there it was to the accompaniment of a peevish muttering or occasionally a violent outburst.

'Would you believe it?' he grunted as I came in. 'Henry Bransom—more than two years since we saw a penny of his money, yet he lives like a sultan. Never misses a market for miles around, gets as tight as an owl several nights a week and I saw him putting ten pounds on a horse at the races last month.'

He banged the piece of paper down and went on with his job, breathing deeply. Then he froze over another account. 'And look at this one! Old Summers of Low Ness. I bet he's got thousands of pounds hidden under his bed but by God he won't part with any of it to me.'

He was silent for a few moments as he transferred several sheets to the main pile then he swung round on me with a loud cry, waving a paper in my face.

'Oh no! Oh Christ, James, this is too much! Bert Mason here owes me twenty-seven and sixpence. I must have spent more than that sending him bills year in year out and do you know I saw him driving past the surgery yesterday in a brand new car. The bloody scoundrel!'

He hurled the bill down and started his scrutiny again. I noticed he was using only one hand while the other churned among his hair. I hoped fervently that he might hit upon a seam of good payers because I didn't think his nervous system could take much more. And it seemed that my hopes were answered because several minutes went by with only the quiet lifting and laying of the paper sheets. Then Siegfried stiffened suddenly in his chair and sat quite motionless as he stared down at his desk. He lifted an account and held it for several seconds at eye level. I steeled myself. This must be a beauty.

But to my surprise Siegfried began to giggle softly, then

he threw back his head and gave a great bellow of laughter. He laughed until he seemed to have no strength to laugh any more, then he turned to me.

'It's the Major, James,' he said weakly. 'The dear old gallant Major. You know, you can't help admiring him. He owed my predecessor a fair bit when I bought the practice and he still owes it. And I've never had a sou for all the work I've done for him. The thing is he's the same with everybody and yet he gets away with it. He's a genuine artist —these others are just fumbling amateurs by comparison.'

He got up, reached up into the glass-fronted cupboard above the mantelpiece and pulled out the whisky bottle and two glasses. He carelessly tipped a prodigal measure into each glass and handed one to me, then he sank back into his chair, still grinning. The major had magically restored his good humour.

Sipping my drink, I reflected that there was no doubt Major Bullivant's character had a rich, compelling quality. He presented an elegant, patrician front to the world; beautiful Shakespearean actor voice, impeccable manners and an abundance of sheer presence. Whenever he unbent sufficiently to throw me a friendly word I felt honoured even though I knew I was doing his work for nothing.

He had a small, cosy farm, a tweed-clad wife and several daughters who had ponies and were active helpers for the local hunt. Everything in his entire ménage was right and fitting. But he never paid anybody.

He had been in the district about three years and on his arrival the local tradesmen, dazzled by his façade, had fallen over each other to win his custom. After all, he appeared to be just their type because they preferred inherited wealth in Darrowby. In contrast to what I had always found in Scotland, the self-made man was regarded with deep suspicion and there was nothing so damning among the townsfolk as the darkly muttered comment: 'He had nowt when he first came 'ere.'

Of course, when the scales had fallen from their eyes they

fought back, but ineffectually. The local garage impounded the Major's ancient Rolls Royce and hung on to it fiercely for a while but he managed to charm it back. His one failure was that his telephone was always being cut off; it seemed that the Postmaster General was one of the few who were immune to his blandishments.

But time runs out for even the most dedicated expert. I was driving one day through Hollerton, a neighbouring market town about ten miles away, and I noticed the Bullivant girls moving purposefully among the shops armed with large baskets. The Major, it seemed, was having to cast his net a little wider and I wondered at the time if perhaps he was ready to move on. He did, in fact, disappear from the district a few weeks later leaving a lot of people licking their wounds. I don't know if he ever paid anybody before he left but Siegfried didn't get anything.

Even after his departure Siegfried wasn't at all bitter, preferring to regard the Major as a unique phenomenon, a master of his chosen craft. 'After all, James,' he said to me once, 'putting ethical considerations to one side, you must admit that anybody who can run up a bill of fifty pounds for shaves and haircuts at the Darrowby barber's shop must command a certain amount of respect.'

Siegfried's attitude to his debtors was remarkably ambivalent. At times he would fly into a fury at the mention of their names, at others he would regard them with a kind of wry benevolence. He often said that if ever he threw a cocktail party for the clients he'd have to invite the non-payers first because they were all such charming fellows.

Nevertheless he waged an inexorable war against them by means of a series of letters graduated according to severity which he called his P.N.S. system (Polite, Nasty, Solicitor's) and in which he had great faith. It was a sad fact, however, that the system seldom worked with the real hard cases who were accustomed to receiving threatening letters with their morning mail. These people yawned over the polite and nasty ones and were unimpressed by the solicitor's because they knew from experience that Siegfried always shrank from following through to the limit of the law.

When the P.N.S. system failed Siegfried was inclined to come up with some unorthodox ideas to collect his hard-earned fees. Like the scheme he devised for Dennis Pratt. Dennis was a tubby, bouncy little man and his high opinion of himself showed in the way he always carried his entire five feet three inches proudly erect. He always seemed to be straining upwards, his chest thrust forward, his fat little bottom stuck out behind him at an extraordinary angle.

Dennis owed the practice a substantial amount and about eighteen months ago had been subjected to the full rigour of the P.N.S. system. This had induced him to part with five pounds 'on account' but since then nothing more had been forthcoming. Siegfried was in a quandary because he didn't like getting tough with such a cheerful, hospitable man.

Dennis was always either laughing or about to laugh. I remember when we had to anaesthetize a cow on his farm to remove a growth from between its cleats. Siegfried and I went to the case together and on the way we were talking about something which had amused us. As we got out of the car we were both laughing helplessly and just then the farm-house door opened and Dennis emerged.

We were at the far end of the yard and we must have been all of thirty yards away. He couldn't possibly have heard anything of our conversation but when he saw us laughing he threw back his head immediately and joined in at the top of his voice. He shook so much on his way across the yard that I thought he would fall over. When he arrived he was wiping the tears from his eyes.

After a job he always asked us in to sample Mrs Pratt's baking. In fact on cold days he used to keep a Thermos of hot coffee ready for our arrival and he had an endearing habit of sloshing rum freely into each cup before pouring in the coffee.

'You can't put a man like that in court,' Siegfried said. 'But we've got to find some way of parting him from his brass.' He looked ruminatively at the ceiling for a few moments then thumped a fist into his palm.

'I think I've got it, James! You know it's quite possible it just never occurs to Dennis to pay a bill. So I'm going to pitch him into an environment where it will really be brought home to him. The accounts have just gone out and I'll arrange to meet him in here at two o'clock next market day. I'll say I want to discuss his mastitis problem. He'll be right in the middle of all the other farmers paying their bills and I'll deliberately leave him with them for half an hour or so. I'm sure it will give him the notion.'

I couldn't help feeling dubious. I had known Siegfried long enough to realize that some of his ideas were brilliant and others barmy; and he had so many ideas and they came in such a constant torrent that I often had difficulty in deciding which was which. Clearly in this case he was working on the same lines as a doctor who turns a water tap on full to induce a pent-up patient to urinate into a bottle.

The scheme may have merit—it was possible that the flutter of cheque books, the chink of coins, the rustle of notes might tap the long-buried well of debt in Dennis and bring it gushing from him in a mighty flood; but I doubted it.

My doubts must have shown on my face because Siegfried laughed and thumped me on the shoulder. 'Don't look so worried—we can only try. And it'll work. Just you wait.'

After lunch on market day I was looking out of the window when I saw Dennis heading our way. The street was busy with the market bustle but he was easy to pick out. Chin in air, beaming around him happily, every springing step taking him high on tiptoe, he was a distinctive figure. I let him in at the front door and he strutted past me along the passage, the back of his natty sports jacket lying in a neat fold over his protruding buttocks.

Siegfried seated him strategically by Miss Harbottle's elbow, giving him an unimpeded view of the desk. Then he excused himself, saying he had a dog to attend to in the operating room. I stayed behind to answer the clients' queries and to watch developments. I hadn't long to wait; the farmers began to come in, a steady stream of them, clutching their cheque books. Some stood patiently by the desk, and others sat in the chairs along the walls waiting their turn.

It was a typical bill-paying day with the usual quota of moans. The most common expression was that Mr Farnon had been 'ower heavy wi' t'pen' and many of them wanted a 'bit knockin' off'. Miss Harbottle used her discretion in these matters and if the animal had died or the bill did seem unduly large she would make some reduction.

There was one man who didn't get away with it. He had truculently demanded a 'bit of luck' on an account and Miss Harbottle fixed him with a cold eye.

'Mr Brewiss,' she said. 'This account has been owing for over a year. You should really be paying us interest. I can only allow discount when a bill is paid promptly. It's too bad of you to let it run on for this length of time.'

Dennis, sitting bolt upright, his hands resting on his knees, obviously agreed with every word. He pursed his lips in disapproval as he looked at the farmer and turned towards me with a positively scandalized expression.

Among the complaints was an occasional bouquet. A stooping old man who had received one of the polite letters was full of apologies. 'I'm sorry I've missed paying for a few months. The vets allus come out straight away when I send for them so I reckon it's not fair for me to keep them waiting for their money.'

I could see that Dennis concurred entirely with this sentiment. He nodded vigorously and smiled benevolently at the old man.

Another farmer, a hard-looking character, was walking out without his receipt when Miss Harbottle called him back. 'You'd better take this with you or we might ask you to pay again,' she said with a heavy attempt at roguishness.

The man paused with his hand on the door knob. 'I'll tell you summat, missis, you're bloody lucky to get it once—you'd never get it twice.'

Dennis was right in the thick of it all. Watching closely as the farmers slapped their cheque books on the desk for Miss Harbottle to write (they never wrote their own cheques) then signed them slowly and painstakingly. He looked with open fascination at the neat bundles of notes being tucked away in the desk drawer and I kept making little provocative remarks like 'It's nice to see the money coming in. We can't carry on without that, can we?'

The queue began to thin out and sometimes we were left alone in the room. On these occasions we conversed about many things—the weather, Dennis's stock, the political situation. Finally, Siegfried came in and I left to do a round.

When I got back, Siegfried was at his evening meal. I was eager to hear how his scheme had worked out but he was strangely reticent. At length I could wait no longer.

'Well, how did it go?' I asked.

Siegfried speared a piece of steak with his fork and applied some mustard. 'How did what go?'

'Well—Dennis. How did you make out with him?'

'Oh, fine. We went into his mastitis problem very thoroughly. I'm going out there on Tuesday morning to infuse every infected quarter in the herd with acriflavine solution. It's a new treatment—they say it's very good.'

'But you know what I mean. Did he show any sign of paying his bill?'

Siegfried chewed impassively for a few moments and swallowed. 'No, never a sign.' He put down his knife and fork, his face taking on a haggard look. 'It didn't work, did it?'

'Oh well, never mind. As you said, we could only try.' I hesitated. 'There's something else, Siegfried. I'm afraid you're going to be annoyed with me. I know you've told me never to dish out stuff to people who don't pay, but he talked me into letting him have a couple of bottles of fever drink. I don't know what came over me.'

'He did, did he?' Siegfried stared into space for a second then gave a wintry smile. 'Well, you can forget about that. He got six tins of stomach powder out of me.'

Chapter Twenty-Five

THERE WAS ONE CLIENT who would not have been invited to the debtors' cocktail party. He was Mr Horace Dumbleby, the butcher of Aldgrove. As an inveterate non-payer he fulfilled the main qualification for the function but he was singularly lacking in charm.

His butcher shop in the main street of picturesque Aldgrove village was busy and prosperous but most of his trade was done in the neighbouring smaller villages and among the scattered farmhouses of the district. Usually the butcher's wife and married daughter looked after the shop while Mr Dumbleby himself did the rounds. I often saw his blue van standing with the back doors open and a farmer's wife waiting while he cut the meat, his big, shapeless body hunched over the slab. Sometimes he would look up and I would catch a momentary glimpse of a huge, bloodhound face and melancholy eyes.

Mr Dumbleby was a farmer himself in a small way. He sold milk from six cows which he kept in a tidy little byre behind his shop and he fattened a few bullocks and pork pigs which later appeared as sausages, pies, roasting cuts and chops in his front window. In fact Mr Dumbleby seemed to be very nicely fixed and it was said he owned property all over the place. But Siegfried had only infrequent glimpses of his money.

All the slow payers had one thing in common—they would not tolerate slowness from the vets. When they were in trouble they demanded immediate action. 'Will you come at once?', 'How long will you be?', 'You won't keep me waiting, will you?', 'I want you to come out here straight away'. It used to alarm me to see the veins swelling on Siegfried's forehead, the knuckles whitening as he gripped the phone.

After one such session with Mr Dumbleby at ten o'clock on a Sunday night he had flown into a rage and unleashed the full fury of the P.N.S. system on him. It had no loosening effect on the butcher's purse strings but it did wound his feelings deeply. He obviously considered himself a wronged man. From that time on, whenever I saw him with his van out in the country he would turn slowly and direct a blank stare at me till I was out of sight. And strangely, I seemed to see him more and more often — the thing became unnerving.

And there was something worse. Tristan and I used to frequent the little Aldgrove pub where the bar was cosy and the beer measured up to Tristan's stringent standards. I had never taken much notice of Mr Dumbleby before although he always occupied the same corner, but now, every time I looked up, the great sad eyes were trained on me in disapproval. I tried to forget about him and listen to Tristan relating his stories from the backs of envelopes but all the time I could feel that gaze upon me. My laughter would trail away and I would have to look round. Then the excellent bitter would be as vinegar in my mouth.

In an attempt to escape, I took to visiting the snug instead of the bar and Tristan, showing true nobility of soul, came with me into an environment which was alien to him; where there was a carpet on the floor, people sitting around at little shiny tables drinking gin and hardly a pint in sight. But even this sacrifice was in vain because Mr Dumbleby changed his position in the bar so that he could look into the snug through the communicating hatch. The odd hours I was able to spend there took on a macabre quality. I was like a man trying desperately to forget. But quaff the beer as I might, laugh, talk, even sing, half of me was waiting in a state of acute apprehension for the moment when I knew I would have to look round. And when I did, the great sombre face looked even more forbidding framed by the wooden surround of the hatch. The hanging jowls, the terraced chins, the huge, brooding eyes—all were dreadfully magnified by their isolation in that little hole in the wall.

It was no good, I had to stop going to the place. This was very sad because Tristan used to wax lyrical about a certain unique, delicate nuttiness which he could discern in the draught bitter. But it had lost its joy for me; I just couldn't take any more of Mr Dumbleby.

In fact I did my best to forget all about the gentleman, but he was brought back forcibly into my mind when I heard his voice on the phone at 3 a.m. one morning. It was nearly always the same thing when the bedside phone exploded in your ear in the small hours—a calving.

Mr Dumbleby's call was no exception but he was more peremptory than might have been expected. There was no question about apologizing about ringing at such an hour as most farmers would do. I said I would come immediately but that wasn't good enough—he wanted to know exactly in minutes how long I would be. In a sleepy attempt at sarcasm I started to recite a programme of so many minutes to get up and dressed, so many to go downstairs and get the car out etc., but I fear it was lost on him.

When I drove into the sleeping village a light was showing in the window of the butcher's shop. Mr Dumbleby almost trotted out into the street and paced up and down, muttering, as I fished out my ropes and instruments from the boot. Very impatient, I thought, for a man who hadn't paid his vet bill for over a year.

We had to go through the shop to get to the byre in the rear. My patient was a big, fat white cow which didn't seem particularly perturbed by her situation. Now and then she strained, pushing a pair of feet a few inches from her vulva. I took a keen look at those feet—it is the vet's first indication of how tough the job is going to be. Two huge hooves sticking out of a tiny heifer have always been able to wipe the smile off my face. These feet were big enough but not out of

186

the way, and in truth the mother looked sufficiently roomy. I wondered what was stopping the natural sequence.

'I've had me hand in,' said Mr Dumbleby. 'There's a head there but I can't shift owt. I've been pulling them legs for half an hour.'

As I stripped to the waist (it was still considered vaguely cissy to wear a calving overall) I reflected that things could be a lot worse. So many of the buildings where I had to take my shirt off were primitive and draughty but this was a modern cow house and the six cows provided a very adequate central heating. And there was electricity in place of the usual smoke-blackened oil lamp.

When I had soaped and disinfected my arms I made my first exploration and it wasn't difficult to find the cause of the trouble.

There was a head and two legs all right, but they belonged to different calves.

'We've got twins here,' I said. 'These are hind legs you've been pulling—a posterior presentation.'

'Arse fust, you mean?'

'If you like. And the calf that's coming the right way has both his legs back along his sides. I'll have to push him back out of the way and get the other one first.'

This was going to be a pretty tight squeeze. Normally I like a twin calving because the calves are usually so small, but these seemed to be quite big. I put my hand against the little muzzle in the passage, poked a finger into the mouth and was rewarded by a jerk and flip of the tongue; he was alive, anyway.

I began to push him steadily back into the uterus, wondering at the same time what the little creature was making of it all. He had almost entered the world—his nostrils had been a couple of inches from the outside air—and now he was being returned to the starting post.

The cow didn't think much of the idea either because she started a series of straining heaves with the object of frustrating me. She did a pretty fair job, too, since a cow is a lot stronger than a man, but I kept my arm rigid against the calf and though each heave forced me back I maintained a steady pressure till I had pushed him to the brim of the pelvis.

I turned to Mr Dumbleby and gasped: 'I've got this head out of the way. Get hold of those feet and pull the other calf out.'

The butcher stepped forward ponderously and each of his big, meaty hands engulfed a foot. Then he closed his eyes and with many facial contortions and noises of painful effort he began to go through the motions of tugging. The calf didn't move an inch and my spirits drooped. Mr Dumbleby was a grunter. (This expression had its origin in an occasion when Siegfried and a farmer had a foot apiece at a calving and the farmer was making pitiful sounds without exerting himself in the slightest. Siegfried had turned to him and said: 'Look, let's come to an arrangement—you do the pulling and I'll do the grunting.')

It was clear I was going to get no help from the big butcher and decided to have one go by myself. I might be lucky. I let go the muzzle and made a quick grab for those hind feet, but the cow was too quick for me. I had just got a slippery grasp when she made a single expulsive effort and pushed calf number two into the passage again. I was back where I started.

Once more I put my hand against the wet little muzzle and began the painful process of repulsion. And as I fought against the big cow's straining I was reminded that it was 4 a.m. when none of us feels very strong. By the time I had worked the head back to the pelvic inlet I was feeling the beginning of that deadly creeping weakness and it seemed as though somebody had removed most of the bones from my arm.

This time I took a few seconds to get my breath back before I made my dive for the feet, but it was no good. The cow beat me easily with a beautifully timed contraction. Again that intruding head was jammed tight in the passage.

188

I had had enough. And it occurred to me that the little creature inside must also be getting a little tired of this back and forth business. I shivered my way through the cold, empty shop out into the silent street and collected the local anaesthetic from the car. Eight cc's into the epidural space and the cow, its uterus completely numbed, lost all interest in the proceedings. In fact she pulled a little hay from her rack and began to chew absently.

From then on it was like working inside a mail bag; whatever I pushed stayed put instead of surging back at me. The only snag was that once I had got everything straight there were no uterine contractions to help me. It was a case of pulling. Leaning back on a hind leg and with Mr Dumbleby panting in agony on the other, the posterior presentation was soon delivered. He had inhaled a fair amount of placental fluid but I held him upside down till he had coughed it up. When I laid him on the byre floor he shook his head vigorously and tried to sit up.

Then I had to go in after my old friend the second calf. He was lying well inside now, apparently sulking. When I finally brought him snuffling and kicking into the light I couldn't have blamed him if he had said 'Make up your mind, will you!'

Towelling my chest I looked with the sharp stab of pleasure I always felt at the two wet little animals wriggling on the floor as Mr Dumbleby rubbed them down with a handful of straw.

'Big 'uns for twins,' the butcher muttered.

Even this modest expression of approval surprised me and it seemed I might as well push things along a bit.

'Yes, they're two grand calves. Twins are often dead when they're mixed up like that—good job we got them out alive.' I paused a moment. 'You know, those two must be worth a fair bit.'

Mr Dumbleby didn't answer and I couldn't tell whether the shaft had gone home.

I got dressed, gathered up my gear and followed him out

of the byre and into the silent shop past the rows of beef cuts hanging from hooks, the trays of offal, the mounds of freshly-made sausages. Near the outside door the butcher halted and stood, irresolute, for a moment. He seemed to be thinking hard. Then he turned to me.

'Would you like a few sausages?'

I almost reeled in my astonishment. 'Yes, thank you very much, I would.' It was scarcely credible but I must have touched the man's heart.

He went over, cut about a pound of links, wrapped them quickly in grease-proof paper and handed the parcel to me.

I looked down at the sausages, feeling the cold weight on my hand. I still couldn't believe it. Then an unworthy thought welled in my mind. It wasn't fair, I know—the poor fellow couldn't have known the luxury of many generous impulses—but some inner demon drove me to put him to the test. I put a hand in my trouser pocket, jingled my loose change and looked him in the eye.

'Well, how much will that be?' I asked.

Mr Dumbleby's big frame froze suddenly into immobility and he stood for a few seconds perfectly motionless. His face, as he stared at me, was almost without expression, but a single twitch of the cheek and a slowly rising anguish in the eyes betrayed the internal battle which was raging. When he did speak it was in a husky whisper as though the words had been forced from him by a power beyond his control.

'That,' he said, 'will be two and sixpence.'

Chapter Twenty-Six

IT WAS A NEW EXPERIENCE for me to be standing outside
the hospital waiting for the nurses to come off duty, but it
was old stuff to Tristan who was to be found there several
nights a week. His experience showed in various ways, but
mainly in the shrewd position he took up in a dark corner
of the doorway of the gas company office just beyond the
splash of light thrown by the street lamp. From there he
could look straight across the road into the square entrance
of the hospital and the long white corridor leading to the
nurses' quarters. And there was the other advantage that if
Siegfried should happen to pass that way, Tristan would be
invisible and safe.

At half past seven he nudged me. Two girls had come out
of the hospital and down the steps and were standing expectantly in the street. Tristan looked warily in both directions
before taking my arm. 'Come on, Jim, here they are. That's
Connie on the left—the coppery blonde—lovely little thing.'

We went over and Tristan introduced me with characteristic charm. I had to admit that if the evening had indeed
been arranged for therapeutic purposes I was beginning to
feel better already. There was something healing in the way
the two pretty girls looked up at me with parted lips and
shining eyes as though I was the answer to every prayer they
had ever offered.

They were remarkably alike except for the hair. Brenda
was very dark but Connie was fair with a deep, fiery glow
where the light from the doorway touched her head. Both of
them projected a powerful image of bursting health—fresh

cheeks, white teeth, lively eyes and something else which I found particularly easy to take; a simple desire to please.

Tristan opened the back door of the car with a flourish. 'Be careful with him in there Connie, he looks quiet but he's a devil with women. Known far and wide as a great lover.'

The girls giggled and studied me with even greater interest. Tristan leaped into the driver's seat and we set off at breakneck speed.

As the dark countryside hastened past the windows I leaned back in the corner and listened to Tristan who was in full cry; maybe in a kindly attempt to cheer me or maybe because he just felt that way, but his flow of chatter was unceasing. The girls made an ideal audience because they laughed in delight at everything he said. I could feel Connie shaking against me. She was sitting very close with a long stretch of empty seat on the other side of her. The little car swayed round a sharp corner and threw her against me and she stayed there quite naturally with her head on my shoulder. I felt her hair against my cheek. She didn't use much perfume but smelt cleanly of soap and antiseptic. My mind went back to Helen—I didn't think much about her these days. It was just a question of practice; to scotch every thought of her as soon as it came up. I was getting pretty good at it now. Anyway, it was over—all over before it had begun.

I put my arm round Connie and she lifted her face to me. Ah well, I thought as I kissed her. Tristan's voice rose in song from the front seat, Brenda giggled, the old car sped over the rough road with a thousand rattles.

We came at last to Poulton, a village on the road to nowhere. Its single street straggled untidily up the hillside to a dead end where there was a circular green with an ancient stone cross and a steep mound on which was perched the institute hall.

This was where the dance was to be held, but Tristan had other plans first. 'There's a lovely little pub here. We'll just have a toothful to get us in the mood.'

We got out of the car and Tristan ushered us into a low stone building.

There was nothing of the olde worlde about the place; just a large, square, whitewashed room with a black cooking range enclosing a bright fire and a long high-backed wooden settle facing it. Over the fireplace stretched a single immense beam, gnarled and pitted with the years and blackened with smoke. We hurried over to the settle, feeling the comfort of it as a screen against the cold outside. We had the place to ourselves.

The landlord came in. He was dressed informally—no jacket, striped, collarless shirt, trousers and braces which were reinforced by a broad, leather belt around his middle. His cheerful round face lit up at the sight of Tristan. 'Now then, Mr Farnon, are you very well?'

'Never better, Mr Peacock, and how are you?'

'Nicely, sir, very nicely. Can't complain. And I recognize the other gentleman. Been in my place before, haven't you?'

I remembered then. A day's testing in the Poulton district and I had come in here for a meal, freezing and half starved after hours of wrestling with young beasts on the high moor. The landlord had received me unemotionally and had set to immediately with his frying-pan on the old black range while I sat looking at his shirt back and the braces and the shining leather belt. The meal had taken up the whole of the round oak table by the fire—a thick steak of home cured ham overlapping the plate with two fresh eggs nestling on its bosom, a newly baked loaf with the knife sticking in it, a dish of farm butter, some jam, a vast pot of tea and a whole Wensleydale cheese, circular, snow white, about eighteen inches high.

I could remember eating unbelievingly for a long time and finishing with slice after slice of the moist, delicately flavoured cheese. The entire meal had cost me half a crown.

'Yes, Mr Peacock, I have been here before and if I'm ever starving on a desert island I'll think of that wonderful meal you gave me.'

The landlord shrugged, 'Well it was nowt much, sir. Just t'usual stuff.' But he looked pleased.

'That's fine, then,' Tristan said impatiently. 'But we haven't come to eat, we've come for a drink and Mr Peacock keeps some of the finest draught Magnet in Yorkshire. I'd welcome your opinion on it, Jim. Perhaps you would be kind enough to bring us up two pints and two halves, Mr Peacock.'

I noticed there was no question of asking the girls what they would like to have, but they seemed quite happy with the arrangement. The landlord reappeared from the cellar, puffing slightly. He was carrying a tall, white enamelled jug from which he poured a thin brown stream, varying the height expertly till he had produced a white, frothy head on each glass.

Tristan raised his pint and looked at it with quiet reverence. He sniffed it carefully and then took a sip which he retained in his mouth for a few seconds while his jaw moved rapidly up and down. After swallowing he smacked his lips a few times with the utmost solemnity then closed his eyes and took a deep gulp. He kept his eyes closed for a long time and when he opened them they were rapturous, as though he had seen a beautiful vision.

'It's an experience coming here,' he whispered. 'Keeping beer in the wood is a skilful business, but you, Mr Peacock, are an artist.' The landlord inclined his head modestly and Tristan, raising his glass in salute, drained it with an easy upward motion of the elbow.

Little oohs of admiration came from the girls but I saw that they, in their turn, had little difficulty in emptying their glasses. With an effort I got my own pint down and the enamel jug was immediately in action again.

I was always at a disadvantage in the company of a virtuoso like Tristan, but as the time passed and the landlord kept revisiting the cellar with his jug it seemed to become easier. In fact, a long time later, as I drew confidently on my eighth pint, I wondered why I had ever had difficulty with large amounts of fluid. It was easy and it soothed and comforted. Tristan was right—I had been needing this.

It puzzled me that I hadn't realized until now that Connie was one of the most beautiful creatures I had ever seen. Back there in the street outside the hospital she had seemed attractive, but obviously the light had been bad and I had failed to notice the perfection of her skin, the mysterious greenish depths of her eyes and the wonderful hair catching lights of gold and deep red-bronze from the flickering fire. And the laughing mouth, shining, even teeth and little pink tongue—she hardly ever stopped laughing except to drink her beer. Everything I said was witty, brilliantly funny in fact, and she looked at me all the time, peeping over the top of her glass in open admiration. It was profoundly re-assuring.

As the beer flowed, time slowed down and finally lurched to a halt and there was neither past nor future, only Connie's face and the warm, untroubled present.

I was surprised when Tristan pulled at my arm, I had for-gotten he was there and when I focused on him it was the same as with Connie—there was just the face swimming dis-embodied in an empty room. Only this face was very red and puffy and glassy-eyed.

'Would you care for the mad conductor?' the face said.

I was deeply touched. Here was another sign of my friend's concern for me. Of all Tristan's repertoire his imitation of a mad conductor was the most exacting. It involved tremen-dous expenditure of energy and since Tristan was unused to any form of physical activity, it really took it out of him. Yet here he was, ready and willing to sacrifice himself. A wave of treacly sentiment flooded through me and I won-dered for a second if it might not be the proper thing to burst into tears; but instead I contented myself with wringing Tristan's hand.

'There's nothing I would like more, my dear old chap, I said thickly. 'I greatly appreciate the kind thought. And may I take this opportunity of telling you that I consider that in all Yorkshire there is no finer gentleman breathing than T. Farnon.'

The big red face grew very solemn. 'You honour me with those words, old friend.'

'Not a bit of it,' I slurred. 'My stumbling sentences cannot hope to express my extremely high opinion of you.'

'You are too kind,' hiccupped Tristan.

'Nothing of the sort. It's a privlish, a rare privlish to know you.'

'Thank you, thank you,' Tristan nodded gravely at me from a distance of about six inches. We were staring into each other's eyes with intense absorption and the conversation might have gone on if Brenda hadn't broken in.

'Hey, when you two have finished rubbing noses I'd rather like another drink.'

Tristan gave her a cold look. 'You'll have to wait just a few minutes. There's something I have to do.' He rose, shook himself and walked with dignity to the centre of the floor. When he turned to face his audience he looked exalted. I felt that this would be an outstanding performance.

Tristan raised his arms and gazed imperiously over his imaginary orchestra, taking in the packed rows of strings, the woodwind, brass and tympani in one sweeping glance. Then with a violent downswing he led them into the overture. Rossini this time I thought, or maybe Wagner, as I watched him throwing his head about, bringing in the violins with a waving clenched fist or exhorting the trumpets with a glare and a trembling, outstretched hand.

It was somewhere near the middle of the piece that the rot always set in and I watched enthralled as the face began to twitch and the lips to snarl. The arm waving became more and more convulsive then the whole body jerked with uncontrollable spasms. It was clear that the end was near—Tristan's eyes were rolling, his hair hung over his face and he had lost control of the music which crashed and billowed about him. Suddenly he grew rigid, his arms fell to his sides and he crashed to the floor.

I was joining in the applause and laughter when I noticed that Tristan was very still. I bent over him and found that he had struck his head against the heavy oak leg of the settle and was almost unconscious. The nurses were quickly into action. Brenda expertly propped up his head while Connie ran for a basin of hot water and a cloth. When he opened his eyes they were bathing a tender lump above his ear. Mr Peacock hovered anxiously in the background. 'Ista all right? Can ah do anything?'

Tristan sat up and sipped weakly at his beer. He was very pale. 'I'll be all right in a minute and there is something you can do. You can bring us one for the road and then we must be getting on to this dance.'

The landlord hurried away and returned with the enamel jug brimming. The final pint revived Tristan miraculously and he was soon on his feet. Then we shook hands affectionately with Mr Peacock and took our leave. After the brightness of the inn the darkness pressed on us like a blanket and we groped our way up the steep street till we could see the institute standing on its grassy mound. Faint rays of light escaped through the chinks in the curtained windows and we could hear music and a rhythmic thudding.

A cheerful young farmer took our money at the door and when we went into the hall we were swallowed up in a tight mass of dancers. The place was packed solidly with young men in stiff-looking dark suits and girls in bright dresses all sweating happily as they swayed and wheeled to the music.

On the low platform at one end, four musicians were playing their hearts out—piano, accordion, violin and drums. At the other end, several comfortable, middle-aged women stood behind a long table on trestles, presiding over the thick sandwiches of ham and brawn, home made pies, jugs of milk and trifles generously laid with cream.

All round the walls more lads were standing, eyeing the unattached girls. I recognized a young client. 'What do you call this dance?' I yelled above the din.

'The Eva Three Step,' came back the reply.

This was new to me but I launched out confidently with Connie. There was a lot of twirling and stamping and when the men brought their heavy boots down on the boards the hall shook and the noise was deafening. I loved it—I was right on the peak and I whirled Connie effortlessly among the throng. I was dimly aware of bumping people with my shoulders but, try as I might, I couldn't feel my feet touching the floor. The floating sensation was delicious. I decided that I had never been so happy in my life.

After half a dozen dances I felt ravenous and floated with Connie towards the food table. We each ate an enormous wedge of ham and egg pie which was so exquisite that we had the same again. Then we had some trifle and plunged again into the crush. It was about half way through a St Bernard's Waltz that I began to feel my feet on the boards again—quite heavy and dragging somewhat. Connie felt heavy, too. She seemed to be slumped in my arms.

She looked up. Her face was very white. 'Jus' feeling a bit queer—'scuse me.' She broke away and began to tack erratically towards the ladies' room. A few minutes later she came out and her face was no longer white. It was green. She staggered over to me. 'Could do with some fresh air. Take me outside.'

I took her out into the darkness and it was as if I had stepped aboard a ship; the ground pitched and heaved under my feet and I had to straddle my legs to stay upright. Holding Connie's arm, I retreated hastily to the wall of the institute and leaned my back against it. This didn't help a great deal because the wall, too, was heaving about. Waves of nausea swept over me. I thought of the ham and egg pie and groaned loudly.

Open mouthed, gulping in the sharp air, I looked up at the clean, austere sweep of the night sky and at the ragged clouds driving across the cold face of the moon. 'Oh God,' I moaned at the unheeding stars, 'Why did I drink all that bloody beer?'

But I had to look after Connie. I put my arm round her.

'Come on, we'd better start walking.' We began to reel blindly round the building, pausing after every two or three circuits while I got my breath back and shook my head violently to try to clear my brain. But our course was erratic and I forgot that the institute was perched on a little steep-sided hill. There was an instant when we were treading on nothing, then we were sprawling down a muddy bank. We finished in a tangled heap on the hard road at the bottom. I lay there peacefully till I heard a pitiful whimpering near by. Connie! Probably a compound fracture at least; but when I helped her up I found she was unhurt and so, surprisingly, was I. After our large intake of alcohol we must have been as relaxed as rag dolls when we fell.

We went back into the institute and stood just inside the door. Connie was unrecognizable; her beautiful hair hung across her face in straggling wisps, her eyes were vacant and tears coursed slowly through the muddy smears on her cheeks. My suit was plastered with clay and I could feel more of it drying on one side of my face. We stood close, leaning miserably on each other in the doorway. The dancers were a shapeless blur. My stomach heaved and tossed.

Then I heard somebody say 'Good evening'. It was a woman's voice and very close. There were two figures looking at us with interest. They seemed to have just come through the door.

I concentrated fiercely on them and they swam into focus for a few seconds. It was Helen and a man. His pink, scrubbed-looking face, the shining fair hair plastered sideways across the top of his head was in keeping with the spotless British warm overcoat. He was staring at me distastefully. They went out of focus again and there was only Helen's voice. 'We thought we would just look in for a few moments to see how the dance was going. Are you enjoying it?'

Then, unexpectedly, I could see her clearly. She was smiling her kind smile but her eyes were strained as she looked from me to Connie and back again. I couldn't speak but stood gazing at her dully, seeing only her calm beauty in the crush and noise. It seemed, for a moment, that it would be the most natural thing in the world to throw my arms around her but I discarded the idea and, instead, just nodded stupidly.

'Well then, we must be off,' she said and smiled again. 'Good night.'

The fair-haired man gave me a cold nod and they went out.

Chapter Twenty-Seven

IT LOOKED as though I was going to make it back to the road all right. And I was thankful for it because seven o'clock in the morning with the wintry dawn only just beginning to lighten the eastern rim of the moor was no time to be digging my car out of the snow.

This narrow, unfenced road skirted a high tableland and gave on to a few lonely farms at the end of even narrower tracks. It hadn't actually been snowing on my way out to this early call—a uterine haemorrhage in a cow—but the wind had been rising steadily and whipping the top surface from the white blanket which had covered the fell-tops for weeks. My headlights had picked out the creeping drifts; pretty, pointed fingers feeling their way inch by inch across the strip of tarmac.

This was how all blocked roads began, and at the farm as I injected pituitrin and packed the bleeding cervix with a clean sheet I could hear the wind buffeting the byre door and wondered if I would win the race home.

On the way back the drifts had stopped being pretty and lay across the road like white bolsters; but my little car had managed to cleave through them, veering crazily at times, wheels spinning, and now I could see the main road a few hundred yards ahead, reassuringly black in the pale light.

But just over there on the left, a field away, was Cote House. I was treating a bullock there—he had eaten some frozen turnips—and a visit was fixed for today. I didn't fancy trailing back up here if I could avoid it and there was a light in the kitchen window. The family were up, anyway. I turned and drove down into the yard.

The farmhouse door lay within a small porch and the wind had driven the snow inside forming a smooth, two-foot heap against the timbers. As I leaned across to knock, the surface of the heap trembled a little, then began to heave. There was something in there, something quite big. It was eerie standing in the half light watching the snow parting to reveal a furry body. Some creature of the wild must have strayed in, searching for warmth—but it was bigger than a fox or anything else I could think of.

Just then the door opened and the light from the kitchen streamed out. Peter Trenholm beckoned me inside and his wife smiled at me from the bright interior. They were a cheerful young couple.

'What's that?' I gasped, pointing at the animal which was shaking the snow vigorously from its coat.

'That?' Peter grinned, 'That's awd Tip.'

'Tip? Your dog? But what's he doing under a pile of snow?'

'Just blew in on him, I reckon. That's where he sleeps, you know, just outside back door.'

I stared at the farmer. 'You mean he sleeps there, out in the open, every night?'

'Aye, allus. Summer and winter. But don't look at me like that Mr Herriot—it's his own choice. The other dogs have a warm bed in the cow house but Tip won't entertain it. He's fifteen now and he's been sleeping out there since he were a pup. I remember when me father was alive he tried all ways to get t'awd feller to sleep inside but it was no good.'

I looked at the old dog in amazement. I could see him more clearly now; he wasn't the typical sheep dog type, he was bigger-boned, longer in the hair, and he projected a bursting vitality that didn't go with his fifteen years. It was difficult to believe that any animal living in these bleak uplands should choose to sleep outside—and thrive on it. I had to look closely to see any sign of his great age. There was the slightest stiffness in his gait as he moved around, perhaps a fleshless look about his head and face, and of course the tell-tale lens opacity in the depths of his eyes. But the general impression was of an unquenchable jauntiness.

He shook the last of the snow from his coat, pranced jerkily up to the farmer and gave a couple of reedy barks. Peter Trenholm laughed. 'You see he's ready to be off—he's a beggar for work is Tip.' He led the way towards the buildings and I followed, stumbling over the frozen ruts, like iron under the snow, and bending my head against the knife-like wind. It was a relief to open the byre door and escape into the sweet bovine warmth.

There was a fair mixture of animals in the long building. The dairy cows took up most of the length, then there were a few young heifers, some bullocks and finally, in an empty stall deeply bedded with straw, the other farm dogs. The cats were there, too, so it had to be warm. No animal is a better judge of comfort than a cat and they were just visible as furry balls in the straw. They had the best place, up against the wooden partition where the warmth came through from the big animals.

Tip strode confidently among his colleagues—a young dog and a bitch with three half-grown pups. You could see he was boss.

One of the bullocks was my patient and he was looking a bit better. When I had seen him yesterday his rumen (the big first stomach) had been completely static and atonic following an over eager consumption of frozen turnips. He had been slightly bloated and groaning with discomfort. But today as I leaned with my ear against his left side I could hear the beginnings of the surge and rumble of the normal rumen instead of the deathly silence of yesterday. My gastric lavage had undoubtedly tickled things up and I felt that another of the same would just about put him right. Almost lovingly I got together the ingredients of one of my favourite treatments, long since washed away in the flood of progress; the ounce of formalin, the half pound of common salt, the can of black treacle from the barrel which you used to find in most cow houses, all mixed up in a bucket with two gallons of hot water.

I jammed the wooden gag into the bullock's mouth and buckled it behind the horns, then as Peter held the handles I passed the stomach tube down into the rumen and pumped in the mixture. When I had finished the bullock opened his eyes wide in surprise and began to paddle his hind legs. Listening again at his side, I could hear the reassuring bubbling of the stomach contents. I smiled to myself in satisfaction. It worked, it always worked.

Wiping down the tube I could hear the hiss-hiss as Peter's brother got on with the morning's milking, and as I prepared to leave he came down the byre with a full bucket on the way to the cooler. As he passed the dogs' stall he tipped a few pints of the warm milk into their dishes and Tip strolled forward casually for his breakfast. While he was drinking, the young dog tried to push his way in but a soundless snap from Tip's jaws missed his nose by a fraction and he retired to another dish. I noticed, however, that the old dog made no protest as the bitch and pups joined him. The cats, black and white, tortoise-shell, tabby grey, appeared, stretching, and advanced in a watchful ring. Their turn would come.

Mrs Trenholm called me in for a cup of tea and when I came out it was full daylight. But the sky was burdened grey and the sparse trees near the house strained their bare branches against the wind which drove in long, icy gusts over the white empty miles of moor. It was what the Yorkshiremen called a 'thin wind' or sometimes a 'lazy wind'— the kind that couldn't be bothered to blow round you but went straight through instead. It made me feel that the best place on earth was by the side of that bright fire in the farmhouse kitchen.

Most people would have felt like that, but not old Tip. He was capering around as Peter loaded a flat cart with some hay bales for the young cattle in the outside barns; and as Peter shook the reins and the cob set off over the fields, he leapt on to the back of the cart.

As I threw my tackle into the boot I looked back at the old dog, legs braced against the uneven motion, tail waving, barking defiance at the cold world. I carried away the memory of Tip who scorned the softer things and slept in what he considered the place of honour—at his master's door.

A little incident like this has always been able to brighten my day and fortunately I have the kind of job where things of this kind happened. And sometimes it isn't even a happening—just a single luminous phrase.

As when I was examining a cow one morning while its neighbour was being milked. The milker was an old man and he was having trouble. He was sitting well into the cow, his cloth-capped head buried in her flank, the bucket gripped tightly between his knees, but the stool kept rocking about as the cow fidgeted and weaved. Twice she kicked the bucket over and she had an additional little trick of anointing her tail with particularly liquid faeces then lashing the old man across the face with it.

Finally he could stand it no longer. Leaping to his feet he dealt a puny blow at the cow's craggy back and emitted an exasperated shout.

'Stand still, thou shittin' awd bovril!'

Or the day when I had to visit Luke Benson at his small-holding in Hillom village. Luke was a powerful man of about sixty and had the unusual characteristic of speaking always through his clenched teeth. He literally articulated every word by moving only his lips, showing the rows of square, horse-like incisors clamped tightly together. It lent a peculiar intensity to his simplest utterance; and as he spoke, his eyes glared.

Most of his conversation consisted of scathing remarks about the other inhabitants of Hillom. In fact he seemed to harbour a cordial dislike of the human race in general. Yet strangely enough I found him a very reasonable man to deal with; he accepted my diagnoses of his animals' ailments without question and appeared to be trying to be friendly by addressing me repeatedly as 'Jems', which was the nearest he could get to my name with his teeth together.

His fiercest hatred was reserved for his neighbour and fellow smallholder, a little lame man called Gill to whom Luke referred invariably and unkindly as 'Yon 'oppin youth'. A bitter feud had raged between them for many years and I had seen Luke smile on only two occasions—once when Mr Gill's sow lost its litter and again when he had a stack burnt down.

When Mr Gill's wife ran away with a man who came round the farms selling brushes it caused a sensation. Nothing like that had ever happened in Hillom before and a wave of delighted horror swept through the village. This, I thought, would have been the high point of Luke Benson's life and when I had to visit a heifer of his I expected to find him jubilant. But Luke was gloomy.

As I examined and treated his animal he remained silent and it wasn't until I went into the kitchen to wash my hands that he spoke. He glanced round warily at his wife, a gaunt, grim-faced woman who was applying blacklead to the grate.

'You'll have heard about yon 'oppin youth's missus runnin' off?' he said.

'Yes,' I replied. 'I did hear about it.' I waited for Luke to gloat but he seemed strangely ill at ease. He fidgeted until I had finished drying my hands then he glared at me and bared his strong teeth.

'Ah'll tell you something, Jems,' he ground out. 'Ah wish somebody would tek MA bugger!'

And there was that letter from the Bramleys—that really made me feel good. You don't find people like the Bramleys now; radio, television and the motor-car have carried the outside world into the most isolated places so that the simple people you used to meet on the lonely farms are rapidly becoming like people anywhere else. There are still a few left, of course—old folk who cling to the ways of their fathers—and when I come across any of them I like to make some excuse to sit down and talk with them and listen to the old Yorkshire words and expressions which have almost disappeared.

But even in the thirties when there were many places still untouched by the flood of progress the Bramleys were in some ways unique. There were four of them; three brothers, all middle-aged bachelors, and an old sister, also unmarried, and their farm lay in a wide, shallow depression in the hills. You could just see the ancient tiles of Scar House through the top branches of the sheltering trees if you stood outside the pub in Drewburn village and in the summer it was possible to drive down over the fields to the farm. I had done it a few times, the bottles in the boot jingling and crashing as the car bounced over the rig and furrow. The other approach to the place was right on the other side through Mr Broom's stackyard and then along a track with ruts so deep that only a tractor could negotiate it.

There was, in fact, no road to the farm, but that didn't bother the Bramleys because the outside world held no great attraction for them. Miss Bramley made occasional trips to Darrowby on market days for provisions, and Herbert, the middle brother, had come into town in the spring of 1929 to have a tooth out, but apart from that they stayed contentedly at home.

A call to Scar House always came as rather a jolt because it meant that at least two hours had been removed from the working day. In all but the driest weather it was safer to leave the car at Mr Broom's and make the journey on foot. One February night at about eight o'clock I was splashing my way along the track, feeling the mud sucking at my wellingtons; it was to see a horse with colic and my pockets were stuffed with the things I might need—arecoline, phials of morphia, a bottle of Paraphyroxia. My eyes were half closed against the steady drizzle but about half a mile ahead I could see the lights of the house winking among the trees.

After twenty minutes of slithering in and out of unseen

puddles and opening a series of broken, string-tied gates, I reached the farm yard and crossed over to the back door. I was about to knock when I stopped with my hand poised. I found I was looking through the kitchen window and in the interior, dimly lit by an oil lamp, the Bramleys were sitting in a row.

They weren't grouped round the fire but were jammed tightly on a long, high-backed wooden settle which stood against the far wall. The strange thing was the almost exact similarity of their attitudes; all four had their arms folded, chins resting on their chests, feet stretched out in front of them. The men had removed their heavy boots and were stocking-footed, but Miss Bramley wore an old pair of carpet slippers.

I stared, fascinated by the curious immobility of the group. They were not asleep, not talking or reading or listening to the radio—in fact they didn't have one—they were just sitting.

I had never seen people just sitting before and I stood there for some minutes to see if they would make a move or do anything at all, but nothing happened. It occurred to me that this was probably a typical evening; they worked hard all day, had their meal, then they just sat till bedtime.

A month or two later I discovered another unsuspected side of the Bramleys when they started having trouble with their cats. I knew they were fond of cats but the number and variety which swarmed over the place and perched confidently on my car bonnet on cold days with their unerring instinct for a warm place. But I was unprepared for the family's utter desolation when the cats started to die. Miss Bramley was on the doorstep at Skeldale House nearly every day carrying an egg basket with another pitiful patient—a cat or sometimes a few tiny kittens—huddling miserably inside.

Even today with the full range of modern antibiotics, the treatment of feline enteritis is unrewarding and I had little success with my salicylates and non-specific injections. I did my best. I even took some of the cats in and kept them at the surgery so that I could attend them several times a day, but the mortality rate was high.

The Bramleys were stricken as they saw their cats diminishing. I was surprised at their grief because most farmers look on cats as pest killers and nothing more. But when Miss Bramley came in one morning with a fresh consignment of invalids she was in a sorry state. She stared at me across the surgery table and her rough fingers clasped and unclasped on the handle of the egg basket.

'Is it going to go through 'em all?' she quavered.

'Well, it's very infectious and it looks as though most of your young cats will get it anyway.'

For a moment Miss Bramley seemed to be struggling with herself, then her chin began to jerk and her whole face twitched uncontrollably. She didn't actually break down but her eyes brimmed and a couple of tears wandered among the network of wrinkles on her cheeks. I looked at her helplessly as she stood there, wisps of grey hair straggling untidily from under the incongruous black beret which she wore pulled tightly over her ears.

'It's Topsy's kittens I'm worried about,' she gasped out at length. 'There's five of 'em and they're the best we've got.'

I rubbed my chin. I had heard a lot about Topsy, one of a strain of incomparable ratters and mousers. Her last family were only about ten weeks old and it would be a crushing blow to the Bramleys if anything happened to them. But what the devil could I do? There was, as yet, no protective vaccine against the disease—or wait a minute, was there? I remembered that I'd heard a rumour that Burroughs Wellcome were working on one.

I pulled out a chair. 'Just sit down a few minutes, Miss Bramley. I'm going to make a phone call.' I was soon through to the Wellcome Laboratory and half expected a sarcastic reply. But they were kind and co-operative. They had had encouraging results with the new vaccine and would be glad to let me have five doses if I would inform them of the result.

I hurried back to Miss Bramley. 'I've ordered something for your kittens. I can't guarantee anything but there's nothing else to do. Have them down here on Tuesday morning.'

The vaccine arrived promptly and as I injected the tiny creatures Miss Bramley extolled the virtues of the Topsy line. 'Look at the size of them ears! Did you ever see bigger 'uns on kittens?'

I had to admit that I hadn't. The ears were enormous, sail-like and they made the ravishingly pretty little faces look even smaller.

Miss Bramley nodded and smiled with satisfaction. 'Aye, you can allus tell. It's the sure sign of a good mouser.'

The injection was repeated a week later. The kittens were still looking well.

'Well that's it,' I said. 'We'll just have to wait now. But remember I want to know the outcome of this, so please don't forget to let me know.'

I didn't hear from the Bramleys for several months and had almost forgotten about the little experiment when I came upon a grubby envelope which had apparently been pushed under the surgery door. It was the promised report and was, in its way, a model of conciseness. It communicated all the information I required without frills or verbiage.

It was in a careful, spidery scrawl and said simply: 'Dere Sir, Them kittens is now big cats. Yrs trly, R. Bramley.'

Chapter Twenty-Eight

AS I STOPPED MY CAR by the group of gipsies I felt I was
looking at something which should have been captured by a
camera. The grass verge was wide on this loop of the road
and there were five of them squatting round the fire; it
seemed like the mother and father and three little girls.
They sat very still, regarding me blankly through the drifting smoke while a few big snowflakes floated across the scene
and settled lazily on the tangled hair of the children. Some
unreal quality in the wild tableau kept me motionless in my
seat, staring through the glass, forgetful of the reason for my
being here. Then I wound down the window and spoke to
the man.

'Are you Mr Myatt? I believe you have a sick pony.' The
man nodded. 'Aye, that's right. He's over here.' It was a
strange accent with no trace of Yorkshire in it. He got up
from the fire, a thin, dark-skinned unshaven little figure, and
came over to the car holding out something in his hand. It
was a ten shilling note and I recognized it as a gesture of
good faith.

The gipsies who occasionally wandered into Darrowby
were always regarded with a certain amount of suspicion.
They came, unlike the Myatts, mainly in the summer to
camp down by the river and sell their horses and we had
been caught out once or twice before. A lot of them seemed
to be called Smith and it wasn't uncommon to go back on the
second day and find that patient and owner had gone. In
fact Siegfried had shouted to me as I left the house this morning: 'Get the brass if you can.' But he needn't have worried
—Mr Myatt was on the up and up.

211

I got out of the car and followed him over the grass, past the shabby, ornate caravan and the lurcher dog tied to the wheel, to where a few horses and ponies were tethered. My patient was easy to find; a handsome piebald of about thirteen hands with good clean legs and a look of class about him. But he was in a sorry state. While the other animals moved around on their tethers, watching us with interest, the piebald stood as though carved from stone.

Even from a distance I could tell what was wrong with him. Only acute laminitis could produce that crouching posture and as I moved nearer I could see that all four feet were probably affected because the pony had his hind feet right under his body in a desperate attempt to take his full weight on his heels.

I pushed my thermometer into the rectum. 'Has he been getting any extra food, Mr Myatt?'

'Aye, he getten into a bag of oats last night.' The little man showed me the big, half-empty sack in the back of the caravan. It was difficult to understand him but he managed to convey that the pony had broken loose and gorged himself on the oats. And he had given him a dose of castor oil —he called it 'casta ile'

The thermometer read 104 and the pulse was rapid and bounding. I passed my hand over the smooth, trembling hooves, feeling the abnormal heat, then I looked at the taut face, the dilated notrils and terrified eyes. Anybody who has had an infection under a finger-nail can have an inkling of the agony a horse goes through when the sensitive laminae of the foot are inflamed and throbbing against the unyielding wall of the hoof.

'Can you get him to move?' I asked.

The man caught hold of the head collar and pulled, but the pony refused to budge.

I took the other side of the collar. 'Come on, it's always better if they can get moving.'

We pulled together and Mrs Myatt slapped the pony's rump. He took a couple of stumbling steps but it was as though the ground was red hot and he groaned as his feet came down. Within seconds he was crouching again with his weight on his heels.

'It seems he just won't have it.' I turned and went back to the car. I'd have to do what I could to give him relief and the first thing was to get rid of as much as possible of that bellyful of oats. I fished out the bottle of arecoline and gave an injection into the muscle of the neck, then I showed the little man how to tie cloths round the hooves so that he could keep soaking them with cold water.

Afterwards I stood back and looked again at the pony. He was salivating freely from the arecoline and he had cocked his tail and evacuated his bowel; but his pain was undiminished and it would stay like that until the tremendous inflammation subsided—if it ever did. I had seen cases like this where serum had started to ooze from the coronet; that usually meant shedding of the hooves—even death.

As I turned over the gloomy thoughts the three little girls went up to the pony. The biggest put her arms round his neck and laid her cheek against his shoulder while the others stroked the shivering flanks. There were no tears, no change in the blank expressions, but it was easy to see that that pony really meant something to them.

Before leaving I handed over a bottle of tincture of aconite mixture. 'Get a dose of this down him every four hours, Mr Myatt, and be sure to keep putting cold water on the feet. I'll come and see him in the morning.'

I closed the car door and looked through the window again at the slow-rising smoke, the drifting snowflakes and the three children with their ragged dresses and uncombed hair still stroking the pony.

'Well, you got the brass, James,' Siegfried said at lunch, carelessly stuffing the ten shilling note into a bulging pocket. 'What was the trouble?'

'Worst case of laminitis I've ever seen. Couldn't move the pony at all and he's going through hell. I've done the usual things but I'm pretty sure they won't be enough.'

'Not a very bright prognosis, then?'

'Really black. Even if he gets over the acute stage he'll have deformed feet, I'd like to bet. Grooved hooves, dropped soles, the lot. And he's a grand little animal, lovely piebald. I wish to God there was something else I could do.'

Siegfried sawed two thick slices off the cold mutton and dropped them on my plate. He looked thoughtfully at me for a moment. 'You've been a little distrait since you came back. These are rotten jobs, I know, but it's no good worrying.'

'Ach, I'm not worrying, exactly, but I can't get it off my mind. Maybe it's those people—the Myatts. They were something new to me. Right out of the world. And three raggedy little girls absolutely crazy about that pony. They aren't going to like it at all.'

As Siegfried chewed his mutton I could see the old glint coming into his eyes; it showed when the talk had anything to do with horses. I knew he wouldn't push in but he was waiting for me to make the first move. I made it.

'I wish you'd come along and have a look with me. Maybe there's something you could suggest. Do you think there could be?'

Siegfried put down his knife and fork and stared in front of him for a few seconds, then he turned to me. 'You know, James, there just might be. Quite obviously this is a right pig of a case and the ordinary remedies aren't going to do any good. We have to pull something out of the bag and I've got an idea. There's just one thing.' He gave me a crooked smile. 'You may not like it.'

'Don't bother about me,' I said. 'You're the horseman. If you can help this pony I don't care what you do.'

'Right, eat up then and we'll go into action together.' We finished our meal and he led me through to the instrument room. I was surprised when he opened the cupboard where old Mr Grant's instruments were kept. It was a kind of museum.

When Siegfried had bought the practice from the old vet

who had worked on into his eighties these instruments had come with it and they lay there in rows, unused but undisturbed. It would have been logical to throw them out, but maybe Siegfried felt the same way about them as I did. The polished wooden boxes of shining, odd-shaped scalpels, the enema pumps and douches with their perished rubber and brass fittings, the seaton needles, the ancient firing irons—they were a silent testament to sixty years of struggle. I often used to open the cupboard door and try to picture the old man wrestling with the same problems as I had, travelling the same narrow roads as I did. He had done it absolutely on his own and for sixty years. I was only starting but I knew a little about the triumphs and disasters, the wondering and worrying, the hopes and disappointments—and the hard labour. Anyway, Mr Grant was dead and gone, taking with him all the skills and knowledge I was doggedly trying to accumulate.

Siegfried reached to the back of the cupboard and pulled out a long flat box. He blew the dust from the leather covering and gingerly unfastened the clasp. Inside, a fleam, glittering on its bed of frayed velvet, lay by the side of a round, polished blood stick.

I looked at my employer in astonishment. 'You're going to bleed him, then?'

'Yes, my boy, I'm going to take you back to the Middle Ages.' He looked at my startled face and put a hand on my arm. 'But don't start beating me over the head with all the scientific arguments against blood-letting. I've no strong views either way.'

'But have you ever done it? I've never seen you use this outfit.'

'I've done it. And I've seen some funny things after it, too.' Siegfried turned away as if he wanted no more discussion. He cleaned the fleam thoroughly and dropped it into the sterilizer. His face was expressionless as he stood listening to the hiss of the boiling water.

The gipsies were again hunched over the fire when we

got there and Mr Myatt, sensing that reinforcements had arrived, scrambled to his feet and shuffled forward, holding out another ten shilling note.

Siefried waved it away. 'Let's see how we get on, Mr Myatt,' he grunted. He strode across the grass to where the pony still trembled in his agonized crouch. There was no improvement; in fact the eyes stared more wildly and I could hear little groans as the piebald carefully eased himself from foot to foot.

Siegfried spoke softly without looking at me, 'Poor beggar. You weren't exaggerating, James. Bring that box from the car, will you?'

When I came back he was tying a choke rope round the base of the pony's neck. 'Pull it up tight,' he said. As the jugular rose up tense and turgid in its furrow he quickly clipped and disinfected a small area and inserted a plaque of local anaesthetic. Finally he opened the old leather-covered box and extracted the fleam, wrapped in sterile lint.

Everything seemed to start happening then. Siegfried placed the little blade of the fleam against the bulging vein and without hesitation gave it a confident smack with the stick. Immediately an alarming cascade of blood spouted from the hole and began to form a dark lake on the grass. Mr Myatt gasped and the little girls set up a sudden chatter. I could understand how they felt. In fact I was wondering how long the pony could stand this tremendous outflow without dropping down.

It didn't seem to be coming out fast enough for Siegfried, however, because he produced another stick from his pocket, thrust it into the pony's mouth and began to work the jaws. And as the animal champed, the blood gushed more fiercely.

When at least a gallon had come away Siegfried seemed satisfied. 'Slacken the rope, James,' he cried, then rapidly closed the wound in the neck with a pin suture. Next he trotted over the grass and looked over a gate in the roadside wall.

'Thought so,' he shouted. 'There's a little beck in that

field. We've got to get him over to it. Come on, lend a hand everybody!'

He was clearly enjoying himself and his presence was having its usual effect. The Myatts were spurred suddenly into action and began to run around aimlessly, bumping into each other. I was gripped by a sudden tension and preparedness and even the pony seemed to be taking an interest in his surroundings for the first time.

All five of the gipsies pulled at the halter, Siegfried and I looped our arms behind the pony's thighs, everybody gave encouraging shouts and at last he began to move forward. It was a painful process but he kept going—through the gate and across the field to where the shallow stream wandered among its rushes. There were no banks to speak of and it was easy to push him out into the middle. As he stood there with the icy water rippling round his inflamed hooves I fancied I could read in his eyes a faint dawning of an idea that things were looking up at last.

'Now he must stand in there for an hour,' Siegfried said. 'And then you'll have to make him walk round the field. Then another hour in the beck. As he gets better you can give him more and more exercise but he must come back to the beck. There's a lot of work for somebody here, so who's going to do it?'

The three little girls came shyly round him and looked up, wide-eyed, into his face. Siegfried laughed. 'You three want the job, do you? Right, I'll tell you just what to do.'

He pulled out the bag of peppermint drops which was an ever-present among his widely-varied pocket luggage and I settled myself for a long wait. I had seen him in action with the children on the farms and when that bag of sweets came out, everything stopped. It was the one time Siegfried was never in a hurry.

The little girls each solemnly took a sweet, then Siegfried squatted on his heels and began to address them like a professor with his class. They soon began to thaw and put a word in for themselves. The smallest launched into a barely intelligible account of the remarkable things the pony had done when he was a foal and Siegfried listened intently, nodding his head gravely now and then. There was all the time in the world.

His words obviously went home because, over the next few days whenever I passed the gipsy camp I could see the three wild little figures either grouped around the pony in the beck or dragging him round the field on a long halter shank. I didn't need to butt in—I could see he was improving all the time.

It was about a week later that I saw the Myatts on their way out of Darrowby, the red caravan rocking across the market place with Mr Myatt up front wearing a black velvet cap, his wife by his side. Tethered to various parts of the caravan the family of horses clopped along and right at the rear was the piebald, a bit stiff perhaps, but going very well. He'd be all right.

The little girls were looking out of the back door and as they spotted me I waved. They looked back at me unsmilingly until they had almost turned the corner into Hallgate then one of them shyly lifted her hand. The others followed suit and my last sight was of them waving eagerly back.

I strolled into the Drovers and took a thoughtful half pint into a corner. Siegfried had done the trick there all right but I was wondering what to make of it because in veterinary practice it is difficult to draw definite conclusions even after spectacular results. Was it my imagination or did that pony seem to feel relief almost immediately after the bloodletting? Would we ever have got him moving without it? Was it really the right thing in these cases to bash a hole in the jugular and release about a bucketful of the precious fluid? I still don't have the answers because I never dared try it for myself.

Chapter Twenty-Nine

'COULD MR HERRIOT see my dog, please?'

Familiar enough words coming from the waiting-room but it was the voice that brought me to a slithering halt just beyond the door.

It couldn't be, no of course it couldn't, but it sounded just like Helen. I tiptoed back and applied my eye without hesitation to the crack in the door. Tristan was standing there looking down at somebody just beyond my range of vision. All I could see was a hand resting on the head of a patient sheep dog, the hem of a tweed skirt and two silk stockinged legs.

They were nice legs—not skinny—and could easily belong to a big girl like Helen. My cogitations were cut short as a head bent over to speak to the dog and I had a close-up in profile of the small straight nose and the dark hair falling across the milky smoothness of the cheek.

I was still peering, bemused, when Tristan shot out of the room and collided with me. Stifling an oath, he grabbed my arm and hauled me along the passage into the dispensary. He shut the door and spoke in a hoarse whisper.

'It's her! The Alderson woman! And she wants to see you! Not Siegfried, not me, but you, Mr Herriot himself!'

He looked at me wide-eyed for a few moments, then as I stood hesitating he opened the door and tried to propel me into the passage.

'What the hell are you waiting for?' he hissed.

'Well, it's a bit embarrassing, isn't it? After that dance, I mean. Last time she saw me I was a lovely sight—so pie-eyed I couldn't even speak.'

Tristan struck his forehead with his hand. 'God help us! You worry about details, don't you? She's asked to see you —what more do you want? Go on, get in there!'

I was shuffling off irresolutely when he raised a hand. 'Just a minute. Stay right there.' He trotted off and returned in a few seconds holding out a white lab coat.

'Just back from the laundry,' he said as he began to work my arms into the starched sleeves. 'You'll look marvellous in this, Jim—the immaculate young surgeon.'

I stood unresisting as he buttoned me into the garment but struck away his hand when he started to straighten my tie. As I left him he gave me a final encouraging wave before heading for the back stairs.

I didn't give myself any more time to think but marched straight into the waiting-room. Helen looked up and smiled. And it was just the same smile. Nothing behind it. Just the same friendly, steady-eyed smile as when I first met her. We faced each other in silence for some moments then when I didn't say anything she looked down at the dog.

'It's Dan in trouble this time,' she said. 'He's our sheep dog but we're so fond of him that he's more like one of the family.'

The dog wagged his tail furiously at the sound of his name but yelped as he came towards me. I bent down and patted his head. 'I see he's holding up a hind leg.'

'Yes, he jumped over a wall this morning and he's been like that ever since. I think it's something quite bad—he can't put any weight on the leg.'

'Right, bring him through to the other room and I'll have a look at him. But take him on in front of me, will you, and I'll be able to watch how he walks.'

I held the door open and she went through ahead of me with the dog.

Watching how Helen walked distracted me over the first few yards, but it was a long passage and by the time we had reached the second bend I had managed to drag my attention back to my patient.

And glory be, it was a dislocated hip. It had to be, with that shortening of the limb and the way he carried it underneath his body with the paw just brushing the ground.

My feelings were mixed. This was a major injury but on the other hand the chances were I could put it right quickly and look good in the process. Because I had found, in my brief experience, that one of the most spectacular procedures in practice was the reduction of a dislocated hip. Maybe I had been lucky, but with the few I had seen I had been able to convert an alarmingly lame animal into a completely sound one as though by magic.

In the operating room I hoisted Dan on to the table. He stood without moving as I examined the hip. There was no doubt about it at all—the head of the femur was displaced upwards and backwards, plainly palpable under my thumb.

The dog looked round only once—when I made a gentle attempt to flex the limb—but turned away immediately and stared resolutely ahead. His mouth hung open a little as he panted nervously but like a lot of the placid animals which arrived on our surgery table he seemed to have resigned himself to his fate. I had the strong impression that if I started to cut his head off he wouldn't make much fuss.

'Nice, good-natured dog,' I said. 'And a bonny one, too.'

Helen patted the handsome head with the broad blaze of white down the face; the tail wagged slowly.

'Yes,' she said. 'He's just as much a family pet as a working dog. I do hope he hasn't hurt himself too badly.'

'Well, he has a dislocated hip. It's a nasty thing but with a bit of luck I ought to be able to put it back.'

'What happens if it won't go back?'

'He'd have to form a false joint up there. He'd be very lame for several weeks and probably always have a slightly short leg.'

'Oh dear, I wouldn't like that,' Helen said. 'Do you think he'll be all right?'

I looked at the docile animal still gazing steadfastly to his front. 'I think he's got a good chance, mainly because you haven't hung about for days before bringing him in. The sooner these things are tackled the better.'

'Oh good. When will you be able to start on him?'

'Right now.' I went over to the door. 'I'll just give Tristan a shout. This is a two man job.'

'Couldn't I help?' Helen said. 'I'd very much like to if you wouldn't mind.'

I looked at her doubtfully. 'Well, I don't know. You mightn't like playing tug of war with Dan in the middle. He'll be anaesthetized of course but there's usually a lot of pulling.'

Helen laughed. 'Oh, I'm quite strong. And not a bit squeamish. I'm used to animals, you know, and I like working with them.'

'Right,' I said. 'Slip on this spare coat and we'll begin.'

The dog didn't flinch as I pushed the needle into his vein and as the Nembutal flowed in, his head began to slump against Helen's arm and his supporting paw to slide along the smooth top of the table. Soon he was stretched unconscious on his side.

I held the needle in the vein as I looked down at the sleeping animal. 'I might have to give him a bit more. They have to be pretty deep to overcome the muscular resistance.'

Another cc. and Dan was as limp as any rag doll. I took hold of the affected leg and spoke across the table. 'I want you to link your hands underneath his thigh and try to hold him there when I pull. O.K.? Here we go, then.'

It takes a surprising amount of force to pull the head of a displaced femur over the rim of the acetabulum. I kept up a steady traction with my right hand, pressing on the head of the femur at the same time with my left. Helen did her part efficiently, leaning back against the pull, her lips pushed forward in a little pout of concentration.

I suppose there must be a foolproof way of doing this job —a method which works the very first time—but I have never been able to find it. Success has always come to me only after a fairly long period of trial and error and it was the same today. I tried all sorts of angles, rotations and twists on the flaccid limb, trying not to think of how it would look if this just happened to be the one I couldn't put back. I was wondering what Helen, still hanging on determinedly to her end, must be thinking of this wrestling match when I heard the muffled click. It was a sweet and welcome sound.

I flexed the hip joint once or twice. No resistance at all now. The femoral head was once more riding smoothly in its socket.

'Well that's it,' I said. 'Hope it stays put—we'll have to keep our fingers crossed. The odd one does pop out again but I've got a feeling this is going to be all right.'

Helen ran her hand over the silky ears and neck of the sleeping dog. 'Poor old Dan. He wouldn't have jumped over that wall this morning if he'd known what was in store for him. How long will it be before he comes round?'

'Oh, he'll be out for the rest of the day. When he starts to wake up tonight I want you to be around to steady him in case he falls and puts the thing out again. Perhaps you'd give me a ring. I'd like to know how things are.'

I gathered Dan up in my arms and was carrying him along the passage, staggering under his weight, when I met Mrs Hall. She was carrying a tray with two cups.

'I was just having a drink of tea, Mr Herriot,' she said. 'I thought you and the young lady might fancy a cup.'

I looked at her narrowly. This was unusual. Was it possible she had joined Tristan in playing Cupid? But the broad, dark-skinned face was as unemotional as ever.

'Well, thanks very much, Mrs Hall. I'll just put this dog outside first.' I went out and settled Dan on the back seat of Helen's car; with only his eyes and nose sticking out from under a blanket he looked at peace with the world.

Helen was already sitting with a cup in her lap and I thought of the other time I had drunk tea in this room with a girl. On the day I had arrived in Darrowby. She had been one of Siegfried's followers and toughest of them all.

This was a lot different. During the struggle in the operating room I had been able to observe Helen at close range and I had discovered that her mouth turned up markedly at the corners as though she was just going to smile or had just been smiling; also that the deep warm blue of the eyes under the smoothly arching brows made a dizzying partnership with the rich black-brown of her hair.

And this time the conversation didn't lag. Maybe it was because I was on my own ground—perhaps I never felt fully at ease unless there was a sick animal involved somewhere, but at any rate I found myself prattling effortlessly just as I had done up on that hill when we had first met.

Mrs Hall's teapot was empty and the last of the biscuits gone before I finally saw Helen off and started on my round.

The same feeling of easy confidence was on me that night when I heard her voice on the phone.

'Dan is up and walking about,' she said. 'He's still a bit wobbly but he's perfectly sound on that leg.'

'Oh great, he's got the first stage over. I think everything's going to be fine.'

There was a pause at the other end of the line, then: 'Thank you so much for what you've done. We were terribly worried about him, especially my young brother and sister. We're very grateful.'

'Not at all, I'm delighted too. He's a grand dog.' I hesitated for a moment—it had to be now. 'Oh, you remember we were talking about Scotland today. Well, I was passing the Plaza this afternoon and I see they're showing a film about the Hebrides. I thought maybe . . . I wondered if perhaps, er . . . you might like to come and see it with me.'

Another pause and my heart did a quick thud-thud.

'All right,' Helen said. 'Yes, I'd like that. When? Friday night? Well, thank you—goodbye till then.'

I replaced the receiver with a trembling hand. Why did I make such heavy weather of these things? But it didn't matter—I was back in business.

Chapter Thirty

RHEUMATISM is a terrible thing in a dog. It is painful enough in humans but an acute attack can reduce an otherwise healthy dog to terrified, screaming immobility.

Very muscular animals suffered most and I went carefully as my fingers explored the bulging triceps and gluteals of the little Staffordshire bull terrier. Normally a tough little fellow, afraid of nothing, friendly, leaping high in an attempt to lick people's faces; but today, rigid, trembling, staring anxiously in front of him. Even to turn his head a little brought a shrill howl of agony.

Mercifully it was something you could put right, and quickly too. I pulled the Novalgin into the syringe and injected it rapidly. The little dog, oblivious to everything but the knife-like stabbing of the rheumatism did not stir at the prick of the needle. I counted out some salicylate tablets into a box, wrote the directions on the lid and handed the box to the owner.

'Give him one of those as soon as the injection has eased him, Mr Tavener. Then repeat in about four hours. I'm pretty sure he'll be greatly improved by then.'

Mrs Tavener snatched the box away as her husband began to read the directions. 'Let me see to it,' she snapped. 'No doubt I'll be the one who has the job to do.'

It had been like that all the time, ever since I had entered the beautiful house with the terraced gardens leading down to the river. She had been at him ceaselessly while he was holding the dog for me. When the animal had yelped she had cried: 'Really, Henry, don't grip the poor thing like that, you're hurting him!' She had kept him scuttling about for this and that and when he was out of the room she said: 'You know, this is all my husband's fault. He will let the dog swim in the river. I knew this would happen.'

Half-way through, daughter Julia had come in and it was clear from the start she was firmly on Mama's side. She helped out with plenty of 'How could you, Daddy!' and 'For God's sake, Daddy!' and generally managed to fill in the gaps when her mother wasn't in full cry.

The Taveners were in their fifties. He was a big, floridly handsome man who had made millions in the Tyneside shipyards before pulling out of the smoke to this lovely place. I had taken an instant liking to him; I had expected a tough tycoon and had found a warm, friendly, curiously vulnerable man, obviously worried sick about his dog.

I had reservations about Mrs Tavener despite her still considerable beauty. Her smile had a switched-on quality and there was a little too much steel in the blue of her eyes. She had seemed less concerned about the dog than with the necessity of taking it out on her husband.

Julia, a scaled-down model of her mother, drifted about the room with the aimless, bored look of the spoiled child; glancing blankly at the dog or me, staring without interest through the window at the smooth lawns, the tennis court, the dark band of river under the trees.

I gave the terrier a final reassuring pat on the head and got up from my knees. As I put away the syringe, Tavener took my arm. 'Well, that's fine, Mr Herriot. We're very grateful to you for relieving our minds. I must say I thought the old boy's time had come when he started yelling. And now you'll have a drink before you go.'

The man's hand trembled on my arm as he spoke. It had been noticeable, too, when he had been holding the dog's head and I had wondered; maybe Parkinson's disease, or nerves, or just drink. Certainly he was pouring a generous measure of whisky into his glass, but as he tipped up the bottle his hand was seized by an even more violent tremor and he slopped some spirit on to the polished sideboard.

'Oh God! Oh God!' Mrs Tavener burst out. There was a bitter note of oh no, not again, in her cry and Julia struck her forehead with her hand and raised her eyes to heaven. Tavener shot a single hunted look at the women then grinned as he handed me my glass.

'Come and sit down, Mr Herriot,' he said. 'I'm sure you have time to relax for a few minutes.'

We moved over to the fireside and Tavener talked pleasantly about dogs and the countryside and the pictures which hung on the walls of the big room. Those pictures were noted in the district; many of them were originals by famous painters and they had become the main interest in Tavener's life. His other passion was clocks and as I looked round the room at the rare and beautiful timepieces standing among elegant period furniture it was easy to believe the rumours I had heard about the wealth within these walls.

The women did not drink with us; they had disappeared when the whisky was brought out, but as I drained my glass the door was pushed open and they stood there, looking remarkably alike in expensive tweed coats and fur-trimmed hats. Mrs Tavener pulling on a pair of motoring gloves, looked with distaste at her husband. 'We're going into Brawton,' she said. 'Don't know when we'll be back.'

Behind her, Julia stared coldly at her father; her lip curled slightly.

Tavener did not reply. He sat motionless as I listened to the roar of the car engine and the spatter of whipped-up gravel beyond the window; then he looked out, blank-faced, empty-eyed at the drifting cloud of exhaust smoke in the drive.

There was something in his expression which chilled me. I put down my glass and got to my feet. 'Afraid I must be moving on, Mr Tavener. Thanks for the drink.'

He seemed suddenly to be aware of my presence; the friendly smile returned. 'Not at all. Thank you for looking after the old boy. He seems better already.'

In the driving mirror, the figure at the top of the steps looked small and alone till the high shrubbery hid him from my view.

The next call was to a sick pig, high on Marstang Fell. The road took me at first along the fertile valley floor, winding under the riverside trees past substantial farmhouses and rich pastures; but as the car left the road and headed up a steep track the country began to change. The transition was almost violent as the trees and bushes thinned out and gave way to the bare, rocky hillside and the miles of limestone walls.

And though the valley had been rich with the fresh green of the new leaves, up here the buds were unopened and the naked branches stretched against the sky still had the look of winter.

Tim Alton's farm lay at the top of the track and as I pulled up at the gate I wondered as I always did how the man could scrape a living from those few harsh acres with the grass flattened and yellowed by the wind which always blew. At any rate, many generations had accomplished the miracle and had lived and struggled and died in that house with its outbuildings crouching in the lee of a group of stunted, wind-bent trees, its massive stones crumbling under three centuries of fierce weathering.

Why should anybody want to build a farm in such a place? I turned as I opened the gate and looked back at the track threading between the walls down and down to where the white stones of the river glittered in the spring sunshine. Maybe the builder had stood here and looked across the green vastness and breathed in the cold, sweet air and thought it was enough.

I saw Tim Alton coming across the yard. There had been no need to lay down concrete or cobbles here; they had just swept away the thin soil and there, between house and buildings was a sloping stretch of fissured rock. It was more than a durable surface—it was everlasting.

'It's your pig this time, then, Tim,' I said and the farmer nodded seriously.

'Aye, right as owt yesterday and laid flat like a dead 'un this morning. Never looked up when I filled his trough and by gaw when a pig won't tackle his grub there's summat far wrong.' Tim dug his hands inside the broad leather belt which encircled his oversized trousers and which always seemed to be about to nip his narrow frame in two and led the way gloomily into the sty. Despite the bitter poverty of his existence he was a man who took misfortune cheerfully. I had never seen him look like this and I thought I knew the reason; there is something personal about the family pig.

Smallholders like Tim Alton made their meagre living from a few cows; they sold their milk to the big dairies or made butter. And they killed a pig or two each year and cured it themselves for home consumption. On the poorer places it seemed to me that they ate little else; whatever meal I happened to stumble in on, the cooking smell was always the same—roasting fat bacon.

It appeared to be a matter of pride to make the pig as fat as possible; in fact, on these little wind-blown farms where the people and the cows and the dogs were lean and spare, the pig was about the only fat thing to be seen.

I had seen the Alton pig before. I had been stitching a cow's torn teat about a fortnight ago and Tim had patted me on the shoulder and whispered: 'Now come along wi' me, Mr Herriot and I'll show tha summat.' We had looked into the sty at a twenty-five-stone monster effortlessly emptying a huge trough of wet meal. I could remember the pride in the farmer's eyes and the way he listened to the smacking and slobbering as if to great music.

It was different today. The pig looked, if possible, even more enormous as it lay on its side, eyes closed, filling the entire floor of the sty like a beached whale. Tim splashed a stick across the untouched meal in the trough and made encouraging noises but the animal never stirred. The farmer looked at me with haggard eyes.

'He's bad, Mr Herriot. It's serious whatever it is.'

I had been taking the temperature and when I read the thermometer I whistled. 'A hundred and seven. That's some fever.'

The colour drained from Tim's face. 'Oh 'ell! A hundred and seven! It's hopeless, then. It's ower with him.'

I had been feeling along the animal's side and I smiled reassuringly. 'No, don't worry, Tim. I think he's going to be all right. He's got erysipelas. Here, put your fingers along his back. You can feel a lot of flat swellings on his skin— those are the diamonds. He'll have a beautiful rash within a few hours but at the moment you can't see it, you can only feel it.'

'And you can make him better?'

'I'm nearly sure I can. I'll give him a whacking dose of serum and I'd like to bet you he'll have his nose in that trough in a couple of days. Most of them get over it all right.'

'Well that's a bit o' good news, any road,' said Tim, a smile flooding over his face. 'You had me worried there with your hundred and seven, dang you!'

I laughed. 'Sorry, Tim, didn't mean to frighten you. I'm often happier to see a high temperature than a low one. But it's a funny time for erysipelas. We usually see it in late summer.'

'All right, I'll let ye off this time. Come in and wash your hands.'

In the kitchen I ducked my head but couldn't avoid bumping the massive side of bacon hanging from the beamed ceiling. The heavy mass rocked gently on its hooks; it was about eight inches thick in parts—all pure white fat. Only by close inspection was it possible to discern a thin strip of lean meat.

Mrs Alton produced a cup of tea and as I sipped I looked across at Tim who had fallen back into a chair and lay with his hands hanging down; for a moment he closed his eyes and his face became a mask of weariness. I thought for the hundredth time about the endless labour which made up the lives of these little farmers. Alton was only forty but his body was already bent and ravaged by the constant demands he made on it; you could read his story in the corded forearm, the rough, work-swollen fingers. He told me once that the last time he missed a milking was twelve years ago and that was for his father's funeral.

I was taking my leave when I saw Jennie. She was the Altons' eldest child and was pumping vigorously at the tyre of her bicycle which was leaning against the wall just outside the kitchen door.

'Going somewhere?' I asked and the girl straightened up quickly, pushing back a few strands of dark hair from her forehead. She was about eighteen with delicate features and large, expressive eyes; in her wild, pinched prettiness there was something of the wheeling curlews, the wind and sun, the wide emptiness of the moors.

'I'm going down to t'village.' She stole a glance into the kitchen. 'I'm going to get a bottle of Guinness for dad.'

'The village! It's a long way to go for a bottle of Guinness. It must be two miles and then you've got to push back up this hill. Are you going all that way just for one bottle?'

'Ay, just one,' she whispered, counting out a sixpence and some coppers into her palm with calm absorption. 'Dad's been up all night waiting for a heifer to calve—he's tired out. I won't be long and he can have his Guinness with his dinner. That's what he likes.' She looked up at me conspiratorially. 'It'll be a surprise for him.'

As she spoke, her father, still sprawled in the chair, turned his head and looked at her; he smiled and for a moment I saw a serenity in the steady eyes, a nobility in the seamed face.

Jennie looked at him for a few seconds, a happy secret look from under her lowered brows; then she turned quickly, mounted her bicycle and began to pedal down the track at surprising speed.

I followed her more slowly, the car, in second gear, bumping and swaying over the stones. I stared straight ahead, lost in thought. I couldn't stop my mind roaming between the two houses I had visited; between the gracious mansion by the river and the crumbling farmhouse I had just left; from Henry Tavener with his beautiful clothes, his well-kept hands, his rows of books and pictures and clocks, to Tim Alton with his worn, chest-high trousers nipped in by that great belt, his daily, monthly, yearly grind to stay alive on that unrelenting hilltop.

But I kept coming back to the daughters; to the contempt in Julia Tavener's eyes when she looked at her father and the shining tenderness in Jennie Alton's.

It wasn't so easy to work out as it seemed; in fact it became increasingly difficult to decide who was getting the most out of their different lives. But as I guided the car over the last few yards of the track and pulled on to the smooth tarmac of the road it came to me with unexpected clarity. Taking it all in all, if I had the choice to make, I'd settle for the Guinness.

Chapter Thirty-One

TRISTAN was unpacking the U.C.M.'s. These bottles contained a rich red fluid which constituted our last line of defence in the battle with animal disease. Its full name, Universal Cattle Medicine, was proclaimed on the label in big black type and underneath it pointed out that it was highly efficacious for coughs, chills, scours, garget, milk fever, pneumonia, felon and bloat. It finished off on a confident note with the assurance: 'Never Fails to Give Relief' and we had read the label so often that we half believed it.

It was a pity it didn't do any good because there was something compelling about its ruby depths when you held it up to the light and about the solid camphor-ammonia jolt when you sniffed at it and which made the farmers blink and shake their heads and say 'By gaw, that's powerful stuff,' with deep respect. But our specific remedies were so few and the possibilities of error so plentiful that it was comforting in cases of doubt to be able to hand over a bottle of the old standby. Whenever an entry of Siegfried's or mine appeared in the day book stating 'Visit attend cow, advice, 1 U.C.M.' it was a pretty fair bet we didn't know what was wrong with the animal.

The bottles were tall and shapely and they came in elegant white cartons, so much more impressive than the unobtrusive containers of the antibiotics and steroids which we use today. Tristan was lifting them out of the tea chest and stacking them on the shelves in deep rows. When he saw me he ceased his labours, sat on the chest and pulled out a packet of Woodbines. He lit one, pulled the smoke a long way down then fixed me with a non-committal stare.

'You're taking her to the pictures, then?'

Feeling vaguely uneasy under his eye, I tipped a pocketful of assorted empties into the waste basket. 'Yes, that's right. In about an hour.'

'Mm.' He narrowed his eyes against the slowly escaping smoke. 'Mm, I see.'

'Well what are you looking like that for?' I said defensively. 'Anything wrong with going to the pictures?'

'No-no. No-no-no. Nothing at all, Jim. Nothing, nothing. A very wholesome pursuit.'

'But you don't think I should be taking Helen there.'

'I never said that. No, I'm sure you'll have a nice time. It's just that . . .' He scratched his head. 'I thought you might have gone in for something a bit more . . . well . . . enterprising.'

I gave a bitter laugh. 'Look, I tried enterprise at the Reniston. Oh, I'm not blaming you, Triss, you meant well, but as you know it was a complete shambles. I just don't want anything to go wrong tonight. I'm playing safe.'

'Well, I won't argue with you there,' Tristan said. 'You couldn't get much safer than the Darrowby Plaza.'

And later, shivering in the tub in the vast, draughty bathroom, I couldn't keep out the thought that Tristan was right. Taking Helen to the local cinema was a form of cowardice, a shrinking away from reality into what I hoped would be a safe, dark intimacy. But as I towelled myself, hopping about to keep warm, and looked out through the fringe of wistaria at the darkening garden there was comfort in the thought that it was another beginning, even though a small one.

And as I closed the door of Skeldale House and looked along the street where the first lights of the shops beckoned in the dusk I felt a lifting of the heart. It was as though a breath from the near-by hills had touched me. A fleeting fragrance which said winter had gone. It was still cold—it was always cold in Darrowby until well into May—but the promise was there of sunshine, warm grass and softer days.

You had to look closely or you could easily miss the Plaza, tucked in as it was between Pickersgills the ironmongers and Howarths the chemists. There had never been much attempt at grandeur in its architecture and the entrance was hardly wider than the average shop front. But what puzzled me as I approached was that the place was in darkness. I was in good time but the show was due to start in ten minutes or so and there was no sign of life.

I hadn't dared tell Tristan that my precautions had extended as far as arranging to meet Helen here. With a car like mine there was always an element of doubt about arriving anywhere in time or indeed at all and I had thought it prudent to eliminate all transport hazards.

'Meet you outside the cinema.' My God, it wasn't very bright was it? It took me back to my childhood, to the very first time I had taken a girl out. I was just fourteen and on my way to meet her I tendered my only half-crown to a bloody-minded Glasgow tram conductor and asked for a penny fare. He vented his spleen on me by ransacking his bag and giving me change entirely in halfpennies. So when the cinema queue reached the pay box I had to stand there with my little partner and everybody else watching while I paid for our shilling tickets with great handfuls of copper. The shame of it left a scar—it was another four years before I took out a girl again.

But the black thoughts were dispelled when I saw Helen picking her way across the market-place cobbles. She smiled and waved cheerfully as if being taken to the Darrowby Plaza was the biggest treat a girl could wish for, and when she came right up to me there was a soft flush on her cheeks and her eyes were bright.

Everything was suddenly absolutely right. I felt a surging conviction that this was going to be a good night—nothing was going to spoil it. After we had said hello she told me that Dan was running about like a puppy with no trace of a limp and the news was another wave on the high tide of my euphoria.

The only thing that troubled me was the blank, uninhabited appearance of the cinema entrance.

'Strange there's nobody here,' I said. 'It's nearly starting time. I suppose the place is open?'

'Must be,' Helen said. 'It's open every night but Sunday. Anyway, I'm sure these people are waiting too.'

I looked around. There was no queue as such but little groups were standing here and there; a few couples, mostly middle-aged, a bunch of small boys rolling and fighting on the pavement. Nobody seemed worried.

And indeed there was no cause. Exactly two minutes before the picture was due to start a figure in a mackintosh coat pedalled furiously round the corner of the street, head down, legs pistoning, the bicycle lying over at a perilous angle with the ground. He came to a screeching halt outside the entrance, inserted a key in the lock and threw wide the doors. Reaching inside, he flicked a switch and a single neon strip flickered fitfully above our heads and went out. It did this a few times and seemed bent on mischief till he stood on tiptoe and beat it into submission with a masterful blow of his fist. Then he whipped off the mackintosh revealing faultless evening dress. The manager had arrived.

Soon a very fat lady appeared from nowhere and wedged herself into the pay box. The show was ready to roll.

We all began to shuffle inside. The little boys put down their ninepences and punched each other as they passed through a curtain into the stalls, while the rest of us proceeded decorously upstairs to the one-and-sixpenny seats in the balcony. The manager, his white shirt front and silk lapels gleaming, bowed with great courtesy as we passed.

We paused at a row of pegs at the top of the stairs while some people hung up their coats. I was surprised to see Maggie Robinson the blacksmith's daughter there, taking the tickets, and she appeared to be intrigued by the sight of us. She simpered and giggled, darted glances at Helen and did everything but dig me in the ribs. Finally she parted the curtains and we went inside.

It struck me immediately that the management were determined that their patrons wouldn't feel cold because if it hadn't been for the all-pervading smell of old sofas we might have been plunging into a tropical jungle. Maggie steered us through the stifling heat to our places and as I sat down I noticed there was no arm between the two seats.

'Them's the courting seats,' she blurted out and fled with her hand to her mouth.

The lights were still on and I looked round the tiny balcony. There were only about a dozen people dotted here and there sitting in patient silence under the plain distempered walls. By the side of the screen the hands of a clock stood resolutely at twenty past four.

But it was all right sitting there with Helen. I felt fine except for a tendency to gasp like a goldfish in the airless atmosphere. I was settling down cosily when a little man seated in front of us with his wife turned slowly round. The mouth in the haggard face was pursed grimly and he fixed his eyes on mine in a long, challenging stare. We faced each other for several silent moments before he finally spoke.

'She's dead,' he said.

A thrill of horror shot through me. 'Dead?'

'Aye, she is. She's dead.' He dragged the word out slowly with a kind of mournful satisfaction while his eyes still stared into mine.

I swallowed a couple of times. 'Well, I'm sorry to hear that. Truly sorry.'

He nodded grimly and continued to regard me with a peculiar intensity as though he expected me to say more. Then with reluctance he turned and settled in his seat.

I looked helplessly at the rigid back, at the square, narrow shoulders muffled in a heavy overcoat. Who in God's name was this? And what was he talking about? I knew the face from somewhere—must be a client. And what was dead? Cow? Ewe? Sow? My mind began to race over the cases I had seen during the past week but that face didn't seem to fit in anywhere.

237

Helen was looking at me questioningly and I managed a wan smile. But the spell was shattered. I started to say something to her when the little man began to turn again with menacing deliberation.

He fixed me once more with a hostile glare. 'Ah don't think there was ever owt wrong with her stomach,' he declared.

'You don't, eh?'

'No, young man, ah don't.' He dragged his eyes unwillingly from my face and turned towards the screen again.

The effect of this second attack was heightened because the lights went off suddenly and an incredible explosion of noise blasted my ear-drums. It was the Gaumont News. The sound machine, like the heating system, had apparently been designed for something like the Albert Hall and for a moment I cowered back under the assault. As a voice bellowed details of fortnight-old events I closed my eyes and tried again to place the man in front of me.

I often had trouble identifying people outside their usual environment and had once discussed the problem with Siegfried. He had been airy. 'There's an easy way, James. Just ask them how they spell their names. You'll have no trouble at all.'

I had tried this on one occasion and the farmer had looked at me strangely, replied 'S-M-I-T-H' and hurried away. So there seemed nothing to do now but sit sweating with my eyes on the disapproving back and search through my memory. When the news finished with a raucous burst of music I had got back about three weeks without result.

There was a blessed respite of a few seconds before the uproar broke out again. This was the main feature—the film about Scotland was on later—and was described outside as a tender love story. I can't remember the title but there was a lot of embracing which would have been all right except that every kiss was accompanied by a chorus of long-drawn sucking noises from the little boys downstairs. The less romantic blew raspberries.

And all the time it got hotter. I opened my jacket wide and unbuttoned my shirt collar but I was beginning to feel decidedly light-headed. The little man in front, still huddled in his heavy coat, seemed unperturbed. Twice the projector broke down and we stared for several minutes at a blank screen while a storm of whistling and stamping came up from the stalls.

Maggie Robinson, standing in the dim light by the curtain, still appeared to be fascinated by the sight of Helen and me. Whenever I looked up I found her eyes fixed upon us with a knowing leer. About half-way through the film, however, her concentration was disturbed by a commotion on the other side of the curtain and she was suddenly brushed aside as a large form burst through.

With a feeling of disbelief I recognized Gobber Newhouse. I had had previous experience of his disregard of the licensing laws and it was clear he had been at it again. He spent most afternoons in the back rooms of the local pubs and here he was, come to relax after a rough session.

He reeled up the aisle, turned, to my dismay, into our row, rested briefly on Helen's lap, trod on my toe and finally spread his enormous carcass over the seat on my left. Fortunately it was another courting seat with no central arm to get in his way but for all that he had great difficulty in finding a comfortable position. He heaved and squirmed about and the wheezing and snuffling and grunting in the darkness might have come from a pen of bacon pigs. But at last he found a spot and with a final cavernous belch composed himself for slumber.

The tender love story never did have much of a chance but Gobber sounded its death knell. With his snores reverberating in my ear and a dense pall of stale beer drifting over me I was unable to appreciate the delicate nuances.

It was a relief when the last close-up came to an end and the lights went up. I was a bit worried about Helen. I had noticed as the evening wore on that her lips had a tendency to twitch occasionally and now and then she drew her brows down in a deep frown. I wondered if she was upset. But Maggie appeared providentially with a tray round her neck and stood over us, still leering, while I purchased two chocolate ices.

I had taken only one bite when I noticed a stirring under the overcoat in front of me. The little man was returning to the attack. The eyes staring from the grim mask were as chilling as ever.

'Ah knew,' he said. 'Right from start, that you were on the wrong track.'

'Is that so?'

'Aye, I've been among beasts for fifty years and they never go on like that when it's the stomach.'

'Don't they? You're probably right.'

The little man twisted higher in his seat and for a moment I thought he was going to climb over at me. He raised a forefinger. 'For one thing a beast wi' a bad stomach is allus hard in its muck.'

'I see.'

'And if you think back, this un's muck was soft, real soft.'

'Yes, yes, quite,' I said hastily, glancing across at Helen. This was great—just what I needed to complete the romantic atmosphere.

He sniffed and turned away and once again, as if the whole thing had been stage-managed, we were plunged into blackness and the noise blasted out again. I was lying back quivering when it came through to me that something was wrong. What was this strident Western music? Then the title flashed on the screen. Arizona Guns.

I turned to Helen in alarm. 'What's going on? This is supposed to be the Scottish film, isn't it? The one we came to see?'

'It's supposed to be.' Helen paused and looked at me with a half-smile. 'But I'm afraid it isn't going to be. The thing is they often change the supporting film without warning. Nobody seems to mind.'

I slumped wearily in my seat. Well I'd done it again. No

dance at the Reniston, wrong picture tonight. I was a genius in my own way.

'I'm sorry,' I said. 'I hope you don't mind too much.'

She shook her head. 'Not a bit. Anyway, let's give this one a chance. It may be all right.'

But as the ancient horse opera crackled out its cliché-ridden message I gave up hope. This was going to be another of those evenings. I watched apathetically as the posse galloped for the fourth time past the same piece of rock and I was totally unprepared for the deafening fusillade of shots which rang out. It made me jump and it even roused Gobber from his sleep.

' 'Ello! 'ellow! 'ellow!' he bawled jerking upright and thrashing around him with his arms. A backhander on the side of the head drove me violently against Helen's shoulder and I was beginning to apologize when I saw that her twitching and frowning had come on again. But this time it spread and her whole face seemed to break up. She began to laugh, silently and helplessly.

I had never seen a girl laugh like this. It was as though it was something she had wanted to do for a long time. She abandoned herself utterly to it, lying back with her head on the back of the seat, legs stretched out in front of her, arms dangling by her side. She took her time and waited until she had got it all out of her system before she turned to me.

She put her hand on my arm. 'Look,' she said faintly. 'Next time, why don't we just go for a walk?'

I settled down. Gobber was asleep again and his snores, louder than ever, competed with the bangs and howls from the screen. I still hadn't the slightest idea who that little man in front could be and I had the feeling he wasn't finished with me yet. The clock still stood at twenty past four. Maggie was still staring at us and a steady trickle of sweat ran down my back.

The environment wasn't all I could have desired, but never mind. There was going to be a next time.

Chapter Thirty-Two

SIEGFRIED had a habit of pulling at the lobe of his ear and staring blankly ahead when preoccupied. He was doing it now, his other hand, outstretched, crumbling a crust of bread on his plate.

I didn't usually pry into my boss's meditations and anyway, I wanted to be off on the morning round, but there was something portentous in his face which made me speak.

'What's the matter? Something on your mind?'

Siegfried turned his head slowly and his eyes glared sightlessly for a few moments until recognition dawned. He stopped his lobe-pulling, got to his feet, walked over to the window and looked out at the empty street.

'There is, James, there is indeed. In fact, I was just about to ask your advice. It's about this letter I got this morning.' He ransacked his pockets impatiently, pulling out handkerchiefs, thermometers, crumpled bank-notes, lists of calls, till he found a long blue envelope. 'Here, read it.'

I opened the envelope and quickly scanned the single sheet.

I looked up, puzzled. 'Sorry, I don't get it. All it says here is that H. W. St. J. Ransom, Maj. Gen., would like the pleasure of your company at Brawton races on Saturday. No problem there, is there? You like racing.'

'Ah, but it's not so simple as that,' Siegfried said, starting again on the lobe. 'This is in the nature of a trial. General Ransom is one of the big boys in the North West Racing Circuit and he's bringing one of his pals along on Saturday to vet me. They're going to examine me for soundness.'

I must have looked alarmed because he grinned. 'Look, I'd better start at the beginning. And I'll cut it short. The officials of the North West Circuit are looking for a veterinary surgeon to supervise all meetings. You know the local man attends if there's a racecourse in his town and he is on call in case of injury to the horses, but this would be different. This supervisory vet would deal with cases of suspected doping and the like—in fact he'd have to be a bit of a specialist. Well I've had a whisper that they think I might be the man for the job and that's what Saturday's about. I know old Ransom but I haven't met his colleague. The idea is to have a day at the races with me and size me up.'

'If you got the job would it mean giving up general practice?' I asked. And a chill wind seemed to creep around me at the idea.

'No, no, but it would mean spending something like three days a week on racecourses and I'm wondering if that wouldn't be just a bit much.'

'Well, I don't know,' I finished my coffee and pushed back my chair. 'I'm not really the one to advise you on this. I haven't had a lot of experience with racehorses and I'm not interested in racing. You'll have to make up your own mind. But you've often talked of specializing in horse work and you love the atmosphere of a racecourse.'

'You're right there, James, I do. And there's no doubt the extra money would come in very useful. It's what every practice needs—a contract of some sort, a regular income from somewhere to make you less dependent on the farmers paying their bills.' He turned away from the window. 'Anyway, I'll go to Brawton races with them on Saturday and we'll see how it turns out. And you must come too.'

'Me! Why?'

'Well it says in the letter "and partner".'

'That means some woman. They'll have their wives with them, no doubt.'

'Doesn't matter what it means, James, you're coming with

me. A day out and a bit of free food and booze will do you good. Tristan can hold the fort for a few hours.'

It was nearly noon on Saturday when I answered the door bell. As I walked along the passage it was easy to identify the people beyond the glass door.

General Ransom was short and square with a moustache of surprising blackness thrusting aggressively from his upper lip. Colonel Tremayne was tall, hawk-nosed and stooping but he shared with his companion the almost tangible aura of authority which comes from a lifetime of command. Two tweedy women stood behind them on the lower step.

I opened the door, feeling my shoulders squaring and my heels coming together under the battery of fierce, unsmiling glares.

'Mr Farnon!' barked the general. 'Expectin' us, I think.'

I retreated a pace and opened the door. 'Oh yes, certainly, please come in.'

The two women swept in first, Mrs Ransom as squat and chunky and even tougher-looking than her husband, then Mrs Tremayne, much younger and attractive in a hard-boiled fashion. All of them completely ignored me except the colonel who brought up the rear and fixed me for a moment with a fishy eye.

I had been instructed to dispense sherry, and once inside the sitting-room I began to pour from a decanter. I was half-way up the second glass when Siegfried walked in. I spilt some of the sherry. My boss had really spruced up for the occasion. His lean frame was draped in cavalry twill of flawless cut; the long, strong-boned face was freshly shaven, the small sandy moustache neatly clipped. He swept off a brand-new bowler as he came in and I put down my decanter and gazed at him with proprietary pride. Maybe there had been a few dukes or the odd earl in Siegfried's family tree but be that as it may, the two army men seemed in an instant to have become low bred and a trifle scruffy.

There was something almost ingratiating in the way the

general went up to Siegfried. 'Farnon, my dear feller, how are you? Good to see you again. Let me introduce you to me wife, Mrs Tremayne, Colonel Tremayne.'

The colonel astonishingly dug up a twisted smile, but my main interest was in the reaction of the ladies. Mrs Ransom, looking up at Siegfried as he bent over her, just went to pieces. It was unbelievable that this formidable fortress should crumble at the first shot, but there it was; the tough lines melted from her face and she was left with a big sloppy smile looking like anybody's dear old mum.

Mrs Tremayne's response was different but no less dramatic. As the steady grey eyes swept her she seemed to wither and it was as if a spasm of exquisite pain twisted her cheeks. She controlled herself with an effort but looked after Siegfried with wistful hunger as he turned back to the men.

I began to slosh the sherry violently into the glasses. Damn it, there it was again. The same old thing. And yet he didn't do anything. Just looked at them. Hell, it wasn't fair.

Sherry over, we moved outside and installed ourselves in Siegfried's Rover on which an immaculate coach-building job had been done since the disaster of last summer. It was an impressive turnout. The car, after a morning's forced labour by Tristan with hose and leather, shone like a mirror. Siegfried, in the driver's seat, extended an elegant arm to his brother as we drove away. I couldn't help feeling that the only superfluous object was myself, squatting uncomfortably on a little let-down seat, facing the two army men who sat to attention in the back seat, their bowlers pointing rigidly to the front. Between them Mrs Tremayne stared wonderingly at the back of Siegfried's head.

We lunched on the course, Siegfried comfortably at home with the smoked salmon, the cold chicken and the champagne. There was no doubt he had scored a tremendous success during the meal, discussing racing knowledgeably with the men and dispensing charm equally to their wives. The tough Mrs Ransom positively simpered as he marked her card for her. It was quite certain that if the new appointment hung upon his behaviour today, a vote at this time would have seen him home and dry.

After lunch we went down to the paddock and had a look at the horses parading for the first race. I could see Siegfried expanding as he took in the scene; the jostling crowds, the shouting bookies, the beautiful animals pacing round, the jockeys, tiny, colourful, durable, chatting to the trainers out in the middle. He had got through enough champagne at lunch to sharpen his appreciation and he was the very picture of a man who just knew he was going to have a successful day.

Merryweather, the course vet, joined us to watch the first race. Siegfried knew him slightly and they were chatting after the race when the 'vet wanted' sign went up. A man hurried up to Merryweather. 'That horse that slipped at the last bend is still down and doesn't look like getting up.'

The vet started for his car which was parked in readiness near the rails. He turned towards us. 'You two want to come?' Siegfried looked inquiringly at his party and received gracious nods of assent. We hurried after our colleague.

Within seconds we were racing down the course towards the last bend. Merryweather, hanging on to the wheel as we sped over the grass, grunted half to himself: 'Hell, I hope this thing hasn't got a fracture—if there's one thing that I mortally hate it's shooting horses.'

It didn't look good when we got to the spot. The sleek animal lay flat on its side showing no movement apart from the laboured rise and fall of its ribs. The jockey, blood streaming from a cut brow, knelt by its head. 'What do you think, sir? Has he broken a leg?'

'Let's have a look.' Merryweather began to palpate the extended limbs, running strong fingers over one bone then another, carefully flexing the joints of fetlock, knee, shoulder, hock. 'Nothing wrong there. Certainly no fracture.' Then he pointed suddenly at the head. 'Look at his eyes.'

We looked; they were glazed and there was a slight but unmistakable nystagmus.

'Concussion?' Siegfried said.

'That's it, he's just had a bang on the head.' Merryweather got off his knees, looking happier. 'Come on, we'll push him on to his chest. I think he ought to be able to get up with a bit of help.'

There were plenty of helpers from the crowd and the horse was rolled easily till he rested on his sternum, forelegs extended forward. After a couple of minutes in this position he struggled to his feet and stood swaying slightly. A stable lad walked him away.

Merryweather laughed. 'Well, that wasn't so bad. Good horse that. I think he'll be all right after a rest.'

Siegfried had started to reply when we heard a 'Psst, psst!' from beyond the rails. We looked up and saw a stout, red-faced figure gesturing at us eagerly. 'Hey! Hey!' it was saying. 'Come over here a minute.'

We went over. There was something about the face which Siegfried seemed to find intriguing. He looked closer at the grinning, pudgy features, the locks of oily black hair falling over the brow and cried out in delight.

'God help us! Stewie Brannon! Here, James, come and meet another colleague—we came through college together.'

Siegfried had told me a lot about Stewie Brannon. So much, in fact, that I seemed to be shaking hands with an old, well-remembered friend. Sometimes, when the mood was on us, Siegfried and I would sit up nearly till dawn over a bottle in the big room at Skeldale House chewing over old times and recalling the colourful characters we had known. I remembered he had told me he had overtaken Stewie about half way through the course and had qualified while Stewie was still battling in his third year. Siegfried had described him as totally unambitious, averse to study, disinclined to wash or shave; in fact, his idea of the young man least likely to succeed. But there had been something about him; he had the ingenuousness of a child, a huge, all-embracing affection for his fellow humans, an impregnable cheerfulness.

Siegfried called over to Merryweather. 'Will you give my apologies to my friends when you go back? There's a chap here I have to see—I'll only be a few minutes.'

Merryweather waved, got into his car and drove back up the course as we ducked under the rails.

Siegfried seized the bulky figure by the arm. 'Come on, Stewie, where can we get a drink?'

Chapter Thirty-Three

WE WENT into a long, low bar under the stand and I experienced a slight shock of surprise. This was the four and six-penny end and the amenities were rather different from the paddock. The eating and drinking was done mainly in the vertical position and the cuisine seemed to consist largely of pies and sausage rolls.

Siegfried fought his way to the bar and collected three whiskies. We sat down at one of the few available tables—an unstable, metal-topped structure. At the next table a sharp-faced character studied the 'Pink 'Un' while he took great swigs at a pint and tore savagely at a pork pie.

'Now, my lad,' Siegfried said. 'What have you been doing for the past six years?'

'Well, let's see,' said Stewie, absently downing his whisky at a gulp. 'I got into finals shortly after you left and I didn't do so bad at all, really. Pipped them both first go, then I had a bit of bother with surgery a couple of times, but I was launched on the unsuspecting animal population four years ago. I've been around quite a lot since then. North, South, even six months in Ireland. I've been trying to find a place with a living wage. This three or four quid a week lark isn't much cop when you have a family to keep.'

'Family? You're married then?'

'Not half. You remember little Meg Hamilton—I used to bring her to the college dances. We got married when I got into final year. We've got five kids now and another on the way.'

Siegfried choked on his whisky. 'Five kids! For God's sake, Stewie!'

'Ah, it's wonderful really, Siegfried. You probably wonder how we manage to exist. Well I couldn't tell you. I don't know myself. But we've kept one jump ahead of ruin and we've been happy, too. I think we're going to be O.K. now. I stuck up my plate in Hensfield a few months ago and I'm doing all right. Been able to clear the housekeeping and that's all that matters.'

'Hensfield, eh?' Siegfried said. I pictured the grim West Riding town. A wilderness of decaying brick bristling with factory chimneys. It was the other Yorkshire. 'Mainly small animals, I suppose?'

'Oh yes. I earn my daily bread almost entirely by separating the local tom cats from their knackers. Thanks to me, the feline females of Hensfield can walk the streets unmolested.'

Siegfried laughed and caught the only waitress in the place lightly by the arm as she hurried by. She whipped round with a frown and an angry word but took another look and smiled. 'Yes, sir?'

Siegfried looked into her face seriously for a few moments, still holding her arm. Then he spoke quietly. 'I wonder if you'd be kind enough to bring us three large whiskies and keep repeating the order whenever you see our glasses are empty. Would you be able to do that?'

'Certainly, sir, of course.' The waitress was over forty but she was blushing like a young girl.

Stewie's chins quivered with silent laughter. 'You old bugger, Farnon. It does me good to see you haven't changed.'

'Really? Well that's rather nice, isn't it?'

'And the funny thing is I don't think you really try.'

'Try? Try what?'

'Ah, nothing. Forget it—here's our whisky.'

As the drinks kept coming they talked and talked. I didn't butt in—I sat listening, wrapped in a pleasant euphoria and pushing every other glassful unobtrusively round to Stewie who put it out of sight with a careless jerk of the wrist.

As Siegfried sketched out his own progress, I was struck by the big man's total absence of envy. He was delighted to hear about the rising practice, the pleasant house, the assistant. Siegfried had described him as plump in the old days but he was fat now, despite his hard times. And I had heard about that overcoat; it was the 'navy nap' which had been his only protection through the years at college. It couldn't have looked so good then, but it was a sad thing now, the seams strained to bursting by the bulging flesh.

'Look, Stewie.' Siegfried fumbled uncomfortably with his glass. 'I'm sure you're going to do well at Hensfield but if by some mischance things got a bit rough, I hope you wouldn't hesitate to turn to me. I'm not so far off in Darrowby, you know. In fact.' He paused and swallowed. 'Are you all right now? If a few quid would help, I've got 'em here.'

Stewie tossed back what must have been the tenth double whisky and gazed at his old friend with gentle benevolence. 'You're a kind old bugger, Siegfried, but no thanks. As I said we're clearing the housekeeping and we'll be O.K. But I appreciate it—you always were kind. A strange old bugger, but kind.'

'Strange?' Siegfried was interested.

'No, not strange. Wrong word. Different. That's it, you were as different as hell.'

'Different?' queried Siegfried, swallowing his whisky as if it had stopped tasting of anything a long time ago. 'I'm sure you're wrong there, Stewie '

'Don't worry your head about it,' Stewie said, and reached across the table to thump his friend on the shoulder. But his judgement was way out and instead he swept Siegfried's bowler from his head. It rolled to the feet of the man at the next table.

During the conversation I had been aware of this gentleman rushing out and trailing slowly back to resume his study of the 'Pink 'Un' and renew his attack on the food and drink. The man looked down at the hat. His face was a picture of misery and frustration born of too much beer, semi-masticated pork pies and unwise investment. Convulsively he lashed out with a foot at the bowler and looked better immediately.

The hat, deeply dented, soared back to Siegfried who caught it and replaced it on his head with unruffled aplomb. He didn't seem in the least annoyed; apparently considered the man's reaction perfectly normal.

We all stood up and I was mildly surprised by a slight swaying and blurring of my surroundings. When things came to rest I had another surprise; the big bar was nearly empty. The beer machines were hidden by white cloths. The barmaids were collecting the empty glasses.

'Stewie,' Siegfried said. 'The meeting's over. Do you realize we've been nattering here for over two hours?'

'And very nice, too. Far better than giving the hard-earned coppers to the bookies.' As Stewie rose to his feet he clutched at the table and stood blinking for a few seconds.

'There's one thing, though,' Siegfried said. 'My friends. I came here with a party and they must be wondering where I've got to. Tell you what, come and meet them. They'll understand when they realize we haven't seen each other for years.'

We worked our way round to the paddock. No sign of the general and company. We finally found them in the car park grouped unsmilingly around the Rover. Most of the other cars had gone. Siegfried strode up confidently, his dented bowler cocked at a jaunty angle.

'I'm sorry to have left you but a rather wonderful thing happened back there. I would like to present Mr Stewart Brannon, a professional colleague and a very dear friend.'

Four blank stares turned on Stewie. His big, meaty face was redder than ever and he smiled sweetly through a faint dew of perspiration. I noticed that he had made a lopsided job of buttoning the navy nap overcoat; there was a spare buttonhole at the top and a lack of alignment at the bottom. It made the straining, tortured garment look even more grotesque.

The general nodded curtly, the colonel appeared to be grinding his teeth, the ladies froze visibly and looked away.

'Yes, yes, quite,' grunted the general. 'But we've been waitin' here some time and we want to be gettin' home.' He stuck out his jaw and his moustache bristled.

Siegfried waved a hand. 'Certainly, certainly, by all means. We'll leave right away.' He turned to Stewie. 'Well, goodbye for now, my lad. We'll get together again soon. I'll ring you.'

He began to feel through his pockets for his ignition key. He started quite slowly but gradually stepped up his pace. After he had explored the pockets about five times he stopped, closed his eyes and appeared to give himself over to intense thought. Then, as though he had decided to do the thing systematically, he commenced to lay out the contents of his pockets one by one, using the car bonnet as a table, and as the pile grew so did my conviction that doom was very near.

It wasn't just the key that worried me. Siegfried had consumed a lot more whisky than I had and with its usual delayed action it had begun to creep up on him. He was swaying slightly, his dented bowler had slid forward over one eyebrow and he kept dropping things as he pulled them from his pocket and examined them owlishly.

A man with a long brush and a handcart was walking slowly across the car park when Siegfried grabbed his arm. 'Look, I want you to do something for me. Here's five bob.'

'Right, mister.' The man pocketed the money. 'What d'you want me to do?'

'Find my car key.'

The man began to peer round Siegfried's feet. 'I'll do me best. Dropped it round 'ere, did you?'

'No, no. I've no idea where I dropped it.' Siegfried waved vaguely. 'It's somewhere on the course.'

The man looked blank for a moment then he gazed out

over the acres of littered ground, the carpet of discarded race cards, torn up tickets. He turned back to Siegfried and giggled suddenly, then he walked away, still giggling.

I stole a glance at our companions. They had watched the search in stony silence and none of them seemed to be amused. The general was the first to explode.

'Great heavens, Farnon, have you got the blasted key or haven't you? If the damn thing's lost, then we'd better make other arrangements. Can't keep the ladies standing around here.'

A gentle cough sounded in the background. Stewie was still there. He shambled forward and whispered in his friend's ear and after a moment Siegfried wrung his hand fervently.

'By God, Stewie, that's kind of you! You've saved the situation.' He turned back to the party. 'There's nothing to worry about—Mr Brannon has kindly offered to provide us with transport. He's gone to get his car from the other park.' He pointed triumphantly at the shiny back of the bulging navy overcoat navigating unsteadily through the gate.

Siegfried did his best to keep a conversation going but it was hard slogging. Nobody replied to any of his light sallies and he stopped abruptly when he saw a look of rage and disbelief spread over the general's face. Stewie had come back.

The car was a tiny Austin Seven dwarfed even further by the massive form in the driver's seat. I judged from the rusted maroon paintwork and cracked windows that it must be one of the very earliest models, a 'tourer' whose hood had long since disintegrated and been replaced by a home-made canvas cover fastened to the twisted struts by innumerable loops of string.

Stewie struggled out, dragged open the passenger door and inclined his head with modest pride. He motioned towards a pile of sacks which lay on the bare boards where the passenger seat should have been; there were no seats in the back either, only a couple of rough wooden boxes bearing coloured labels with the legend 'Finest American Apples'. From the boxes peeped a jumble of medicine bottles, stethoscopes, powders, syringe cases.

'I thought,' said Stewie. 'If we put the sacks on top of the boxes...'

The general didn't let him finish. 'Dammit, is this supposed to be a joke?' His face was brick red, the veins on his neck were swelling dangerously. 'Are you tryin' to insult me friend and these ladies? You want horsewhippin' for this afternoon's work, Farnon. That's what you want—horsewhippin'!'

He was halted by a sudden roar from the Rover's engine. The colonel, a man of resource as befitted his rank, had shorted the ignition. Fortunately the doors were not locked.

The ladies took their places in the back with the colonel and I slunk miserably on to my little seat. The general had regained control of himself. 'Get in! I'll drive!' he barked at Siegfried as though addressing an erring lance-corporal.

But Siegfried held up a restraining hand. 'Just one moment,' he slurred. 'The windscreen is very dirty. I'll give it a rub for you.'

The ladies watched him silently as he weaved round to the back of the car and began to rummage in the boot. The love light had died from their eyes. I don't know why he took the trouble; possibly it was because, through the whisky mists, he felt he must re-establish himself as a competent and helpful member of the party.

But the effort fell flat; the effect was entirely spoiled. He was polishing the glass with a dead hen.

It was a couple of weeks later, again at the breakfast table that Siegfried, reading the morning paper with his third cup of coffee, called out to me.

'Ah, I see Herbert Jarvis M.R.C.V.S., one time Captain R.A.V.C., has been appointed to the North West Circuit as supervisory veterinary surgeon. I know Jarvis. Nice chap. Just the man for the job.'

I looked across at my boss for some sign of disappointment or regret. I saw none.

Siegfried put down his cup, wiped his lips on his napkin and sighed contentedly. 'You know, James, everything happens for the best. Old Stewie was sent by providence or heaven or anything you like. I was never meant to get that job and I'd have been as miserable as hell if I had got it. Come on, lad, let's get off into those hills.'